Politics of North East India

With Special Reference to Assam

Deepan Das

Asstt. Prof., Department of Political Science
R.G. Baruah College, Guwahati

CONCEPT PUBLISHING COMPANY PVT. LTD.
NEW DELHI-110059

Politics of North East India: With Special Reference to ASSAM by **Dr. Deepan Das,** Astt. Prof., Deptt. of Political Science, R.G. Baruah College, Guwahati written as per the new Semester System (Major) of Dibrugarh University.

BOOK CODE - ENG. - 2

ISBN-13: 978-93-88937-02-3 (HB)

ISBN-13: 978-93-88937-03-0 (PB)

First Published in 2019

Published and Printed by

Concept
Since 1974

Concept Publishing Company Pvt. Ltd.
A/15-16, Commercial Block, Mohan Garden
New Delhi-110059 (India)
Phones : 25351460, 25351794
Email : publishing@conceptpub.com,
Website: www.conceptpub.com

Preface

This book provides an in-depth study about the Society and Politics of North Eastern States of India with special reference to Assam. As Dibrugarh University has included a paper on Politics of North East India with Special Reference to Assam for the Students of Fourth Semester (Major) under Dibrugarh University, therefore, it is expected that this book will help the students to prepare for the paper.

While writing this book the authors have taken the help from the works of different eminent writers and scholars. The authors are greatly indebted to these personalities whose writings and advices have helped them in completing this book. The authors are also thankful to Mrinal Barua (Ranada).

The authors are also thankful to Sh. Ashok Mittal, Concept Publishing Co. Pvt. Ltd. to bring the book to the light of the day.

Lastly, any suggestions and constructive criticism regarding the improvement of the book from the teachers and the student community are most welcome.

Dibrugarh, January 2019

Author

SYLLABUS

POLITICS OF NORTH EAST INDIA WITH SPECIAL REFERENCE TO ASSAM

TDC (Major): 4th Semester

Paper - 10600 PSCM: Total Marks: 100

(80 Marks for Final Examination and 20 Marks for Internal Assessment)

Objectives: The primary aim of this paper is acquaint with the students with the sensitive peripheral states of India that has attracted the attention of the social scientists since a few year back. Moreover, being the citizens of the North East region it is invariably the concern of the students to have proper understanding of their own area. This is also one of the objective of introducing this paper.

Unit I: Emergence of North East as a Region

- Geo-political features
- Colonial legacy
- Heterogenous character of North East Society and its impact on Politics
- Tribals (both the Hills and Plains) and Non-Tribals Politics

(Lectures 10 and Marks 15)

Unit II: Politics of Autonomy in Assam

- Regionalism and Sub-regionalism
- Demand for Autonomous State and Sixth Schedule
- Demand for Separate State

(Lectures 10 and Marks 15)

Unit III: Politics of Ethnicity in Assam

- Politics of Migration
- Identity Movements
- Language Movement
- Foreign National Movement
- Insurgency and Secessionist Movements

(Lectures 15 and Marks 15)

Unit IV: Electoral Politics

- Emergence of Assamese Middle Class and their role in Politics
- Role of Political Parties—both National and Regional
- Pressure Groups

(Lectures 15 and Marks 15)

Unit V: Border Dispute in North East India with Reference to

- Border dispute between Assam and Nagaland
- Border dispute between Assam and Meghalaya
- Border dispute between Assam and Arunachal Pradesh
- Inter-State Conflicts

(Lectures 10 and Marks 15)

Contents

Unit-I
Emergence of North East as a Region

At present, North East (NE) India is composed of eight states, viz. Arunachal Pradesh, Assam, Manipur, Meghalaya, Mizoram, Nagaland, Sikkim and Tripura. The region covers a geographical area of 2.55 lakh square km. This region is the eastern most part of India and in recent times it is of great significance to the Indian State because of its geographical location. The region is a gateway to South East Asia as it is bordered by Bangladesh, Bhutan, Myanmar, Nepal and China (Rocky, 2013). The abundance of natural resources in the region and its contribution to the economy of India is noteworthy. But it has been alleged that the region has received no major development since independence as a return of its large contributions towards the country's economy.

North East India as a Region

Prior to 1826, there was no such region named as NE India. It was only under the colonial regime of British that the region of North East India emerged within the territory of the British India. In fact the region as well as the country was divided in small and numerous provinces or kingdoms before the advent of East India Company in India. This part of the country was divided by kingdoms like that of the *Ahom*, the *Naga*, the *Kachari*, the *Jaintia*, the *Khasi*, the *Maran* and *Muttock*, the *Koch Rajbongshis* and so on. The *Ahom* had conquered many of the contemporary kingdoms and by the end of 18th century *Ahom* were in a dominant position. But due to internal conspiracy and dissension, the Burmese with the help of some traitor within the *Ahom* invaded the then Assam. The British fearing the onward march of the Burmese helped the *Ahom* and battled against the Burmese which culminated in the Treaty of Yandaboo, 1826.

It should be mentioned here that though the undivided Goalpara District of the region came under the British rule early in 1765 due to the transfer of *Deewani* from Mughals to the British, the rest of the region was independent from British rule for a long period of time. It was only in 1826, that British rule was imposed in the whole region (the then Assam) on account of the signing of the Treaty of Yandaboo (24th February, 1826) between the Burmese and British after a long and expensive war to claim possession over the region.

Both the sides had to pay huge loss due to that devastating and long standing war. But still the East India Company was in a better position than the Burmese because they had the money power and the manpower (both European and the Indian). Burmese had to accept the conditions imposed by the Company and forced to cede to the British the region including Assam, a major part of the upper Burma, *viz.* Rakhine (Arakan), and Taninthayi (Tenasserim) and the then Burmese possessed Manipur. It should be mentioned here that Manipur was an independent kingdom and the border area of Burma and Manipur was rebellion prone area especially the Kabaw Valley. Manipur was a rebellion-prone tributary for the Burmese. Hence, the Burmese send expeditions in 1764-1765, 1768-1770, and 1775-1782 annexed it in 1819 after a rebellion.

Thereafter, the East India Company took the control of the lower Assam by appointing David Scott as the Senior Commissioner of Assam and a Junior Commissioner was appointed for Upper Assam. However, the British installed Purandar Singha the King of Upper Assam in the year 1833 but was replaced in 1838 on vague charge of 'mal-administration' (Chaube, 1999). By 1842 the entire Brahmaputra Valley was under the control of East India Company including Sadiya and the *Muttock* territory (Presently Dibrugarh).

Although a good relation between the *Khasi* Chief and the British as well as between the *Jaintia* King and the British developed due to the British extended protection during the Burmese attack, yet the *Khasi* Chief had to enter into a subordinate alliance with the British Government in 1833 and the *Jaintia* King was removed and his territory was merged with British India. It has to be mentioned here that the chief tribes, viz. the *Khasi, Garo* and *Jaintia* had their own kingdoms in the past until they came under British Administration in the 19th century. Later British incorporated Meghalaya into Assam in 1835. This region enjoyed semi-independent status by virtue of a treaty relationship with the British Crown.

Moreover, governance of Manipur was given to Gambhir Singh, as a reward for his contribution to the East India Company's fight against the Burmese. Then in 1834 on account of his death his son succeeded him in the year 1834 followed by a number of succession. It is believed that Manipur was the last of the independent states to be incorporated into British India in 1891. Thus, it is clearly evident now that the region of North East as a whole came into existence during the British regime. In other words, the NE India was more or less originated during the formation and expansion of British India. It has to be mentioned here that the then NE India incorporates in it a major portion of Burma as already explained above. The following general political map of 1893 of the British Indian Empire will be helpful in this regard.

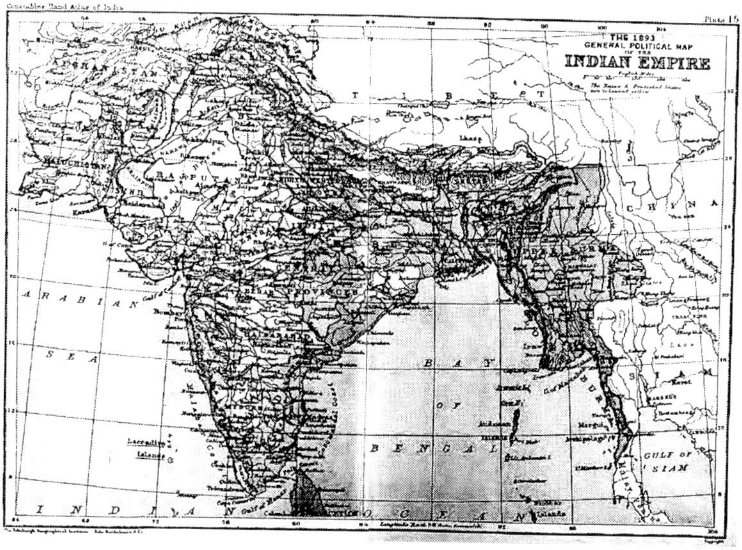

It is also necessary to mention about the Tripura Kingdom, one of the oldest as well as independent princely States in India which is also an important entity in the easternmost part of India. Though, it was an independent princely state and was ruled by their traditional kings of Manikya Dynasty until 1949, its independence was qualified, being subject to the recognition of British. In fact, the Tripuri Kingdom was under the protectorate of the British empire and was known as Hill Tippera.

Thus, when India became independent in 1947, there were only two states in this region of North East, viz. Assam and Manipur. Tripura joined the family of North East Indian states on 15 October, 1949 when Tripura merged with the Indian Union. It is noteworthy that a total of 184 kings ruled Tripura before it merged to Indian Union.

Assam was a much larger state at that time and four new states were carved out of Assam in the decades following independence. Nagaland was the first state that was carved out of Assam in 1963 which was a consequence of the 16-Point Agreement of 1960. It was followed by the creation of Meghalaya in the year 1972. It was the result of the North-Eastern Areas (Reorganization) Act, 1971 of parliament, which conferred full statehood status on the autonomous state of Meghalaya. It was formed by carving out two districts from the state of Assam, viz. the United Khasi Hills and Jaintia Hills, and the Garo Hills. In the same year Mizoram was carved out from Assam as a Union Territory and got statehood in 1987. Before becoming Mizoram it was known as the Mizo Hill District of Assam. In regard to Arunachal Pradesh (then known as North East Frontier Agency by 1954), like Mizoram, was also made a Union Territory carved out of Assam in the year 1972 and then, a full-fledged state in February 1987.

The last state to join North Eastern Region (NER) is the Sikkim in 2002 and came to be known as the young brother of the Seven Sisters. Although Sikkim became a state in India in 1975, it was only in 2002 it was officially declared as a part of the NER.

However, it is important to mention about some other significant developments in the post-colonial period which led to further recognize the NER as an entity or region in the map of India. The creation of North-East Frontier Agency (NEFA) in 1951 by Pandit Jawaharlal Nehru is a great development in this direction. This region as an entity captured more serious attention of Indian leaders in the wake of Indo-China War of 1962 (Ngaihte, 2013: 13). In subsequent time, creation of North Eastern Council (NEC) in 1971 by an Act of Parliament and creation of Ministry of Development of North Eastern Region (MoDONER) in September 2001 gave boost to the claim NER as an entity. Existence of umbrella organizations like North East Student Organization (NESO) and Council of Baptist Churches in North East India (CBCNEI) legitimize NER as an entity. Moreover, establishment of higher institutions of learning like North Eastern Hill University (NEHU) in 1973 and presence of academic bodies like the North East India History Association (NEIHA) and North East India Political Science Association (NEIPSA) testifies the consolidation of NE concept in the academic sphere (*ibid.*). Furthermore, it may be added the recent creation of North East United FC with the slogan of '*Eight States, One United*' in the Indian Super League symbolizes NER as united entity in the national and international platform, although may be from emotional point of view.

Thus the present NE India is a result of long process of evolution. However, the word region has a specific meaning for the students of political science. We can relate the word 'region' with other words such as 'regionalism'. The feeling of regionalism takes place in the mind of a group of people who resides in a particular region. Those people of the particular region think of themselves as having similarity and unity among themselves and also feels that they are differ from the people of other regions. This is particularly true in case of the people of NE India. They differ from the rest of the people of India culturally and biologically. Arguing about the hill people of NE Robert Reid (a retired officer of Indian Civil Service and Governor of Assam from 1937 to 1942) said that "neither racially, historically, culturally, nor linguistically they have any affinity with the people of the plains, or with the people of India proper" (Baruah, 2008).

Concept of Region

In the Social Sciences, a 'region' is a cohesive area that is homogeneous in selected defining criteria and is distinguished fro neighboring areas or regions by those criteris. It is a intellectual construct created by the selection of features relevant to a particular problem and the disregard of other features considered to be irrelevant. A region is distinguished from an area, which is usually a broader concept designting a portion of surface of the Earth. Area boundaries are arbitrary established fro convenience. Regional boundaries are determined by the homogeneity and cohesiveness of the section.

Region may be modal, defined by the organization of activity about some central place (e.g. a town and its hinterland, or tributary area), or uniform, defined by the homogeneous distribution of some phenomena within it (e.g. a tropical rain forest).

Region may also be defined in terms of Single or multiple features or in terms that approach the total content of human occupancy of a area. The most common features in social science are ethnic, cultural, or linguistic (Province), climate or topographical (the Tennessee Valley), industrial or urban economic specialization (the cotton belt of North America), administrative units (Standard government regions in Great Britain), and international political areas (Middle East). The concept of region is currently used in analysis, planning and administration of many National and International Public Programmes. Regionalism, or regional consciousness the ideological correlate of the concept that develop from a sense of identify within the region, is important in many historical, political, and sociological analysis.

Now to define the term 'region' in the context of seven North Eastern states, the question that naturally arises is: Do these units ideally form one planning region? According to J.R. Meyer and H.W. Richard Son, a planning region may be delineated on the basis of any one of the following three considerations:

(1) Homogeneity with respect to topography or climate, natural resources, level of special economic and political development etc.
(2) Modality or polarization centring on some urban metropolitan area.
(3) Administrative coherence or identity.

The North Eastern Region (NER) clearly falls in the first category. Its homogeneous features in the field of topography; rainfall, level of socio-economic development is well marked. Some geographers and regional planning experts have, therefore, included these states into one macro-planning region.

However, the term 'region' as applied to North East India has never been clearly defined. In the words of Sunil Munshi and his colleagnues, "the identification of North East India as a region is primarily a geo-political acid". The lack of a sophisticated definition of the term 'region' in the context of North East India does no longer make the area other than a region. It constitutes a region despite its varied physical features and its different economic, political and social systems.

Geo-political Features of North East India

Before proceeding to discuss the geo-political features of the NER, it is necessary for us to know the implication of geo-politics. What does it imply? Geo-politics is the study of the links between political power and geographic space. Basically, geo-politics is an area of study in International Relation or Politics and it studies the effects of geography (both human and physical) on international politics and international relationship of various countries. It helps in foreign policy analysis which seeks to understand, explain, and predict international political behaviour primarily in terms of geographical variables like physical location, size, climate, topography, demography, natural resources, and technological advances of the state.

Although traditionally the term has applied largely to the impact of geography on politics, now it encompasses wide connotations and it includes the analyses of geography, history, and social science. Geo-politics also studies the interest of the international political actors and their interest focused in a particular area, space, geographical element or ways, relations which create a geo-political system. Geo-politics is multi-disciplinary study and includes a number of subjects with a primary emphasis on political geography, international relations, the territorial aspects of political science and international law. The term "Geo-politics" was coined by Rudolf Kjellén at the beginning of the twentieth century.

The geo-political features of the NER can be discussed as follows:

1. Location and Connectivity to the Rest of India: The region is located to the eastern most part of India and connected to the Indian mainland by a thin 22 km-long land corridor passing through Siliguri in the eastern State of West Bengal. This thin corridor is popularly known as the Chicken Neck Corridor. The Chicken Neck is the only land route for the NE to the rest of the country as well as to the world.

2. International Boundaries: While only 2 per cent of the landmass is connected with mainland India, notably the region (which is of 2,62,174 square kilometres) shares a well sensitive 4,500 km long international border with South and South East Asian Countries (Dutta, 2009) with China in the North, Myanmar in the East, Bangladesh in the South West and Bhutan to the North West.

3. Landlocked: As already mentioned that the Chicken Neck (also known as Siliguri Corridor) is the only land corridor for the NER and the whole region is surrounded by foreign countries of South Asia and South East Asia, the region is considered to be landlocked one. This is because that although the region shares about 98 per cent of its borders with neighbouring countries, but there is not a single formal land at present to establish direct and rapid communication with these countries.

4. Creation of States in NER: Most of the states in NE India were carved out from the greater state of Assam. It was mentioned in the earlier paragraph that at the time of independence there was only three states in the NER, viz. Assam, Manipur and Tripura. It is only a repetition that Nagaland was the first state to be carved out of Assam in 1963. It was followed by the creation of Meghalaya in the year 1972. Mizoram was also carved out of Assam in 1972 and received the status of statehood in 1987. In the same year, Arunachal Pradesh was also received statehood.

5. Boundary Disputes Among the States of NE India: As the states like Arunachal Pradesh, Meghalaya and Nagaland were created by carving out the erstwhile Greater Assam; it is natural to have boundary disputes among them. These three states particularly have disputes with Assam. This may be because of the desire to grab more lands for their own state from the original one. For example, we have Assam-Nagaland boundary dispute (popular Merapani clash and the recent 2014 Uriamghat incidence in Golaghat District, and some incidence in Jorhat and Sivasagar District including the Nagas Claim on the Teok river etc.), one of the most worst boundary dispute in the country. Then we have Assam-Arunachal Pradesh boundary dispute. The Charaipung incidence of 2010 in Sivasagar District is an example of such dispute. In this incidence, the disputed areas are Lahdoigarh Road, Teok river etc. Similarly, we have disputes in the Assam-

Meghalaya border. The disputed areas in Assam-Meghalya boundaries are the Jayantia-Mikir hills boundary, Nongwah-Mawtamur areas, Sonapur-Khanapara areas and the Garo hills, Kamrup and Goalpara District boundary. These border disputes are significant geo-political feature of NER and it influences largely the regional policy making process as well as the national.

Colonial Legacy

Brief discussions about colonial legacy, particularly British Colonialism, have been made in this section titled *Emergence of North East India as a Region*. In fact, the emergence of the region had its root in its colonial legacy. However, it should be mentioned here that it was not only the British East India Company to be ambitious of spreading their colonialism. The Mughals were also interested in extending their kingdom to NE India. Although Mughals were defeated by the Ahoms, they had conquered their first organized attack upon Assam in 1613 and defeated Raja Parikshit of Kamrup. Mughals from time to time have conquered some parts of Assam and they had records of short time reigns. There are evidences to show that the Mughals had ruled in places like Pandu, Guwahati, Kajali, Hajo etc., although for short periods of time. However, it should be mentioned that some places of the region, such as the then Goalpara, which also included the Garo Hills of the region (presently in the state of Meghalaya) was remained a part of Mughal province of Bengal (Baruah, 2008) for a long period of time in comparison and neither the Ahoms nor any other native Kingdoms regained these areas.

Moreover, the discussion on colonial legacy is incomplete without mentioning the devastating rule of the Burmese. The period from 1821 to 1825 was the period of Burmese control over Assam and usually remembered with horror by the people of the region. This short period is generally referred as the *manor din* in Assamese. This short period of Burmese control over the then Kingdom of Assam is important one, as it leads to the historical British Colonialism in the region.

British control in the region started in the year 1826 and lasted till India got independence. However, the then district of Goalpara in western Assam came under the control of the East India Company as early as in 1765 according to the Mughal emperor's *Firman* of August 12 of that year (*Ibid.*). So the British occupation in that western part of the NER was started much earlier than the rest of the region. The British, after getting the rights over Assam, introduced major changes both in administration and economy of the then Assam. The boundaries of the then Assam under

British occupation gradually increased to include most of the areas which constitute the present NER. However, state like Manipur was not a part of the then Assam. But, it can be said that the then Assam constitute a major part of the region. Hence, the terms Assam, particularly the colonial one and NER are often inter-changeably used here.

However, Assam as a colonial province, a Chief Commissionership, was formed in 1874 (*Ibid.*). This Chief Commissioner Province of Assam also included the district of Sylhet and Mymensingh (presently in Bangladesh). The rule of British during 1826 to 1873 in Assam is considered as an appendage of the unwieldy province of Bengal. The decision of making Assam a separate administrative entity was, although, based on the considerations of administrative convenience, the considerations of development of tea, colonial and petroleum industries were also there. These natural assets of the region motivated the British to expand its boundaries as well as the boundaries of the then Assam.

The British, particularly, was interested in developing tea industry in the region. With a view to expand the tea business in the region, the House of Commons in 1854 with legislation encouraged the tea industrialists of Britain to do tea cultivation in Assam. Establishment of Assam Company, a company for private tea business was the product of that encouragement by the House of Commons. Tea cultivation was expanded in Assam by the establishment of *Jorehat Tea Company* in 1857 and *James Phindle Company* in 1861 by occupying thousands of acres of land of indigenous people. The growth of tea industry during British regime gave a new turn to the Assam-Bengal trade. In fact, tea became the most important exportable commodity from Assam.

However, the unfair and arrogant occupation of indigenous lands the indigenous communities, particularly those in the hilly areas. As a result, there were frequent acts of cruelty and violence between the hill people and the people of the tea garden, viz. the owner, the employee and the workers of the tea garden. For instance, Mr. Holcombe was cut into two pieces by the Nagas. It was a reaction by the Nagas against his attitude of expansion of tea cultivation in Naga inhabited areas, particularly the expansion beyond Lahdoigarh. This incident compelled the British Administration to consider the uniqueness in the living style of the hill people. As a result, the Bengal Eastern Frontier Regulation I, 1873, was passed and combined it with 33rd Bengal Act. It was the advent of the Inner Line system in the then Assam which provided certain administrative restrictions in the hill areas and demarcate a line of separation in the hills and the plains. The system of Inner Line was initiated in 1873 and the task was completed in the year 1895.

Besides the Inner-Line system, the British adopted a number of regulations regarding hill areas and people of the NER. For instance, mention may be made about Scheduled Districts Act of 1874, Frontier Tract Regulation Act of 1880 etc. Although the British policy in whole of India was same in general, but yet they considered the uniqueness of the hill tribes of the region and termed them as "primitive tribes" and thus administratively they were kept in excluded tracts (*Ibid.*).

It has to be mentioned here that it was during British regime that while Assam relationship, especially commercial relationship, came closer with Bengal, its trade relationship with its bordering neighbours like that of China decreased significantly. The British observed the economic significance of the region and introduced railways and other communication facilities and thereby enhance the relationship of NER with the rest of British India. In fact, introduction of railways and establishment of commercial relationship between the then Assam and the Bengal or between the then Assam and the rest of India was the beginning of the assimilation of indigenous people and Hindi or Bengali speaking people in the region. As per the data available, a quarter of the population of Assam was non-indigenous in 1901. It is also alleged that the indigenous people of the region did not get benefited from the British developed colonial economy. The benefited revenues arising from tea or coal trade hardly benefit the region or its indigenous people. This is still to some extent evident at present, because the present economy is also the product of the British colonial economy.

While discussing colonial legacy, it is necessary to mention that Eastern Bengal (Presently Bangladesh) was once made a part of Assam. The colonial administrators were highly interested to combine Eastern Bengal and Assam into a single province and it was indeed done in 1905 (Baruah, 2008). This is mainly because of the fact that they were interested in the promising tea industry in Assam and combining Assam with Eastern Bengal would provide them more administrative and transportation convenience. As early as in 1892, some British officials suggested that the Chittagong should be made a part of Assam because having a port like Chittagong in the same province was a great advantage to the European tea planters (*Ibid.*). However, during the time of the decision to combine Eastern Bengal with Assam was taken in 1905, some sections of people proposed that the newly created state should be renamed as North Eastern Province. But, it is important to note that the colonial tea planters greatly defended the name Assam, which by then had developed a serious stake in the name of Assam as the word *Assam* by which the region's tea was known in international markets (*Ibid.*). Finally, the proposal for calling it North

Eastern Province was dropped in favour of the name Eastern Bengal and Assam (*Ibid.*).

The province called Eastern Bengal and Assam was short lived and was reverted to its former status of Chief Commissionership and to its former boundaries that included Sylhet (*Ibid.*). However, in 1921, Assam was upgraded into a Governor's Province as a consequence of the Government of India Act, 1919 and retained its status till independence.

Heterogenous Characters of North East Society and its Impacts on Politics

Despite the fact of having similarity between the states of North Eastern States, the society in this region is heterogenous at present as well as in the past. There are diversity in culture and hence in the society as well. People belonging to various religions, castes and tribes are the inhabitants of this region. The state of Colonial Assam was regarded as a museum of nationalities by many. It was claimed that the *Garos* were migrated from the southern side of central Tibet; *Khasis* (not all of them) were migrated from South East Asia; and the *Nagas* were migrated from the eastern Tibet (Chaube, 1999). Hence, it is natural to find heterogeneity in the society of NER.

The diversity of NER can be judged from the fact that out of 635 tribal communities in India more than 200 communities live here (Dutta, 2009) along with a number of non-tribal communities. Moreover, out of the 325 languages listed in *People of India*, the highest number belongs to the Tibeto-Burman family and 175 communities of NER speaking them (*Ibid.*). An attempt to highlight the social heterogeneity in NER is made below.

The Ahoms: At present, the *Ahoms* are mainly the inhabitant of upper Assam. In Arunachal Pradesh, also a good number of people belonging to *Ahom* Community are found. Originally, they were migrated from Mong Mao (it was a small kingdom which is now located in the Yunnan Province of China) under the leadership of their prince *Sukapha* and reached the Brahmaputra Valley in 1228 after traversing the Patkai hills. *Sukapha* established the *Ahom* Kingdom in the Brahmaputra valley and this kingdom ruled the valley for the next 598 years until the transfer of power to the East India Company in 1826. Although originally these people cherish the ethnic *Tai* religions, most of them are presently the followers of Hinduism. The Hindu *Ahoms* are believed to be belonging to *Kshatriya varna* of the *Varnashram* system of Hinduism as they were the ruling class for a long period of time. A part of the *Ahoms* is also the follower of Buddhism. Moreover, instead of having their own *Tai* Scripts, at present Assamese is their main language of communication. Recently the *Ahom* people of Assam are trying to revive their original *Tai* culture, scripts etc.

The people of *Ahom* community have their unique traditional features. One of such is their tradition of ancestor worship. They worship their ancestors as God because they believe that a person becomes God of the family after his death. They believe that the ancestors must be duly worshipped so that they are being satisfied to keep them safe. Hence, the *Ahom* people offer every first seasonal crop, fruit, vegetable etc. to their deceased ancestors. Moreover, *Ahom* people can be divided in two categories, viz. *Poka*, who use as well as prepare the traditional ethnic wine, and *Kecha,* who do not use it. The *Poka Ahom* people make use of the ethnic wine in various religious and social activities.

The Anals: This is a Scheduled Tribe community of Manipur, found in the Tengnoupal district. They are also known as *Pakan*. This tribe belongs to Tibeto-Burman group of tribes and also considered to be the oldest *Chin-Kuki* tribe of Manipur. They also considered as one of the Naga tribe. The people belonging to this community show best example of concern to their females, particularly to the pregnant one. They culturally rich and well preserved. *Akam* is one of their important festivals, perform to invoke divine blessing.

The *Bengalis:* Bengali people are also in a good number in North East India. They are particularly found in Assam and Tripura of the region. They are similar in respect of living style to the other Bengalis of West Bengal.

The Bodos: The *Bodos* constitute almost half of the total tribal population of the state of Assam. *Bodos* are inhabitants of mainly the districts of Kokrajhar, Chirang, Udalguri, Baksa, Kamrup, Nalbari and a few among them are also live in Cachar, Dima Hasao and Darrang district. They basically reside in plain rural areas and their economy is based on agriculture. They have the practice of storing their agricultural products in common granaries. Every *Bodo* village usually has a common granary. *Bathow puja* is the prime festival of the *Bodo* people. They equally celebrate the Assamese *Bihu* festival.

The Chirus: The *Chiru* is another tribe of Manipur, concentrated in the districts of Senapoti, Tamenglong and Bishnupur. While, their manners, customs etc. reflects *Kuki* origin, at the same time, their physique, hair style, habits, bachelors' quarters appears to be Naga way of life. Their women are empowered and play an important role in agricultural work.

The Dimasas: Dimasas are mainly found in the present district of Dima Hasao. The term *Dimasa* means the son of a river called 'Dima', which is popularly known as Dhansiri River. The unique thing about Dimasa society is that there is the system of division of clans separately for males and females. There is about 40 male clans and 42 female clans.

The Hmars: This tribal community is another dominant community of Manipur and mainly concentrated in the southern region of Manipur at Tipaimukh and Churachandpur. They are also the inhabitants of north and north-eastern part of Mizoram. Some of them are also found in the district of Cachar of Assam. They are considered as a highly educated group in Manipur and basically the followers of Christian religion.

The Kalitas: The *Kalitas* is an upper caste Hindu community next to Brahmins. It appears from the history of Assam that during *Ahom* rule the *Kalita* people served as soldiers, generals, administrators, envoys and judges. Although a wide range of *Kalitas* are peasant at present, there appears a vast range of occupational diversification among the people of *Kalita* community. People of this community are engaged as goldsmith, blacksmith, potter, weaver, gardener etc. The *Kalitas* are found throughout Assam in lesser and greater numbers.

The Kamrupi Brahmins: The various surnames of *Kamrupi Brahmin* People are Sharma, Bhagwati, Bhattacharjee, Mishra, Shashtri, Chakraborty etc. They are also known as *Kamrupi Brahmans* and *Kamrupi Bamon* as well. They were largely settled in Assam during the role of *Varman* dynasty and still live in Assam, particularly in western Assam. They occupy the top rank in the *Varnashram* system. According to *Manusmriti*, pursuit of knowledge is the austerity of a Brahmin.

The Karbis: They are also known as *Mikir* and mainly reside in the districts of Karbi Anglong, Dima Hasao, Golaghat, Kamrup and Nagaon. There are five clans in *Karbi* society, viz. *'Engti'*, '*Enghi*', '*Terang*', '*Timung*' and '*Teran*'. The practice of marriage between the members of same clan is strictly prohibited.

The Khamyang: They are also known as *Shyam* and are primarily found in the Tinsukia district. They follow Theraveda Buddhism. *Khamyang* are closely related to *Khampti*.

The Koivarttas: *Koivartta* is another indigenous community of Assam. It is recognized as one of the Scheduled Caste Community under Constitution (Scheduled Caste) Order, 1950. It is believed that the *Koivarttas* had their origin from *Kshatriya* father and *Sudra* mother. In ancient Assamese etymology, *Koi* means water and *Vartta* means to survive and thus etymologically *Koivartta* implies those people who survive by living near to the sources of water like river. Accordingly, these people are basically dependent on agriculture and fishing activities.

The *Koivartta* community is divided in two categories. The first category of *Koivartta* is known by different names such as *Muttack Koivartta* or *Bhagwatia Koivartta* or *Keots*. This category of *Koivartta* was largely influenced by the saint *Srimanta Sankardeva*. Use of liquor, pork etc. are forbidden among the members of this category. On the other hand, the second category of *Koivartta* is known as *Bamunia Koivartta or Jalua (Fisherman) Koivartta*. This category of people widely follows the rituals dictated by the Brahmins and therefore, they are called as *Bamunia Koivartta*. Both drinking and making of liquor is allowed among the members of this category.

The Konyaks: This tribe is an important tribe of Nagaland. However, a few villages of them are also found in Assam, particularly in Sivasagar District. Moreover, they are also the inhabitants of Tirap and Changlang district of Arunachal Pradesh (*Konyak* tribe of Arunachal Pradesh is known as *Wancho Konyak*). The *Konyaks* are considered to be the most sacred tribe among the *Nagas*. In Nagaland, they have the largest population among the *Nagas*. The unique thing about this tribe is that they follow endogamous principle of marriage, while all the other *Naga* tribes follow exogamous principle of marriage. The *Konyaks* are known as the head hunters of North East India. They were known as war loving tribal community, in the recent past. They frequently attacked the nearby villages of other tribes. It is believed that after conquering the nearby villages, they took the heads of the opposing warriors as trophies and hang those in a communal house called *Morong*. The number of heads indicated the power of the warriors.

The Mishings: The *Mishing* is another Scheduled Tribe community of Assam. They are the inhabitants of the districts of Dhemaji, Dibrugarh, Lakhimmpur, Sivasagar and Jorhat. The clans of *Mishings* are *Doley, Panging, Pait, Padun, Pait, Taid, Kutum* etc. Cultivation is the main occupation of *Mishing* people. The female members of them are good weavers as well as hard workers in the agricultural field. *Mishing* is a democratic society where the chief of the society is known as 'Gam'. They usually reside in *Chang Ghor*. The chief festival of them is *Ali-Ai-Ligang*, which is a festival related with agriculture.

The Pawi or the Lai: This tribal community is a found in Mizoram, but they are also the inhabitants of Manipur, Chin Hills of Burma, Southern Bangladesh etc. *Lai* or the *Pawi* has a number of clans, viz. *Anu, Bawm, Canada, Chuntei, Fanchun, Fanai, Hnamler, Lautu, Khuangsai, Miram, Pang, Sim, Zangiat* etc. In Mizoram, they are presently the inhabitants of Lai Autonomous District. They strictly preserve their ethnic *Lai* language. In order to preserve their language as a symbol of identity, they included the *Lai* language up to Middle School Standard.

The Rabhas: Rabhas live mainly in Goalpara, South of Kamrup, Darrang and Garo hills. A notable portion of *Rabha* population is also found in Baksa District. *Rabhas* are important ethnic group of Assam. *Rabha* society is an agricultural one and notably the *Rabha* women are most active and equally contribute in the field of agriculture.

The Sonowal Kacharis: They are originally a part of greater *Bodo* tribe. During the role of *Ahom* the *Sonowal Kacharis* were entrusted with the task of sieving gold from the river Suwansiri and it is believed they are, therefore, came to be known as *Sonowal.* Presently, *Sonowal Kacharis* are mainly the inhabitants of the districts of Dibrugarh, Lakhimpur and Sivsagar districts of Assam.

The Sutiyas: The *Sutiyas* originally belong to Indo-Tibetan race. At present they are found in the states of Assam and Arunachal Pradesh. They were one of the oldest settled communities in Assam. Once they had a large kingdom in upper Assam. The kingdom was popularly known as Vidarbha and its capital was situated at Kundil (the then Sadiya). The Kingdom, in the sixteenth century expanded from *Parashuram Kund* (a holy place in present Arunachal Pradesh) in the east to *Viswanath* in the west. The original language of the community is also known as *Sutiya*, a language of Tibeto-Burman language group. At present, the *Sutiya* people no longer use this language and speak Assamese. However, the *Sutiya* language is well preserved by the *Deuri* community of Assam. In regards to religion, the *Sutiya* people, at present, follow the Hinduism. But before adopting Hinduism they followed an ancient religion, viz. *Bon*, which was closely related with Buddhism.

The Tiwas: Tiwas are mainly the inhabitants of Morigaon District. *Tiwas* have 12 different clans. They are formerly known as *Lalung*. The main God of *Tiwa* is 'Fa-Mahadeo'. The main festivals of *Tiwa* are Bihu, Sagra, Misawa and Wansua.

The Phake: Phake are mainly found in Dibrugarh and Tinsukia districts. They are Tai-speaking tribal group and it is believed that they were migrated from Thailand in the later part of 18th century. They are followers of Theraveda Buddhism.

There are a huge number communities or tribes in North East India, all of which cannot be included here. Specially, in terms of tribal population, there is extreme heterogeneity in terms of distribution of population, their social structure and cultural pattern. There is spatial variation in the tribal characteristic of a single tribe. For example the sub-divisions of *Khasis*, viz. the *Wars, Khynriams, Pnars* and *Bhois* has different characteristics and identity. Thus it is natural to discover diverse and heterogeneous characters in the whole society of North East India. The various heterogeneous characters can briefly be described as follows:

Language: The communities in different states of NE India speak different languages. Some Communities have their own dialects in place of language. According to the census of 2001 in Assam, people speak Assamese (48.8%), Bengali (27.5%), Bodo (4.8%), Nepali (2.12%), Hindi (5.88%), and others (11.8%). People of Assam also speak native languages like *Deuri, Mishing, Karbi, Rabha, Tiwa* etc. which are of Tibeto-Burman origin. *Rajbongshi*, more popularly known as *Kamatapur* or *Goalparia* is also spoken by the people of Assam. *Tai* languages are also spoken here in Assam and notably four kinds of *Tai* languages are found in Assam, viz. *Tai Phake, Tai Aiton, Khamti,* and *Khamyang. Ahom* and *Turung* were other forms of *Tai* languages which were spoken by the people of Assam, but now these are extinct.

In general in respect of NER, *Assamese* is the main langauge in Assam; *Mizo* is of Mizoram; *Khasi, Pnar* and *Garo* are of Meghalaya; *Manipuri* is of Manipur; *Ao* and *Konyak* are of Meghalaya; *Tripuri* is of Tripura; and *Sikkimese* is the language of Sikkim. Languages and dialects in Arunachal Pradesh are *Dofla, Mishri, Adi Gallong, Monpa* and so on. Besides, there are other languages and dialects in the region, viz. *Missing, Bodo, Karbi, Akka, Nokte, Khamti, Wancho, Bengali, Nepali, Bhutia, Tenyidie* etc.

Religion: Heterogeneity in the society of NE India is also reflected by the fact that people of the region cherish different religions. Most of the tribal people particularly the hill tribes cherish Christianity. Some of them still believed in ancient religions like *Tantrisism, Saktivism* etc. While discussing about the practice of religion in the region, mention must be made about Srimanta Sankardeva of Assam and his Vaishnavism. A major portion of people is belonging to Hinduism. Brahminism was spread in the valley of Manipur and probably reached the valley of Manipur in the fifteenth century. Vaishnavism reached the *Nocte Nagas* of Tirap district of Arunachal Pradesh with the sincere efforts of the followers of Srimanta Sankardeva of Assam. A remarkable portion of the population also belongs to Islamism. Besides, religion like Buddhism, Sikhism also found here. People belonging to these last two categories are truly the minority religious communities here in NER.

Marriage: As there are heterogeneous religious practices among the people of NER, the practice of marriage is also heterogeneous. Different communities in NER have their own practice of marriage. The practice of inter-caste or inter-tribe marriage as well as intra-caste or intra-tribe marriage not common to all. Moreover in the past, male members of some hill tribes in NER used to marry several females at the same time and in a way, the polygamy system of marriage was justified. Recently such practices are abandoned to a great extent.

Family: In respect of family, both joint and single families are found in NER. However, recently due to increasing urbanization and population growth, the number of joint families is decreasing day by day. Whereas there is a increase in the number of single or nuclear families. Unlike the rest of the country, matriarchal families are also found in NE India. The *Khasi* and the *Garo* Communities has such families, which are unique in their type. It reflects the prestigious status of women in NER, particularly in tribal societies.

Culture: All the states of NER is consisting of a number of communities and hence people have their own cultural food habit, dance, song, traditional wearing etc. For example, the *Assamese* women wear *Sadar-Mekhela* as their traditional dress. Likewise the *Bodo* women wear *Dokhona*. To mention about the *Naga* people, the traditional *Shawl* is the most important dress of them. Moreover, Bihu Dance is the cultural symbol of Assamese community. Similarly, *Manipuri* is a classical dance form of Manipur, it actually covers a number of dance form (including *Ras Lila* and *Pung Cholom*) of the region. The *Bagarumba* of the *Bodo* people is another popular traditional dance form of the region. *Nongkrem* is the name of a folkdance of Meghalaya. The *Khasi* people of Meghalaya perform this kind of dance form. Furthermore, *Khuallam* dances a dance form of *Mizo* people of Mizoram. Another popular dance of the *Mizo* people of Mizoram is the *Cheraw* dance which is also popularly known as Bamboo-Dance.

Occupation: Although most of the people are dependent on agriculture, a major portion of people in the region has heterogeneous occupation, like fishing, weaving, handi-crafts, carpentry etc. The various places of the region are enriched with different kind of natural resources and hence the people of those various locations adapted their occupations according to the natural potentiality of their native area.

Uniqueness in Land Ownership Practice: In North East India, the existence of a widely varied customs and traditions of land ownership are found. For example, we can mention about the practice of community land. Community land is the land set apart by a tribe for use of its members without the right of private ownership. Community land is separated into residential areas meant for the settlement of families or individuals where houses were constructed, land lying in the vicinity of residential areas and is kept and used for public purposes; or land located at a farther distance from the residential areas and is meant for carrying out economic activities (Nongkynryh, 2008).

In connection with land ownership diversity we can refer to the Ukhrul district of the state of Manipur, where the *Thangkul* tribe is the majority in population. The village land of *Thangkul* is broadly divided into five categories: (i) *Khalung*—lands allocated for residential purposes; (ii) *Thingkam*—forest lands located in the vicinity of the residential areas;

(iii) *Masalam* or *Shalam* or *Shalui*—semi-private land is village land used for shifting cultivation; (iv) *Yaruilam*—public lands allocated for purpose of farming and shifting cultivation; and (v) *Terraced paddy fields*—this type of lands are private property and the owners of such plots of land can sell or dispose of them as they wish. However, the other tribes of the same area have different rules of land occupation.

From the briefly discussed social features of the region it is evident that the society in NER is heterogeneous, although belong to the same area and had a common history. However, with the passage of time and with modernization and liberalization, these features of traditional societies in NER are changing gradually.

Impact of the Social Heterogeneity in Politics of the Region

As the social system in NE India is not uniform, there are differences among people and in their viewpoints as well. These differences and heterogeneity in society has their impacts on the politics of the region. The division of greater Assam is a suitable example of it.

The impact of language on politics of NER can be cited as an example of the same. Establishment of Official Language Commission in 1956 and State Re-organization Act of 1956 were two important events to be mentioned. The recommendation of the State Re-organization Commission that state should be re-organized on the basis of language had influenced the people of the region as well as the polity. The demand for creation of new states on the basis of language by carving out the erstwhile greater Assam and fulfilment of those demands from time was clearly the impact of language on politics. Moreover, the decision to made *Assamese* as the official language of the state in the 1950s resented people of other communities speaking other languages. These communities were the *Garos, the Bodos, the Nagas, the Khasis, the Karbis, the Bengalis* etc. Mention may be made about agitations led by the *Bengalis* against making *Assamese* the official language of Assam by a resolution of the State Legislative Assembly in the line of Official Language Commission of 1956. The agitation resulted in huge loss of life and property. Many *Bengalis* even bound to leave the state. Incidents like looting, firing, *hartals*, strikes were frequently taking place in the state. In order to satisfy the Bengalis settled in Assam, Official Language Act was suitably amended in 1960 to pacify their feelings (Raj, 2004).

Moreover, like the other parts of the country, caste also influences the politics of the region. Caste politics is particularly evident in Assam. This is because of the exercise vote-bank politics of several leading parties of the country and till date they ably influenced the emotions of the people of certain castes as well as tribes. Political parties used to nominate candidates to a particular constituency keeping in mind the majority caste of that constituency.

Furthermore, the impact of heterogeneous society in NER on its politics can easily be judged from the 'inner-line system' in hill areas. This is recognition to the fact that the society in the hill areas of NER is different from other areas of the region and the country.

Tribal and Non-tribal Politics of the NE States

As no event in the human history is born out of vacuum, tribal and non-tribal politics of today has it root in the past. It is not a product of today, it was in a way is the product of colonial period as discussed earlier in this chapter. Its emergence can be traced back to the British imperialist policy called—*divide et imperia*. While up to the end of nineteenth century, attempts were made in Assam, like other parts of India, for integration of various ethnic communities through the process of *Sanskritization,* the British, with their Machiavellian level-headedness, started discouraging further *Sanskritization,* as they were aware of the fact that a colony can be best ruled if its people remain divided. Keeping in view their policy of divide and rule, they pursued a policy of segregation instead of ethnic assimilation. On recommendations from the Simon Commission they divided the tribal areas of Assam into 'excluded areas' and 'partially excluded areas' and thereby created tribal and non-tribal division. In the policy declaration it was mentioned that it was the primary duty of the administration to maintain the distinct entity of the tribes and educate them to stand on their own feet. Such a subtle policy of the imperialist helped them to keep the tribal people under their wing. On the other hand, they keep the tribal people away from the other developed neighbours which helped the tribal people to preserve their primitiveness more instead of development of the tribal people. Although this policy of segregation had achieved some success in respect of reducing conflicts, but on the negative side, the gap between the tribal and non-tribal was started to widened and thus provided the base for emergence of tribal and non-tribal politics.

As already mentioned that there are more than 200 tribal communities in NER and according to the Census of 2011, among them, there are as many as 23 numbers of tribal groups which are notified as Scheduled Tribes (STs). As there are a number of tribal groups, both hill and plain, here in this region, it is natural to have politics, contests, conflicts etc. between tribal groups or between a tribal group and government. But at present, tribal politics has reached its extreme position in NER because of violent displays, insurgent activities, *bandhs* etc. by tribal groups for achieving their ends. Tribal politics may either aim at securing Scheduled Tribe status for them under the Constitution of India or designed to achieve autonomy either within the Indian Union or outside. Sometimes, in the way of achieving their desired goals, they have to indulge in conflicts with others or may be with neighbouring tribes. For instance, here mention may be made about the *Naga* tribes. The demand for a separate independent *Greater Nagalim* is an outcome of tribal politics, more properly, hill tribal politics. However, we can trace back the emergence of this kind of *Naga* politics to the period of its reorganization as separate state within Indian Union because in 1963 the Indian government was ignorant about the widespread distribution of *Naga* population in NER. *Nagas* are not only the inhabitants of the state of Nagaland but also resides in Assam, Manipur and Arunachal Pradesh. In the interest of achieving goals such as *Greater Nagalim*, National Socialist Council of Nagaland (NSCN), an insurgent organization, was formed on January 31, 1980 by Isak Chisi Swu, Thuingaleng Muivah and S.S. Khaplang. Later during 1988, NSCN split into two fractions due to internal differences. The leadership of one fraction was given by Isak Chisi Swu and Thuingaleng Muivah and accordingly the group came to be known as NSCN(IM). The charge of other group or fraction was taken by S.S. Khaplang and this fraction renamed as NSCN (K).

This is just a single example of insurgency in connection with tribal politics. There are other insurgent groups in the region of NER having tribal politics as the base of their struggle. For example, the National Democratic Front of Bodoland (NDFB) of Assam and the United National Liberation Front (UNLF) of Manipur are such other example in this regard. In fact, Manipur is regarded as the breeding ground for militants because the small state has over 30, insurgent groups within its territory.

However, tribal as well as non-tribal politics is seen in different incarnation in different period of time in the post-independence period. Besides insurgency, tribal politics or we can say tribal and non-tribal politics is visible in the form of riots among indigenous communities or between indigenous communities and other recently settled communities. For example we can refer to the deadly riots of 2012 in Bodoland. This is riot between the Bodo, the indigenous tribal community of that region of Assam and the Bengali speaking Muslims. It was alleged that most of the Bengali speaking Muslim people were Bangladeshi immigrants. The riots were started on 20th July, 2012 and as on 8th August, 2012, 77 people had died in the riots and over 400,000 people were taking shelter in 270 relief camps, after being displaced 400 villages. The *Bodo* militants who were also involved in the riots blamed the continuous immigration from Bangladesh as the major cause behind the riots and demanded a separate state of *Bodoland* so that the identity of *Bodo* tribe can be secured from the non-tribals as well as from the immigrants. Thus, severity of tribal and non-tribal politics is evident from this incident. Moreover, the impact of this incident of riots between tribal and non-tribal politics was also reflected in the 2014 Lok Sabha election. The UPA Government which was in power during that time was receiving all-round criticism for its failure to prevent the massacre. The Bharatiya Janata Party exploited the issue well and even promised the All Bodo Student's Union that it will re-examine the demand for a separate state of *Bodoland*. Hence, it may be claimed that tribal and non-tribal politics of NER have its impact even at the national level.

Tribal and non-tribal politics is also evident in the form of demand to be recognized as Scheduled Tribe under the Constitution of India. It is well known that all tribal communities are not included in the Scheduled Tribe category. Therefore, those communities are continuously demanding the Scheduled Tribe status and even non-tribal communities are demanding the same. Moreover, some non-tribal communities are also demanding Scheduled Tribe status for securing more benefits for their respective community. For example, the *Koch Rajbongshi* community, a non-tribal community of Assam is demanding the Scheduled Tribe status. However, they claim that they belong to the indigenous tribes of Assam and possess all the characteristics to be recognized as a Scheduled Tribe. On the other hand, the Government of India (GOI) continuously rejected their demand by asserting that this community lost its tribal characteristics long ago (Roy, 2014). The general rule of the Central Government is that any community must fulfil the five specific criteria to be recognized as a Scheduled Tribe, viz. primitive traits, distinctive culture, geographical isolation, shyness of contact with community at large and backwardness.

The demand to be recognized as Scheduled Tribe by the *Koch Rajbongshis* was first raised long way back in 1968. However, they did not receive any success and its consequence in generating the feeling of frustration and deep sense of betrayal on part of *Koch Rajbongshi* people. Gradually this frustration led to the formation of demand to carve out a separate state of *Kamatapur*.

From the above detailed discussion, a general conclusion can be drawn that NER represents a mosaic of diverse people belonging to different tribes and communities and diverse geographical features. NER and its diversity can be compared with a 'salad bowl' where suppose the given *bowl* is NER and the different ingredients of the *salad* is its diversity in the form of various communities and tribes as well as various geographical features. In the given '*salad* bowl' the distinct character of each item is clearly visible, though the different ingredients are placed in a single bowl (Ngaihte, 2013: 13). Diversity, in fact, tells the totality of a set or system (*ibid.*).

MODEL QUESTIONS

1. What do you mean by Geo-Politics? Explain the Geo-Political features of North East India.
2. Make an attempt to highlight the heterogeneous character of North East region and its impact on the Politics.
3. Write a note an the relations between the Hills and Plains.
4. Explain the emergence of North East as a Region.
5. Discuss about the post-colonial development of Plains Tribes of Assam with special reference to the Bodos.
6. Explain the administrative changes brought about by the colonial Rulers.
7. Discuss the changes of Land Revenue System in Colonial Assam. What were its implications?
8. Discuss the new social groups of Colonial Assam. How did they contribute the demographic Composition of Assam?
9. Discuss the class structure of colonial Assam with special reference to the Assamese Middle Class.
10. Short Notes:
    a. Colonial Assam
    b. Yandaboo Pact
    c. Colonial Economy
    d. Assamese Middle Class

Unit-II
Politics of Autonomy in Assam

Politics of autonomy in Assam is a broad area of study. The area of political autonomy in Assam can be studied in relation to hill-plain politics as well as in close connection with tribal and non-tribal politics. Politics of autonomy in Assam is also inspired by the quest for identity by different indigenous groups of Assam. It has been alleged that hill-plains or tribal-non-tribal equation in Assam has never been stable (Chaube, 1999 256). The parties in conflict, viz. the hills and plains or the tribal and the non-tribal are complaining each other in the interest of gathering more benefit in the form autonomy.

Factors of Autonomy Movement

The autonomy movements by the tribal's in Assam are not the product of a single factor. It is, rather, an outcome of different factors. Some of the factors are social which is related with the indifferent attitude of upper caste Assamese people towards the tribals. Some of them are economic which include the overall economic backwardness of the tribals. Some of the factors such as emergence middle class, emergence of different political organization etc. are some political factors. After all, the autonomy movement combines different factors social, economic, political, cultural etc. The following is an attempt to highlight various factors of Autonomy Movement.

Historical Factor: Historical factor provides a subtle basis for the tribals of Assam to exert their pressure for autonomy. Historically, the tribals are the earliest community to migrate to this land. Therefore, tribals regarded themselves as the aborigin of Assam and the other communities have no right to prevent the tribals from getting autonomy. Such a justification was reflected in the letter written to the Sentinel in 1991 by an NDFB cadre, Làkhi Basumatary, who questioned the ULFA's legitimacy to demand for independent Assam. Basumatary was of opinion that the ULFA has no right to demand for independent state. For him the Assamese people have "illegally conquered" Assam and therefore, they do not have any right to exploit the tribal people Mr. Basumatary's justification no doubt, emanates from the history of migration of different races. Other tribals also think that they are the "Son of the Soil" and therefore, they must have the right to demand for autonomy.

1. Inhabitant Factor: Inhabitant pattern of the tribal people also contributes towards the emergence of autonomy movement among the tribals of Assam. A particular tribe whether may be the Bodo, Tiwa, Rabha, Mishing or such other tribals concentrated into a particular area. Such concentration of a particular tribe into a particular area helped the tribal people to articulate their grievances among themselves. Thus, the inhabitant pattern of the tribal communities of Assam provided them with an opportunity to mobilise the people for autonomy movement. If the tribal people would have scattered, instead of concentration, then it would have been difficult for them to mobilize the people of a particular community. Therefore, while exploring the factors of autonomy movement one should not leave the inhabitant factor.

2. Demonstrative Factor: Role of the demonstrative factor also cannot be ignored regarding the emergence of autonomy movement of Assam. The movement for autonomy, in fact, is a politics of "role model". It means when the tribal community starts their movement for autonomy, they are being inspired by other such movement for autonomy. Therefore, there is vast similarity regarding the demands, strategy and organizations of different autonomy movement. If for the Bodos the Assam movement is the "Reference movement" then the Bodos become relying point for other plain tribes. Therefore, once a movement for autonomy is succeeded or the demands forwarded by the movement is fulfilled then, other movement also inspired by or rather straight forward similar demanded for fulfilment. That is why all the tribal movement demands for autonomy under Sixth Schedule of the Constitution.

Sixth Schedule of the Constitution: The Sixth Schedule of the Constitution of India also responsible for the emergence of different tribal autonomy movements. During the time of framing of the Constitution the Sixth Schedule of the Constitution was framed to provide autonomy for the tribes of North-East. Gopinath Bordoloi, the first Prime Minister of Assam, was the champion of tribal autonomy under the Sixth Schedule of Constitution. But the plain tribes were not included under the provision of the Sixth Schedule. Therefore, in the post-independent period the plain tribes demanded for autonomy under the Sixth Schedule of the Constitution. Such demand was, for the first time, raised by the Bodos and later on by the other plain tribes of Assam like Tiwas, Rabhas, Mishings etc.

3. Emergence of a Pretty Middle Class in Tribal Societies: The tribal people are generally educationally and economically backward people. Therefore, it took time to the tribals to develop themselves educationally and economically. Gradually a section of tribal people educated themselves. They developed discontent over the backwardness of their own community. Therefore, they felt an urgent necessary of a mass movement for the upliftment of their own communities. They also realised that unless and until the tribals are provided with greater autonomy within a separate political arrangement, it would be difficult to upgrade the tribal people. This section of people came to contact with leaders of different movement, come to know about the political action, strategy for movement, and way of public mobilization and become the leaders of the movement. Thus a vigorous movement for autonomy came into existence.

4. Role of different Tribal Organizations: The plain tribes of Assam had their common political platform even in the pre-independent period. The formation of Plains Tribals League in 1933 was the first attempt in this regard. The Plains Tribal League raised the voices of the plain tribes particularly, regarding the protection of tribal land. However, the Plain Tribal League was not much concerned with the question of tribal autonomy. Therefore, another socio-cultural organization Tribal Sangha was formed in 1954. The question of tribal autonomy did not get much importance in the Tribal Sangha. It was, therefore, with the formation of Plains Tribal Council that the plain tribes developed their political assertion for separate statehood. Gradually almost all plain tribes have formed their separate political organization and started the movement for autonomy.

Economic Factor: Economically the tribal people are the backward people. Agriculture is still a primary sector for the tribals. But, there is no such remarkable effort on the part of the government to improve the agricultural sector. Lack of proper market mechanism, lack of proper and improved communication and transport system, slow processes of modernisation method of cultivation etc. are some major problems with the agriculture sector of Assam. As a result the agricultural based tribal people could not develop themselves. Mentioning about the seriousness of economic conditions of the tribal people, ABSU in its justification for "Why Separate State" has mentioned—"Tribals are suffering from serious economic crisis. Although the percentage of people below poverty line in national level is either 48 or 50, the percentage of tribal people below poverty line shall not be less than 10 per cent." It has also been mentioned "As such, the mode of living of tribal people is also below standard. Due to serious economic crisis, the education of tribal students has also been badly hampered".

Besides, there is also discrimination in the process of employment. There are as many as twenty four tribes and sub-tribes, but there are provisions for only 10 per cent of job reservation for the plain tribes. But very significantly the government does not take any measure to fulfil the vacancies reserved for the tribals. Thus, it can be said that lack of modernization of agricultural sector and low rate of employment of tribal youth, make the tribal people economically backward. Economic backwardness not only affects their economic life but also social, educational and the pattern of livelihood as a whole. But contrary to such deterious conditions of the tribals the government is not keen to adopt any such effort to upgrade the tribal people. Therefore, they lost their faith on the existing system of governance and demanded for a separate governmental mechanism with greater autonomy.

5. Land Problem: Alienation of tribal land is another problem which developed a frustration among the tribals. As the tribal societies are agriculture based, therefore, protection of tribal land is important for tribals. But very significantly the government not only failed to protect the tribal land from the encroachment of the non-tribals but government itself allotted the tribal lands for the purpose of development.

It is, here, deserved to be mentioned that the question of protection of tribal land is an age-old question. The demand for the protection of tribal land was raised even during the pre-independence period to protect the tribal land from the encroachment by the Muslim peasants from East Bengal. As a result the Line System was introduced under which the village were divided into three classes—

(a) Open villages: Where immigrants might settle freely;
(b) Closed villages: Where immigrants could not settle at all; and
(c) Mixed village: Where line was drawn and the immigrants could settle only one side of the line.

However, a substantive measure was taken to protect the tribal lands in 1947 by legislating the "Assam Land and Revenue Regulation, 1886". Under which provision was made to create tribal Belts and Blocks to protect tribal land. Accordingly various tribal Belts and Blocks were created to protect tribal land.

Although all these Belts and Blocks are there yet, encroachment of non-tribals takes place into these Belts and Blocks. In most cases the non-tribal people, by taking the advantage of economic weakness, try to buy the lands of tribal people in the protected areas. After all deprivation of the tribal people from their protected lands has created discontent among them and therefore, protection of tribal land becomes one of the important issues of autonomy movement.

8. Assamese Chauvinism: Chauvinistic attitude of mainstream Assamese people is also responsible for the emergence of different autonomy movements. As it was observed in ABSU's justification for "Why Separate State" that the "Assamese people have never accepted the tribals as a part and parcel of Assamese community and society in real sense, though they give a motivated slogan of "Greater Assamese Nationality". Interestingly, because of the chauvinistic attitude of the Assamese people some of plain tribes, who otherwise have been assimilated with Assamese culture, adopted Assamese language, demanded for revitalization of their own culture, customs, traditions, language etc.

The Assamese chauvinism was first reflected in two successive language movements—Official Language Movement (1960) and Language Movement for Medium of Instruction (1972). Both the movements created an apprehension regarding the intension of the Assamese people towards the linguistic minorities in general and the tribals in particular. The Assam Official Language Act, in fact, paved the way for disintegration of the Hill tribes. Similarly, declaration of Assamese as a medium of Instruction obstructed the tribal students who have done their matriculation in their respective languages for receiving college education. Apart from these, on 28 February, 1986, the Secondary Education Board of Assam published a circular under which Assamese language was made as compulsory third language in Assamese medium schools.

Apart from such linguistic chauvinism, the Assamese people, particularly the upper caste Hindus look down upon towards the tribals in their day-to-day social relations. So, if the Assamese do not think the tribals as the part of Greater Assamese Society and if the Assamese people try to establish their hegemony than what is wrong with the tribals to demand for separate political arrangement or to launch a movement for autonomy?

9. Consciousness of Identity and Self-determination: The plain tribes of Assam have their own culture, own tradition, own language and their own distinct way of celebration which altogether gives them a distinct identity. But under the process of assimilation some of the plain's tribes gradually adopted Assamese culture, language etc. This trend, however, did not continued for ever. Rather a reverse trend has started when most of the tribals become conscious about their distinct identity. They began to think that their identity would be submerged if they do not become conscious about their own identity. Thus, the consciousness for identity has started among the tribals and they started movement for the protection of their identity. Protection of their identity, in fact, becomes one of the subtle justification of the autonomy movements of the tribals.

The political philosophy of self-determination also induced the tribals to start autonomy movement. The issue of self-determination, in fact, a global issue. Not only in Assam but also in different parts of the world the movement of self-determination is going on. The UN meet of Indigenous people is the global forum for the movement of self-determination for the indigenous people. Some of tribal leaders, particularly the Bodo leaders attended the World Indigenous People Meet, and were greatly influenced by the ideology of self-determination. Therefore, they demanded for the self-determination of the tribal people of Assam.

10. Sense of Relative Deprivation: The sense of relative deprivation among the tribals also induced them to start autonomy movement. The tribals of Assam feel that they are being deprived of in the field of economic, educational, cultural, job opportunity and politics. They are not equal with the advanced Assamese people and therefore, to get rid of such deprivation there is need for autonomy for the tribals. This is how the sense of relative deprivation contributed towards the emergence of autonomy movement in Assam.

Forgoing discussion makes it clear that the autonomy movement is the product of different factors. Some of the factors ate objective and rational whereas some factors are subjective in nature. But, whatever may be their nature, the autonomy movement is the product of long days deprivation and backwardness of the tribal people in the field of economy, education, culture and politics.

State, Tribal Politics and Autonomy Movement

The state is regarded as the "legitimate power-structure of a given society". Therefore, being the legitimate power structure, it is expected that, state should come forward to resolve the conflict produced by the sub-systems within a political system or should redress the grievances of various sub-systems. As regards India, in the post-independent period the Indian state was committed to the process of nation building. The basic principle adopted for such purpose was "unity in diversity". Therefore, the state tried to accommodate all distinct social groups within its ambit. However, the state did not hesitate to emerge as a "Coercive apparatus', if the situation demands so. Since independence, therefore, two strict rules have been followed in all dealings with dissident domestic, ethnic, religious, linguistic and cultural groups demands (Brass, 1999:3).

Firstly, the state will not entertain and that any group which takes up a secessionist stance will, while it is weak, be ignored and treated as illegitimate, but, should it develop significant strength, be smashed, with armed force if necessary.

Secondly, there was prohibition against the concession of demands for any form of political recognition of a religious community. Muslims, Sikhs and other religious minorities are free to presence their own personal law, to practice their religion as they see fit, to seek protection for their language and culture, but not to demand either a separate electorates or any form of proportional representation in elected or appointed government bodies.

Thus, in the initial years, the Indian state was strictly committed towards the maintenance of unity and integrity of the nation and therefore, it did not allowed any social group to develop much of strength, which can pause a challenge towards the unity, integrity, and sovereignty of the nation. The state, therefore, did not hesitate to use its "Coercive force" to attain the objective.

However, with the passage of time the state realised the failure of the coercive approach. Because, in spite of state repression, the movements by different groups at different parts of the country continued to exist. Therefore, the state liberalized its approach towards such social groups. The liberalization of the state attitude reflected in the form of re-organisation of states and de-centralisation of financial relation through which the federating units were given greater financial autonomy as it was realised that uneven economic development is the basic cause behind the assertions of such social groups. The state, at the same time, however, continued its coercive approach too. Parallel continuity of coercive as well as liable policy by the state is regarded as "Stick and carrot" policy.

The state's attitude towards the autonomy movements of North East was also the same. In the post-independent period it seemed that the all-Indian leaders were not much concerned about the emerging tribal assertion except Nehru. The whole issue was, therefore, regarded as law and order problem. However, when the secessionist movement used to consolidate, the Indian State used its coercive approach. But, coercive approach of the Indian state did not yield any lasting solution. As a result the Indian state adopted its liberal policy by creating separate states.

While speaking about the attitude of State, an attention is needed to pay on the role of state at periphery level. That is the attitude of Assam Government. In the post-colonial period, the Assam Government dominated by the mainstream Assamese leaders. Therefore, instead of looking the tribal questions genuinely the Assamese leaders, by dint of their dominance in the state government, tried to establish their hegemony over the other minorities. Reflection of such attitudes of the Assam Government reflected in the Official Language Act. Thus, the Assam Government became a platform to show the Chauvinism of the Assamese-speaking people. Even some of the Assamese leaders were not in favour towards the tribal autonomy under the Sixth Schedule of the Constitution and debated against tribal autonomy in the Constituent Assembly Debate. The Assamese chauvinism later on, leads to the creation of separate statehood for the tribals. The state's reluctantness towards the tribal question also reflected in the case of the plain tribes. Because the state did not showed any grave concern over the demands of the plain tribals. It was only in 1993 that the Bodoland Autonomous Council was created. But the formation of BAC was not a lasting solution towards the Bodo problem.

Case was same with other tribals like Tiwas, Rabhas and Mishings when they were given with Autonomous Council in 1995 what they call as "puppet Autonomy". The creation of Bodoland Territorial Council (BTC) seems that the government both at the central as well as state level are realizing the grievances of plains tribes. However, nothing can be predicted right at the movement.

Moreover, the politics of autonomy in Assam can also be understood by approaching the trend of regionalism, sub-regionalism, politics of discrimination, insurgency etc. in the state of Assam. From the discussions in the previous unit it, may be argued that the erstwhile Greater Assam is the mother of the present North Eastern Region (NER). As already mentioned in the Unit I that Nagaland was carved out of Assam in 1963; Meghalaya was carved out in the year 1972; Mizoram was carved out from Assam as a Union Territory in 1972 and got statehood in 1987; and Arunachal Pradesh (then known as North East Frontier Agency by 1954), like Mizoram, was also made a Union Territory carved out of Assam in the year 1972 and then, a full-fledged state in February 1987. The creation of these states by carving out Assam was in a direct or indirect way, the product of politics of autonomy existed in the then Assam. But even after creation of a number of new states, politics of autonomy still existed in Assam. The state is still suffering from new demands of autonomy from various section of greater Assamese community. For instance, the increasing demands of the Bodo people for a separate state of *Bodoland* can be mentioned here. In order to pacify such demands, the government has given the status of Autonomous Council to the four Bodo inhabiting districts of Assam, viz. Kokrajhar, Chirang, Udalguri and Baksa.

Another example is the Karbi Anglong Autonomous Council. More and more Autonomous Councils are increasing in Assam which will be broadly discussed in the section titled *Sub-regionalism*.

Regionalism and Sub-Regionalism

Regionalism is an unavoidable issue in Indian Politics as it has heavy weights on it. It is not only today, but even before independence; regionalism was used as a tool by the British imperialist to promote their policy of keeping India divided (Raj, 2004: 28). The Britishers generally used regionalism as a tool of deliberate encouragement so that the unity could not develop. They compelled the native people of the different parts of the dominion to think in terms of their own region than that of united Indian nation. During that period, people used to hate people of other regions and love their own soil as they were the son of that particular soil.

In the post-independence period, huge efforts were made to unite the people of India as a whole. Leaders like Sardar Ballabh Bhai Patel played an instrumental role in this regard. Constitutional attempts were also made by adopting a single constitution for the whole country with a unified judiciary. Single citizenship is also provided instead of double citizenship, as practiced in federal country like United States of America. Attempts were also made to reorganize the states on the basis of language. The Tamils were the pioneers in advocating for state based on language.

But even after such attempts regionalism thrives in India with a heavy weight. The allegation of discrimination of various states as well as various regions by the Central Government is an apparent evident of it. The rising demands for creation of separate independent country, creation of more states within the country, regional autonomy etc. are the outcome of existing strong regional sentiments. Regionalism is proved to be a big hindrance in the way of having a strong united Indian nation. But, at the same time it can be argued that it is becoming a strong instrument for the underdeveloped and neglected regions of the country to get their demand fulfilled.

Meaning of Regionalism

Regionalism is an ideology and political movement that tries to advance the causes of the regions. To understand the meaning of regionalism, it is necessary to clarify at the outset that there are two different kinds of regionalism, viz. regionalism at the international level and regionalism at the national level. At the international level, regionalism refers to transnational cooperation to achieve a common goal or resolved a shared problem or it refers to a group of countries, such as Western Europe, the Western Balkans, or Southeast Asia, that are linked by geography, history or economic features (Gochhayat, 2014: 10). On the other hand, at the national level, it refers to a territory, i.e. located within or sometimes across the borders of a nation state. At this level different kinds of regions may be distinguished: Political regions, which usually possess some form of elected regional government; Administrative regions, which are geographical entities created for the purpose of administering a service such as a health region or a electricity region; Geographical region which refer to geographical feature, such as mountain regions, island regions, coastal or maritime regions; and finally, economic regions such as agricultural, industrial or declining industrial regions (*Ibid.*).

According to **Seligment and Johnson**, "*Regionalism is a movement to any exaggerated or oppressive from of Centralization*".

Kausar J. Azam defines Regionalism as a subsidiary process of political integration in India. It is a manifestation of those residual elements which do not find expression in the national polity and national culture and being excluded from the centrality of the new polity express themselves in political discontent and political exclusionism. It could force that gravitational or the centripetal forces of a society fail to absorb assimilate and internalize.

Regionalism broadly means articulation of demand for the development of a particular socio-cultural homogenous sub-area having distinct pattern of economic life or ecological personality which results either in the demand for Separate State or Greater State Autonomy.

According to **Achin Banaik**, Regionalism in India is again two-dimension—one relates to existing state as well as inter-state combination whose target is Centre, the other relates to sub-phenomena with ethnic groups as the main actor where state rather than Central Government is the point of reference.

Regionalism can be regarded as a regional loyalty of the people of a particular region towards their narrow identity problems. When the people of a particular region develop their consciousness about their regional problems and thereafter start assertion for the solution of such problems, then it can be regarded as regionalism. Regionalism, generally is the product of the existence of a strong centre in a federation. When in a federation the Central Government becomes more powerful and gives minimum autonomy to the federating units, then the federating units start their movement for greater autonomy. Since, such a movement occurs in a particular region, hence, such movement is regarded as regional movement.

However, it is not easy to define the concept 'regionalism.' As Professor B. Pakem observes, "... regionalism is a noble concept. It is a multi-dimensional phenomena in terms of its components, at once, geographical, historical, cultural, economic, political, administrative and psychic. It has both positive and negative dimensions. The former embodies a quest for self-fulfilment on the part of a people of an area, and later reflects a psyche of relative deprivation on the part of the people of the area not always viable in terms of a national economic analysis let alone prove to rationalization" (Pakem, 1993: 9-10). Pakem's understanding on regionalism implies that regionalism is the product of the self-consciousness of the people of a particular area who feel themselves as being relatively deprived of. The geographical, historical, cultural, economic etc. factors as Pakem believes may contribute towards the emergence of such regional self-consciousness. Some other definitions of regionalism can be straight forwarded in order to understand the concept comprehensively.

In speaking about Indian regionalism Bipin Chandra says, "Defending the federal features of the Constitution is also not to be seen as regionalism. The demand for a separate state within the Indian Union or for an autonomous region within an existing state, or for devolution of power below the state level, or for devolution to on several practical grounds, but not as regionalist, unless it is put forward in a spirit of hostility to the rest of the population of a state. If the interests of one region or state are asserted against the country as a whole or against another region or state in a hostile manner and a conflict is promoted on the basis of such alleged interests, it can be dubbed as regionalism" (Chandra: 2000: 119-120).

The above mentioned definitions provide the meaning of the term regionalism. Nevertheless to contextualize the term regionalism in India it can be said that regionalism is a two dimensional assertion—both subjective and objective. The subjective dimension of regionalism indicates any short of regional assertion which try to protect and promote subjective identities such as caste, language ethnicity, community etc. Thus, the language movement, the caste movement, the ethnic movement etc. are some subjective regional movements. On the other hand, objective dimension of regionalism indicates any objective assertion which tries to protect and promote subjective identities such as greater autonomy, better communication, industrialization etc. These are some issues, which, if once fulfilled, than it will benefit not only to a particular caste, community, language or ethnic group but also all the people of that respective region. However, it is not necessary that a regional movement always will be exclusively subjective or objective. Sometimes, a regional movement may comprise both subjective and objective assertions either in hidden or in manifested form.

Regionalism, broadly means "articulation of demands for the development of a parlicular socio-culture homogenous sub-area having a distinct pattern of economic life or ecalogical personality which results either in the demands for seperate state or greater state autonomy.

To define the term regionalism, it can be said that regionalism can be understood in two senses, i.e. positive and negative. In the positive sense it is the spontaneous love of the people for their own region to which they belong. For example, the inhabitants of Assam love their culture, language etc. and like to see the progress of the same. This natural sentiment and there is nothing unusual about it. In the positive sense we can also include such demands of various states and regions which are against excessive centralism. These positive demands are helpful for the goals of decentralization.

On the other hand, in the negative sense, regionalism implies those demands which are dangerous for national interest and its integration. In other words, this kind of regional demands which are guided by motive of fulfilling the interest of a particular region over and above the interest of the whole country and may be at the cost of other regions.

Regionalism is different from Nationalism. Nationalism subordinates regional or sectional loyalties to the regionalism, whereas in the case of regionalism local or regional loyalties are given precedence over national interests.

Characteristics of Politics of Regionalism

1. A Product of Diversities: India is a land full of diversities. Indians have varied cultures and a number of languages. They observe different customs. Their socio-economic development also varies from state to state and even from one part of a state to the other. Even after the redrawing of maps of the states on the linguistic basis, some areas of certain states are keen for their regional autonomy.

It has resulted in series of agitations for furthering their individual regional interests. A mention may be made of Assam Agitation in Assam which was fought for regional interest.

2. Linguistic Attachment: Linguistic attachment constitutes another salient factor in this regard. The report of Das Commission in 1948 which opposed the creation of the states on the language basis earned appreciation at the hands of Indian National Congress. But soon after the top leaders of the Congress—Sardar Patel and J.L. Nehru endorsed the creation of Telugu speaking state. There was a strong agitation in Madras and the eventual inception of Andhra state in 1953. It opened the Pandora Box. Linguistic groups all over India started to demand reorganization of states on the basis of language. It had also inspired the regional sentiments in Assam. But, like the rest of the country the linguistic principle couldn't be applied for Assam, particularly for the then Assam, mainly because of the existence of a large number of linguistic communities. The Assamese-Bengali riots of 1950s can be cited as a significant reference here.

3. Economic Disparities: Economic disparities among the states of India, resulting in injustice to a certain part of the state aggravates discontent among the people and resentment begins. The protection of interests of Maharashtrians was led by Shiv Sena (formed in 1967) to agitate against the non-Maharashtrians. Later the All Assam Students Union and All Assam Gana Sangram Parishad did the same in Assam to safeguard the interests of the original Assamese. The safeguarding of the interests of the sons of the soil as apparent in the move for separate Telangana state out of Andhra Pradesh, has become an essential ingredient of the politics of regionalism.

4. Rise Against Continuous Social Injustice: Social injustice with a section of people in a part of state compels them to forge a united front and struggle for social equality and social justice. The tribals of Bihar, Orissa and Madhya Pradesh voiced their sentiments for a separate Jharkhand state as they were conscious of social injustices and poor economic plight. Likewise people of Meghalaya and agitationists in Uttarakhand could not stand social inequalities and injustices and fought for separate states. The Gorkhas of Darjeeling ask for Gorkhaland and Bodos of Assam demand Bodoland.

5. Political Aspirations: Regional leaders seek to gain better positions in political hierarchy if they manage to get carved a separate state for catering to their interest. Regionalism is a useful instrument in fulfilment for the same. A minority in bigger state may become a majority in a newly created smaller state. The agitations in Punjab for Punjab Suba and Nagaland in the state of Assam and Gorkhas asking for inclusion of Nepali in VIII Schedule with an eye on Gorkhaland were relevant examples in this regard.

6. Violent and Non-Violent Struggles: Struggles are part and parcel of regionalism. Regional struggles were both violent and amicable in nature. Generally both amicable and violent ways were adopted for fulfilment of same regional interest. For example, Assam agitation was a peaceful regional movement for development of Assam. On the other hand, there are insurgent groups, like United Liberation Front of Assam (ULFA), who claim that regional development of Assam is possible only through violent insurgent activities against the state. For regional development, various regional organizations such as student organizations, regional farmer organizations, regional political parties, insurgent groups etc. play their own card in their own approach.

Regionalism and Assam

Regional sentiments in Assam had its root in the pre-independent period. The Britishers once imposed the Bengali language as Court Language which contributed towards the linguistic consciousness of the Assamese people. The conscious section of Assam couldn't accept the neglect of Assamese language. They feel that Assamese needs recognition like other Indian languages and should not be made a sub-language of a language like Bengali. It has to be mentioned here that Assamese is one of the oldest Indian languages with having their own script. For instance, Madhab Kandali of Assam had written the Ramayana in Assamese language 100 to 150 years before it was written in Indian languages like Hindi, Bengali, Odiya etc. (The fact is quoted from the inaugural speech of Ledo Adhibeshon of Assam Sahitya Sabha, 2012 delivered by Shri Janaki Ballabh Patnaik, the honourable Ex-Governor of Assam). In fact, Assamese can claim of having the oldest Ramayana in their own script in North-India, which no other North-Indian modern language can claim. Thus, when the Bengali was made the Court Language of Assam, people like Ananda Ram Dhekial Phukan, Ambikagiri Rai Choudhury, Maniram Dewan etc. well aware of the above facts, couldn't tolerate it and advocated the language based sub-nationalism. Organizations like *Asom Bhasa Unnati Sadhini Sabha*, *Asom Sahitya Sabha* also played an important role in promoting linguistic consciousness among the Assamese people.

Sub-regionalism

Sub-regionalism can be found within regionalism. Sub-Regionalism is a part of greater regionalism. In broad sense the people of a state is greater regionalism. For instance, Assamese regionalism is an example of sub-regionalism. Because in comparison to India Assamese is a sub-regionalism. But within Assam ethnic groups like Karbis, Bodos and Missing etc. are the glaring example of sub-regionalism. Hence sub-regionalism is nothing but an integral part of greater regionalism.

Regionalism is usually an issue between the centre and the state. Similarly, sub-regionalism is an important issue within a particular state. Sub-regionalism can be better understood in connection with regionalism or by understanding the academic implication of regionalism. In fact, 'Regionalism', to give an academic label, has come in different forms and been accompanied by varying degrees of violence. The first and most legitimate kind of regionalism has demanded a separate space or state of one's own, withal a space or state resting securely within the Union of India. This variety of regionalism was pioneered by the Telugu-speaking residents of the erstwhile Madras Presidency. The forms of protest it used were attacks on state property, and the hunger-fast, most definitively in the case of Potti Sriramulu, who in 1952 died after not eating for fifty-two days, his death leading in the short-term to the creation of the state of Andhra Pradesh and in the long-term to the wholesale redrawing of the map of India on linguistic lines (Guha).

This beginning of linguistic regionalism was based on the allegation that the Central Government was a captive of North Indian Hindi speaking interest. Consequently, it gave birth to a number of regional political parties, viz. Dravida Munnetra Kazhagam, Akali Dal in Punjab, Telugu Desam Party in Andhra Pradesh, Asom Gana Parishad in Assam etc. But even after creation of a number of regional political parties as well as redrawing of the map of India in linguistic line, a huge number of people in different corners of the country remained dissatisfied. It is known to all that there are number of languages as well as communities in different states of India. The attempt of creating states in India on the basis of a single language, usually the mainstream one, has generated a sense of discrimination in the minds of people belonging to existing peripheral languages and communities. This sense of discrimination can be regarded as sub-regionalism in academics. Sub-regionalism may also be regarded as a product of the success of regionalism which acts as a motivating factor for it. In some situation, it is a product of discrimination by the mainstream communities to the peripheral communities of a region. While in some other situation, it may not be understood in terms of region. Efforts for fulfilment of the interest of some specific section of people may also result in emergence of sub-regionalism. For instance, the formation of student unions by different communities like *Kalitas, Koivarttas, Ahoms*, *Bodos* etc., instead of the fact that there is already a regional student union in Assam viz. All Assam, Students Union (AASU) may be regarded as a product of sub-regionalism sentiment.

Demand for Autonomous State and The Sixth Schedule

Demand for autonomous state or district and the Sixth Schedule of the Constitution of India is the product of the wide diversity and heterogeneous characteristics as well as tribal and ethnic mosaic of the North Eastern region of India. The diversity of culture, tradition, language etc. also simultaneously contributes into the creation of different interests among various tribal and ethnic groups. It can be traced back to the immediate post-independence period. The historical connectedness of the region was systematically undermined by the colonial policies of progressive segregation (Upadhyay, 2006: 4993). During 1874 to 1934, the tribal populations in the region were administered under a succession of extraordinary provisions that segregated them into category called "non-regulated", "backward" or excluded areas (*ibid.*). Moreover, the Inner Line Regulation of 1873 (discussed earlier also) prohibit all "outsiders" to enter the hill areas of the then Assam, except those who obtained special permissions from the government. The overall effect was that these areas were remained excluded from the general pattern of administration that prevailed in the rest of the country. Accordingly, the Government of India Act, 1935 kept most of the hill areas of the region in the "excluded" category and made them independent of the provincial legislature. The overriding effects of the policy were twofold, viz. (a) the possibility of a process of integration of the communities and tribes without their willingness, which could be initiated by a common alien administration, was lost; and (b) most of the tribal communities of the region remained alien to the general style of national administration.

The result of all these was that the region which was a mass heterogeneous people before the advent of the British rule, remained basically the same one. The magnitude of ethnic diversity of NER, the colonial legacy of exclusion and seclusion in certain areas had manifold effects in the immediate period of independence such as insurgency, ethnic conflicts and so on. Another contribution of all these made the minority tribes of NER or undivided Assam conscious about their interests and identity. These minority communities began to demand for autonomy and separate homeland from time to time. One of the responses of the Indian state, to the demands of autonomy and separate homelands by different ethnic groups, was the creation of autonomous districts and autonomous regions within the districts often identified with particular tribes, through the constitutional mechanism of the Sixth Schedule (*ibid.*). Therefore, the study of demand for autonomy in NER and the Sixth Schedule is inter-related and should be studied in close connection.

At present, it can be said that grant of political autonomy and statehood is an interesting part of administration and governance in North East India. Currently, there are ten autonomous district councils in NER which are as follows:

Assam

- Bodoland Territorial Council.
- Karbi Anglong Autonomous Council.
- Dima Hasao Autonomous District Council.

Meghalaya

- Garo Hills Autonomous District Council.
- Jaintia Hills Autonomous District Council.
- Khasi Hills Autonomous District Council.

Tripura

- Tripura Tribal Areas Autonomous District Council.

Mizoram

- Chakma Autonomous District Council.
- Lai Autonomous District Council.
- Mara Autonomous District Council.

A Brief Background of the Sixth Schedule

However, these autonomous district councils, which are in a way unique in their existence, are not created in a single day. In fact, the process of uniqueness in administration of NER goes back to the British era when the Interim Government of India had appointed four sub-committees to the Constituent Assembly and the most important to mention about was 'North East Frontier (Assam) Tribal and Excluded Areas Committee' (NEFTEAC) under the Chairmanship of first Assam Chief Minister, Gopinath Bordoloi. The chief objective behind appointing the sub-committee was to study the peculiar conditions of North Eastern Region and its people so that to make necessary arrangements for administration in NER through the Constitution of India. During the period of British Colonialism there were five hill districts, viz. Naga Hills dominated by the *Nagas*, Garo Hills dominated by the *Garos*, United Khasi and Jaintia Hills dominated by *Khasis* and *Jaintias*, Lusai Hills dominated by the *Mizos*, and United Mikir and North Cachar Hill dominated by the *Karbis*. These regions and their tribes had their unique style of society where they are self dependent and produced all their necessary requirements. As already mentioned in the previous unit that these hill peoples were independent from the general administration of the British and separated from the plain people by demarcating the inner line. Thus they used to enjoy an isolated life from the people of British India and lived nearly a primitive life.

It has to be mentioned here that prior to the appointment of NEFTEAC under the chairmanship of Gopinath Bordoloi, the Cabinet Mission was came to Assam in 1946 to find out ways to protect the rights and interests of religious minority communities and tribes. After observing the situation the Mission recommended the Constituent Assembly to set up an Advisory

Committee for further research and recommendations. Accordingly the Constituent Assembly set up an Advisory Committee, viz. 'Fundamental Rights of the Minorities and Tribals and Excluded Areas' under chairmanship of Sardar Ballabh Bhai Patel. It was only after that the NEFTEAC was set up along with other three sub-committees by this Advisory Committee of Sardar Ballabh Bhai Patel. The NEFTEAC was also come to be known as 'Bordoloi Sub-Committee'. The other members of this committee were A.V. Thakkar, Rupnath Brahma, J.J.M. Nicholas Roy and Mayang Nokcha. Mayang Nokcha replaces Aliba Imti, the previous member who was from Naga Hills.

The Bordoloi Committee, in course of its study and visit received support from various tribes of this area and helped them in preparing the recommendations to be sent to the Advisory Committee of the Constituent Assembly. Various representatives from various tribes in form of individual and public organization accompanied them and forwarded reasonable demands and valuable recommendations to them. The committee was assisted by Dr. Guha who was a well known anthropologist of that time. He was of the opinion that these tribes, who had an unique life style and society should not be assimilated with other people of the plain as it might result in break-up of the existing tribal institutions. He also argued that efforts should be made in the evolution of the old institutions and this evolution should come from the tribe itself. However, he also supported the need of contact with the outside world but it should be minimal and should not lead to destruction of the uniqueness of tribes. The Bordoloi Committee welcomed the views of Dr. Guha and later on, in the recommendations of the committee the views of Guha were taken care of.

As a huge number of ethnic groups live here in North East India and majority of them individually can be categorized as a minority group. In this situation, the sub-committee observed that that every ethnic group in NER is conscious of their identity and want to protect the interest of their respective group. Unlike other parts of India, the consciousness of ethnic or tribal identity among the people of NER is significantly high due to some historical factors of the colonial period. The British policy of excluding various "primitive" tribes in NER, particularly those from the *Naga* Hills and the *Abors* of the North East Frontier Agency (present Arunachal Pradesh) whom they found particularly belligerent, had kept the tribes out of the purview of any kind of administration. Moreover, the hill-plain divide created through the Inner Line System, Scheduled Districts Act, Frontier Tract Regulation Act etc. of British period clearly work as motivating factor in building ethnic consciousness among various hill and plain tribes. Thus, during the immediate period of independence, tribes such as the *Nagas* desired to form a separate independent country outside India/Assam. The Naga Nationalist Struggle, at that time, based on the perspective that *Nagas* were never part of India and advocated that yes the *Nagas* were defeated by the British forces and their territory was occupied, but never defeated by India (Prabhakara, 2007). Similar situation was also there in Tripura and Manipur. Thus to satisfy ethnic groups like that of the *Nagas*, the sub-committee had to recommend some extent of autonomy in administration of the tribal areas of Assam.

It is realized that the hill tribes of North East India needed protection and safeguards so that they might preserve their way of life and at the same time participate in the political life of the country. The committee recommended that the hill people should have full power of administrating their own social laws as well as in codifying and modifying them.

Accordingly, the question of adding the Sixth Schedule to the Constitution of India was raised with the objective to ensure that the rights of tribal's who are minorities within a state or geographical area populated by a dominant non-tribal population. The idea of Sixth Schedule was first argued by JJM Nicholas Roy, a *Khasi* from undivided Assam. At that time, he had a vision for his people and other tribes of the region. Nicholas Roy stood his ground amidst the stiff opposition from very senior and learned parliamentarians during the Constituent Assembly debates on the Sixth Schedule. Credit goes to him for he succeeded in persuading parliamentarians of the whole country to support his cause. He is very rightly regarded as an architect of the District Council Autonomy.

One cannot ignore the fact that many tribes who came under the larger rubric of Assam felt suppressed by the authoritative nature of the dominant Assamese caste Hindu rulers, during and before British colonialism. They failed to act as an impartial ruler of all communities and tribes and hence, failed to display the magnanimity expected from them. At the time of drafting of Indian Constitution, all these facts and situations as well as the view points of various people were considered and accordingly, the parliamentarians from across the country were divided into two groups regarding inclusion of Sixth Schedule in the Constitution.

Stiff opposition to the inclusion of Sixth Schedule was forwarded by Parliamentarians like Rohini Kumar Choudhury from Assam and B. Des, one of the members of Constituent Assembly. However, several other members of the Constituent Assembly seemed convinced by Nicholas Roy's arguments that the tribals might be further alienated unless special provisions were made for their development at a pace they understood and could participate in. Finally, the Sixth Schedule was included in the

Constitution mainly because of the passionate articulation of Nicholas Roy and other likeminded members.

The Sixth Schedule was aimed at granting some kind of autonomy to the tribes so that they could be guided by their customary laws and practices. The tribes should not be pushed to conform to a modern system of governance where they might not be able to negotiate their own political space and to grow according to their own genius.

The Sixth Schedule

The Sixth Schedule of the Constitution of India reads as follows:

SIXTH SCHEDULE [ARTICLES 244 (2) AND 275 (1)]

Provisions as to the Administration of Tribal Areas in [the States of Assam, Meghalaya, Tripura and Mizoram]

1. Autonomous districts and autonomous regions.—

(1) Subject to the provisions of this paragraph, the tribal areas in each item of [[Parts I, II and IIA] and in Part III] of the table appended to paragraph 20 of this Schedule shall be an autonomous district.

(2) If there are different Scheduled Tribes in an autonomous district, the Governor may, by public notification, divide the area or areas inhabited by them into autonomous regions.

(3) The Governor may, by public notification,—

(a) Include any area in [any of the Parts] of the said table,

(b) Exclude any area from – [any of the Parts] of the said table,

(c) Create a new autonomous district,

(d) Increase the area of any autonomous district,

(e) Diminish the area of any autonomous district,

(f) unite two or more autonomous districts or parts thereof so as to form one autonomous district, – [(ff) alter the name of any autonomous district,]

(g) Define the boundaries of any autonomous district:

Provided that no order shall be made by the Governor under clauses (c), (d), (e) and (f) of this sub-paragraph except after consideration of the report of a Commission appointed under sub-paragraph (1) of paragraph 14 of this Schedule:

[Provided further that any order made by the Governor under this sub-paragraph may contain such incidental and consequential provisions (including any amendment of paragraph 20 and of any item in any of the Parts of the said table) as appear to the Governor to be necessary for giving effect to the provisions of the order.]

2. Constitution of District Councils and Regional Councils.—

(1) There shall be a District Council for each autonomous district consisting of not more than thirty members, of whom not more than four persons shall be nominated by the Governor and the rest shall be elected on the basis of adult suffrage.

(2) There shall be a separate Regional Council for each area constituted an autonomous region under sub-paragraph (2) of paragraph 1 of this Schedule.

(3) Each District Council and each Regional Council shall be a body corporate by the name respectively of "the District Council of (name of district)" and "the Regional Council of (name of region)", shall have perpetual succession and a common seal and shall by the said name sue and be sued.

(4) Subject to the provisions of this Schedule, the administration of an autonomous district shall, in so far as it is not vested under this Schedule in any Regional Council within such district, be vested in the District Council for such district and the administration of an autonomous region shall be vested in the Regional Council for such region.

(5) In an autonomous district with Regional Councils, the District Council shall have only such powers with respect to the areas under the authority of the Regional Council as may be delegated to it by the Regional Council in addition to the powers conferred on it by this Schedule with respect to such areas.

(6) The Governor shall make rules for the first constitution of District Councils and Regional Councils in consultation with the existing tribal Councils or other representative tribal organisations within the autonomous districts or regions concerned, and such rules shall provide for—

(a) the composition of the District Councils and Regional Councils and the allocation of seats therein;

(b) the delimitation of territorial constituencies for the purpose of elections to those Councils;

(c) the qualifications for voting at such elections and the preparation of electoral rolls therefore;

(d) the qualifications for being elected at such elections as members of such Councils;

(e) the term of office of members of [Regional Councils];

(f) any other matter relating to or connected with elections or nominations to such Councils;

(g) the procedure and the conduct of business [(including the power to act notwithstanding any vacancy)] in the District and Regional Councils;

(h) the appointment of officers and staff of the District and Regional Councils.

[(6A) The elected members of the District Council shall hold office for a term of five years from the date appointed for the first meeting of the Council after the general elections to the Council, unless the District Council is sooner dissolved under paragraph 16 and a nominated member shall hold office at the pleasure of the Governor:

Provided that the said period of five years may, while a Proclamation of Emergency is in operation or if circumstances exist which, in the opinion of the Governor, render the holding of elections impracticable, be extended by the Governor for a period not exceeding one year at a time and in any case where a Proclamation of Emergency is in operation not extending beyond a period of six months after the Proclamation has ceased to operate:

Provided further that a member elected to fill a casual vacancy shall hold office only for the remainder of the term of office of the member whom he replaces.]

(7) The District or the Regional Council may after its first constitution make rules [with the approval of the Governor] with regard to the matters specified in sub-paragraph (6) of this paragraph and may also make rules [with like approval] regulating—

the formation of subordinate local Councils or Boards and their procedure and the conduct of their business; and

generally all matters relating to the transaction of business

pertaining to the administration of the district or region, as the case may be:

Provided that until rules are made by the District or the Regional Council under this sub-paragraph the rules made by the Governor under sub-paragraph (6) of this paragraph shall have effect in respect of elections to, the officers and staff of, and the procedure and the conduct of business in, each such Council.

3. Powers of the District Councils and Regional Councils to make laws.—

(1) The Regional Council for an autonomous region in respect of all areas within such region and the District Council for an autonomous district in respect of all areas within the district except those which are under the authority of Regional Councils, if any,

within the district shall have power to make laws with respect to-

(a) the allotment, occupation or use, or the setting apart, of land, other than any land which is a reserved forest for the purposes of agriculture or grazing or for residential or other non-agricultural purposes or for any other purpose likely to promote the interests of the inhabitants of any village or town: Provided that nothing in such laws shall prevent the compulsory acquisition of any land, whether occupied or unoccupied, for public purposes [by the Government of the State concerned] in accordance with the law for the time being in force authorizing such acquisition;

(b) the management of any forest not being a reserved forest;

(c) the use of any canal or water-course for the purpose of agriculture;

(d) the regulation of the practice of jhum or other forms of shifting cultivation;

(e) the establishment of village or town committees or councils and their powers;

(f) any other matter relating to village or town administration, including village or town police and public health and sanitation;

(g) the appointment or succession of Chiefs or Headmen;

(h) the inheritance of property;

(i) marriage and divorce;

(j) social customs.

(2) In this paragraph, a "reserved forest" means any area which is a reserved forest under the Assam Forest Regulation, 1891, or under any other law for the time being in force in the area in question.

(3) All laws made under this paragraph shall be submitted forthwith to the Governor and, until assented to by him, shall have no effect.

4. Administration of justice in autonomous districts and autonomous regions.—

(1) The Regional Council for an autonomous region in respect of areas within such region and the District Council for an autonomous district in respect of areas within the district other than those which are under the authority of the Regional Councils, if any, within the district may constitute village councils or courts for the trial of suits and cases between the parties all of whom belong to Scheduled Tribes within such areas, other than suits and cases to which the provisons of sub-paragraph (1) of paragraph 5 of this

Schedule apply, to the exclusion of any court in the State, and may appoint suitable persons to be members of such village councils or presiding officers of such courts, and may also appoint such officers as may be necessary for the administration of the laws made under paragraph 3 of this Schedule.

(2) Notwithstanding anything in this Constitution, the Regional Council for an autonomous region or any court constituted in that behalf by the Regional Council or, if in respect of any area within an autonomous district there is no Regional Council, the District Council for such district, or any court constituted in that behalf by the District Council, shall exercise the powers of a court of appeal in respect of all suits and cases triable by a village council or court constituted under sub-paragraph (1) of this paragraph within such region or area, as the case may be, other than those to which the provisions of sub-paragraph (1) of paragraph 5 of this Schedule apply, and no other court except the High Court and the Supreme Court shall have jurisdiction over such suits or cases.

(3) The High Court *** shall have and exercise such jurisdiction over the suits and cases to which the provisions of sub-paragraph (2) of this paragraph apply as the Governor may from time to time by order specify.

(4) A Regional Council or District Council, as the case may be, may with the previous approval of the Governor make rules regulating—

(a) the constitution of village councils and courts and the powers to be exercised by them under this paragraph;

(b) the procedure to be followed by village councils or courts in the trial of suits and cases under sub-paragraph (1) of this paragraph;

(c) the procedure to be followed by the Regional or District Council or any court constituted by such Council in appeals and other proceedings under sub-paragraph (2) of this paragraph;

(d) the enforcement of decisions and orders of such Councils and courts;

(e) all other ancillary matters for the carrying out of the provisions of sub-paragraphs (1) and (2) of this paragraph.

[(5) On and from such date as the President may, [after consulting the Government of the State concerned], by notification appoint in this behalf, this paragraph shall have effect in relation to such autonomous district or region as may be specified in the notification, as if—

(i) in sub-paragraph (1), for the words "between the parties all of whom belong to Scheduled Tribes within such areas, other than suits and cases to which the provisions of sub-paragraph (1) of paragraph 5 of this Schedule apply", the words "not being suits and cases of the nature referred to in sub-paragraph (1) of paragraph (5) of this Schedule, which the Governor may specify in this behalf", had been substituted;

(ii) sub-paragraphs (2) and (3) had been omitted;

(iii) in sub-paragraph (4)—

(a) for the words "A Regional Council or District Council, as the case may be, may with the previous approval of the Governor make rules regulating", the words "the Governor may make rules regulating" had been substituted; and

(b) for clause (a), the following clause had been substituted, namely:—

"(a) the constitution of village councils and courts, the powers to be exercised by them under this paragraph and the courts to which appeals from the decisions of village councils and courts shall lie;";

(c) for clause (c), the following clause had been substituted, namely:

"(c) the transfer of appeals and other proceedings pending before the Regional or District Council or any court constituted by such Council immediately before the date appointed by the President under sub-paragraph (5);"; and

(d) in clause (e), for the words, brackets and figures "sub-paragraphs (1) and (2)", the word, brackets and figure "Sub-paragraph (1)" had been substituted.]

5. Conferment of powers under the Code of Civil Procedure, 1908, and the Code of Criminal Procedure, 1898, on the Regional and District Councils and on certain courts and officers for the trial of certain suits, cases and offences.—

(1) The Governor may, for the trial of suits or cases arising out of any law in force in any autonomous district or region being a law specified in that behalf by the Governor, or for the trial of offences punishable with death, transportation for life, or imprisonment for a term of not less than five years under the Indian Penal Code or

under any other law for the time being applicable to such district or region, confer on the District Council or the Regional Council having authority over such district or region or on courts constituted by such District Council or on any officer appointed in that behalf by the Governor, such powers under the Code of Civil Procedure, 1908, or, as the case may be, the Code of Criminal Procedure, 1898, as he deems appropriate, and thereupon the said Council, Court or officer shall try the suits, cases or offences in exercise of the powers so conferred.

(2) The Governor may withdraw or modify any of the powers conferred on a District Council, Regional Council, court or officer under sub-paragraph (1) of this paragraph.

(3) Save as expressly provided in this paragraph, the Code of Civil Procedure, 1908, and the Code of Criminal Procedure, 1898 shall not apply to the trial of any suits, cases or offences in an autonomous district or in any autonomous region to which the provisions of this paragraph apply.

[(4) On and from the date appointed by the President under sub-paragraph (5) of paragraph 4 in relation to any autonomous district or autonomous region, nothing contained in this paragraph shall, in its application to that district or region, be deemed to authorise the Governor to confer on the District Council or Regional Council or on courts constituted by the District Council any of the powers referred to in sub-paragraph (1) of this paragraph.]

[6. ***Powers of the District Council to establish primary schools, etc.***—

(1) The District Council for an autonomous district may establish, construct, or manage primary schools, dispensaries, markets, _488 [cattle pounds], ferries, fisheries, roads, road transport and waterways in the district and may, with the previous approval of the Governor, make regulations for the regulation and control thereof and, in particular, may prescribe the language and the manner in which primary education shall be imparted in the primary schools in the district.

(2) The Governor may, with the consent of any District Council, entrust either conditionally or unconditionally to that Council or to its officers functions in relation to agriculture, animal husbandry, community projects, co-operative societies, social welfare, village planning or any other matter to which the executive power of the State *** extends.]

7. District and Regional Funds.—

(1) There shall be constituted for each autonomous district, a District Fund and for each autonomous region, a Regional Fund to which shall be credited all moneys received respectively by the District Council for that district and the Regional Council for that region in the course of the administration of such district or region, as the case may be, in accordance with the provisions of this Constitution.

[(2) The Governor may make rules for the management of the District Fund, or, as the case may be, the Regional Fund and for the procedure to be followed in respect of payment of money into the said Fund, the withdrawal of moneys therefrom, the custody of moneys therein and any other matter connected with or ancillary to the matters aforesaid.

(3) The accounts of the District Council or, as the case may be, the Regional Council shall be kept in such form as the Comptroller and Auditor-General of India may, with the approval of the President, prescribe.

(4) The Comptroller and Auditor-General shall cause the accounts of the District and Regional Councils to be audited in such manner as he may think fit, and the reports of the Comptroller and Auditor-General relating to such accounts shall be submitted to the Governor who shall cause them to be laid before the Council.]

8. Powers to assess and collect land revenue and to impose taxes.—

(1) The Regional Council for an autonomous region in respect of all lands within such region and the District Council for an autonomous district in respect of all lands within the district except those which are in the areas under the authority of Regional Councils, if any, within the district, shall have the power to assess and collect revenue in respect of such lands in accordance with the principles for the time being followed [by the Government of the State in assessing lands for the purpose of land revenue in the State generally].

(2) The Regional Council for an autonomous region in respect of areas within such region and the District Council for an autonomous district in respect of all areas in the district except those which are under the authority of Regional Councils, if any, within the district, shall have power to levy and collect taxes on lands and buildings, and tolls on persons resident within such areas.

(3) The District Council for an autonomous district shall have the power to levy and collect all or any of the following taxes within such district, that is to say—
   (a) taxes on professions, trades, callings and employments;
   (b) taxes on animals, vehicles and boats;
   (c) taxes on the entry of goods into a market for sale therein, and tolls on passengers and goods carried in ferries; and
   (d) taxes for the maintenance of schools, dispensaries or roads.

(4) A Regional Council or District Council, as the case may be, may make regulations to provide for the levy and collection of any of the taxes specified in sub-paragraphs (2) and (3) of this paragraph [and every such regulation shall be submitted forthwith to the Governor and, until assented to by him, shall have no effect].

[9. *Licences or leases for the purpose of prospecting for, or extraction of, minerals.*—

(1) Such share of the royalties accruing each year from licences or leases for the purpose of prospecting for, or the extraction of, minerals granted by [the Government of the State] in respect of any area within an autonomous district as may be agreed upon between [the Government of the State] and the District Council of such district shall be made over to that District Council.

(2) If any dispute arises as to the share of such royalties to be made over to a District Council, it shall be referred to the Governor for determination and the amount determined by the Governor in his discretion shall be deemed to be the amount payable under sub-paragraph (1) of this paragraph to the District Council and the decision of the Governor shall be final.

***10. Power of District Council to make regulations for the Control of money-lending and trading by non-tribals.* —**

(1) The District Council of an autonomous district may make regulations for the regulation and control of money-lending or trading within the district by persons other than Scheduled Tribes resident in the district.

(2) In particular and without prejudice to the generality of the foregoing power, such regulations may—
   (a) prescribe that no one except the holder of a licence issued in that behalf shall carry on the business of money-lending;
   (b) prescribe the maximum rate of interest which may be

charged or be recovered by a money-lender;

(c) provide for the maintenance of accounts by money-lenders and for the inspection of such accounts by officers appointed in that behalf by the District Council;

(d) prescribe that no person who is not a member of the Scheduled Tribes resident in the district shall carry on wholesale or retail business in any commodity except under a licence issued in that behalf by the District Council:

Provided that no regulations may be made under this paragraph unless they are passed by a majority of not less than three-fourths of the total membership of the District Council:

Provided further that it shall not be competent under any such regulations to refuse the grant of a licence to a money-lender or a trader who has been carrying on business within the district since before the time of the making of such regulations.

(3) All regulations made under this paragraph shall be submitted forthwith to the Governor and, until assented to by him, shall have no effect.

11. Publication of laws, rules and regulations made under the Schedule.—All laws, rules and regulations made under this Schedule by a District Council or a Regional Council shall be published forthwith in the Official Gazette of the State and shall on such publication have the force of law.

12. [Application of Acts of Parliament and of the Legislature of the State of Assam to autonomous districts and autonomous regions in the State of Assam.—

(1) *Notwithstanding anything in this Constitution*—

(a) no Act of the [Legislature of the State of Assam] in respect of any of the matters specified in paragraph 3 of this Schedule as matters with respect to which a District Council or a Regional Council may make laws, and no Act of the [Legislature of the State of Assam] prohibiting or restricting the consumption of any non-distilled alcoholic liquor shall apply to any autonomous district or autonomous region [in that State] unless in either case the District Council for such district or having jurisdiction over such region by public notification so directs, and the District Council in giving such direction with respect to any Act may direct that the Act shall in its application to such district or region or any part thereof have effect subject to such exceptions or modifications as it thinks fit;

(b) the Governor may, by public notification, direct that any Act of Parliament or of the [Legislature of the State of Assam] to which the provisions of clause (a) of this sub-paragraph do not apply shall not apply to an autonomous district or an autonomous region [in that State] or shall apply to such district or region or any part thereof subject to such exceptions or modifications as he may specify in the notification.

(2) Any direction given under sub-paragraph (1) of this paragraph may be given so as to have retrospective effect.

[12A. Application of Acts of Parliament and of the Legislature of the State of Meghalaya to autonomous districts and autonomous regions in the State of Meghalaya.—

Notwithstanding anything in this Constitution,—

(a) if any provision of a law made by a District or Regional Council in the State of Meghalaya with respect to any matter specified in sub-paragraph (1) of paragraph 3 of this Schedule or if any provision of any regulation made by a District Council or a Regional Council in that State under paragraph 8 or paragraph 10 of this Schedule, is repugnant to any provision of a law made by the Legislature of the State of Meghalaya with respect to that matter, then, the law or regulation made by the District Council or, as the case may be, the Regional Council whether made before or after the law made by the Legislature of the State of Meghalaya, shall, to the extent of repugnancy, be void and the law made by the Legislature of the State of Meghalaya shall prevail;

(b) the President may, with respect to any Act of Parliament, by notification, direct that it shall not apply to an autonomous district or an autonomous region in the State of Meghalaya, or shall apply to such district or region or any part thereof subject to such exceptions or modifications as he may specify in the notification and any such direction may be given so as to have retrospective effect.

[12AA. Application of Acts of Parliament and of the Legislature of the State of Tripura to the autonomous district and autonomous regions in the State of Tripura.—

Notwithstanding anything in this Constitution,—

Act of the Legislature of the State of Tripura in respect of any of the matters specified in paragraph 3 of this Schedule as matters with respect to which a District Council or a Regional Council may make laws, and no Act of the Legislature of the State of Tripura prohibiting or restricting the consumption of any non-distilled alcoholic liquor shall apply to the autonomous district or any autonomous region in that State unless, in either case, the District Council for that district or having jurisdiction over such region by public notification so directs, and the District Council in giving such direction with respect to any Act may direct that the Act shall, in its application to that district or such region or any part thereof, have effect subject to such exceptions or modifications as it thinks fit;

the Governor may, by public notification, direct that any Act of the Legislature of the State of Tripura to which the provisions of clause (a) of this sub-paragraph do not apply, shall not apply to the autonomous district or an autonomous region in that State, or shall apply to that district or such region, or any part thereof, subject to such exceptions or modifications, as he may specify in the notification;

the President may, with respect to any Act of Parliament, by notification, direct that it shall not apply to the autonomous district or an autonomous region in the State of Tripura, or shall apply to such district or region or any part thereof, subject to such exceptions or modifications as he may specify in the notification and any such direction may be given so as to have retrospective effect.

12B. Application of Acts of Parliament and of the Legislature of the State of Mizoram to autonomous districts and autonomous regions in the State of Mizoram.—

Notwithstanding anything in this Constitution,—

(a) no Act of the Legislature of the State of Mizoram in respect of any of the matters specified in paragraph 3 of this Schedule as matters with respect to which a District Council or a Regional Council may make laws, and no Act of the Legislature of the State of Mizoram prohibiting or restricting the consumption of any non-distilled alcoholic liquor shall apply to any autonomous district or autonomous region in that State unless, in either case, the District Council for such district or having jurisdiction over such region, by public notification, so directs, and the District Council, in giving such direction with respect to any Act, may direct that the Act shall, in its application to such district or region or any part thereof, have effect subject to such exceptions or modifications as it thinks fit;

(b) the Governor may, by public notification, direct that any Act of the Legislature of the State of Mizoram to which the provisions of clause (a) of this sub-paragraph do not apply, shall not apply to an autonomous district or an autonomous region in that State, or shall apply to such district or region, or any part thereof, subject to such exceptions or modifications, as he may specify in the notification;

(c) the President may, with respect to any Act of Parliament, by notification, direct that it shall not apply to an autonomous district or an autonomous region in the State of Mizoram, or shall apply to such district or region or any part thereof, subject to such exceptions or modifications as he may specify in the notification and any such direction may be given so as to have retrospective effect.]

13. Estimated receipts and expenditure pertaining to autonomous districts to be shown separately in the annual financial statement.—The estimated receipts and expenditure pertaining to an autonomous district which are to be credited to, or is to be made from, the Consolidated Fund of the State [***] shall be first placed before the District Council for discussion and then after such discussion be shown separately in the annual financial statement of the State to be laid before the Legislature of the State under article 202.

[**14.** ***Appointment of Commission to inquire into and report on the administration of autonomous districts and autonomous regions***—

(1) The Governor may at any time appoint a Commission to examine and report on any matter specified by him relating to the administration of the autonomous districts and autonomous regions in the State, including matters specified in clauses (c), (d), (e) and (f) of sub-paragraph (3) of paragraph 1 of this Schedule, or may appoint a Commission to inquire into and report from time to time on the administration of autonomous districts and autonomous regions in the State generally and in particular on—

(a) the provision of educational and medical facilities and communications in such districts and regions;

(b) the need for any new or special legislation in respect of such districts and regions; and

(c) the administration of the laws, rules and regulations made by the District and Regional Councils; and define the procedure to be followed by such Commission.

(2) The report of every such Commission with the recommendations

of the Governor with respect thereto shall be laid before the Legislature of the State by the Minister concerned together with an explanatory memorandum regarding the action proposed to be taken thereon by [the Government of the State].

(3) In allocating the business of the Government of the State among his Ministers the Governor may place one of his Ministers specially in charge of the welfare of the autonomous districts and autonomous regions in the State.

[15. ***Annulment or suspension of acts and resolutions of District and Regional Councils***—

(1) If at any time the Governor is satisfied that an act or resolution of a District or a Regional Council is likely to endanger the safety of India [or is likely to be prejudicial to public order], he may annul or suspend such act or resolution and take such steps as he may consider necessary (including the suspension of the Council and the assumption to himself of all or any of the powers vested in or exercisable by the Council) to prevent the commission or continuance of such act, or the giving of effect to such resolution.

(2) Any order made by the Governor under sub-paragraph (1) of this paragraph together with the reasons therefore shall be laid before the Legislature of the State as soon as possible and the order shall, unless revoked by the Legislature of the State, continue in force for a period of twelve months from the date on which it was so made:

Provided that if and so often as a resolution approving the continuance in force of such order is passed by the Legislature of the State, the order shall unless cancelled by the Governor continue in force for a further period of twelve months from the date on which under this paragraph it would otherwise have ceased to operate.

*[16. **Dissolution of a District or a Regional Council.***—

[(1)] The Governor may on the recommendation of a Commission appointed under paragraph 14 of this Schedule by public notification order the dissolution of a District or a Regional Council, and'—

(a) direct that a fresh general election shall be held immediately for the reconstitution of the Council, or

(b) subject to the previous approval of the Legislature of the State assume the administration of the area under the authority of such Council himself or place the administration of such area under the Commission appointed under the said paragraph or any other body considered suitable by him for a period not exceeding twelve months:

Provided that when an order under clause (a) of this paragraph has been made, the Governor may take the action referred to in clause (b) of this paragraph with regard to the administration of the area in question pending the reconstitution of the Council on fresh general election:

Provided further that no action shall be taken under clause (b) of this paragraph without giving the District or the Regional Council, as the case may be, an opportunity of placing its views before the Legislature of the State.

[(2) If at any time the Governor is satisfied that a situation has arisen in which the administration of an autonomous district or region cannot be carried on in accordance with the provisions of this Schedule, he may, by public notification, assume to himself all or any of the functions or powers vested in or exercisable by the District Council or, as the case may be, the Regional Council and declare that such functions or powers shall be exercisable by such person or authority as he may specify in this behalf, for a period not exceeding six months:

Provided that the Governor may by a further order or orders extend the operation of the initial order by a period not exceeding six months on each occasion.

(3) Every order made under sub-paragraph (2) of this paragraph with the reasons therefor shall be laid before the Legislature of the State and shall cease to operate at the expiration of thirty days from the date on which the State Legislature first sits after the issue of the order, unless, before the expiry of that period it has been approved by the State Legislature.]

17. Exclusion of areas from autonomous districts in forming constituencies in such districts—For the purposes of elections to [the Legislative Assembly of Assam or Meghalaya] [or Tripura] [or Mizoram], the Governor may by order declare that any area within an autonomous district [in the State of Assam or Meghalaya] [or Tripura] [or Mizoram], as the case may be,] shall not form part of any constituency to fill a seat or seats in the Assembly reserved for any such district but shall form part of a constituency to fill a seat or seats in the Assembly not so reserved to be specified in the order.

19. Transitional provisions—

(1) As soon as possible after the commencement of this Constitution

the Governor shall take steps for the constitution of a District Council for each autonomous district in the State under this Schedule and, until a District Council is so constituted for an autonomous district, the administration of such district shall be vested in the Governor and the following provisions shall apply to the administration of the areas within such district instead of the foregoing provisions of this Schedule, namely—

(a) no Act of Parliament or of the Legislature of the State shall apply to any such area unless the Governor by public notification so directs; and the Governor in giving such a direction with respect to any Act may direct that the Act shall, in its application to the area or to any specified part thereof, have effect subject to such exceptions or modifications as he thinks fit;

(b) the Governor may make regulations for the peace and good government of any such area and any regulations so made may repeal or amend any Act of Parliament or of the Legislature of the State or any existing law which is for the time being applicable to such area.

(2) Any direction given by the Governor under clause (a) of sub-paragraph (1) of this paragraph may be given so as to have retrospective effect.

(3) All regulations made under clause (b) of sub-paragraph (1) of this paragraph shall be submitted forthwith to the President and, until assented to by him, shall have no effect.

***[20. Tribal areas*—**

(1) The areas specified in Parts I, II [IIA] and III of the table below shall respectively be the tribal areas within the State of Assam, the State of Meghalaya [the State of Tripura] and the [State] of Mizoram.

(2) [Any reference in Part I, Part II or Part III of the table below] to any district shall be construed as a reference to the territories comprised within the autonomous district of that name existing immediately before the day appointed under clause (b) of section 2 of the North-Eastern Areas (Reorganisation) Act, 1971:

Provided that for the purposes of clauses (e) and (f) of sub-paragraph (1) of paragraph 3, paragraph 4, paragraph 5, paragraph 6, sub-paragraph (2), clauses (a), (b) and (d) of sub-paragraph (3) and sub-paragraph (4) of paragraph 8 and clause (d) of sub-paragraph (2) of paragraph 10 of this Schedule, no part of the area comprised within the municipality of Shillong shall be deemed to be within the [Khasi Hills District].

[(3) The reference in Part IIA in the table below to the "Tripura Tribal Areas District" shall be construed as a reference to the territory comprising the tribal areas specified in the First Schedule to the Tripura Tribal Areas Autonomous District Council Act, 1979.]

TABLE

Part I

1. The North Cachar Hills District.
2. [The Karbi Anglong District.]

Part II

[1. Khasi Hills District.
2. Jaintia Hills District.]
3. The Garo Hills District.

[Part IIA —Tripura Tribal Areas District.]

Part III

[1. The Chakma District.
[2. The Mara District.
3. The Lai District.]]

[20A. Dissolution of the Mizo District Council—

(1) Notwithstanding anything in this Schedule, the District Council of the Mizo District existing immediately before the prescribed date (hereinafter referred to as the Mizo District Council) shall stand dissolved and cease to exist.

(2) The Administrator of the Union territory of Mizoram may, by one or more orders, provide for all or any of the following matters, namely:

(a) the transfer, in whole or in part, of the assets, rights and liabilities of the Mizo District Council (including the rights and liabilities under any contract made by it) to the Union or to any other authority;

(b) the substitution of the Union or any other authority for the

Mizo District Council, or the addition of the Union or any other authority, as a party to any legal proceedings to which the Mizo District Council is a party;

(c) the transfer or re-employment of any employee of the Mizo District Council to or by the Union or any other authority, the terms and conditions of service applicable to such employees after such transfer or re-employment;

(d) the continuance of any laws, made by the Mizo District Council and in force immediately before its dissolution, subject to such adaptations and modifications, whether by way of repeal or amendment, as the Administrator may make in this behalf, until such laws are altered, repealed or amended by a competent Legislature or other competent authority;

(e) such incidental, consequential and supplementary matters as the Administrator considers necessary.

Explanation.—In this paragraph and in paragraph 20B of this Schedule, the expression "prescribed date" means the date on which the Legislative Assembly of the Union territory of Mizoram is duly constituted under and in accordance with the provisions of the Government of Union Territories Act, 1963.

20B. Autonomous regions in the Union territory of Mizoram to be autonomous districts and transitory provisions consequent thereto—

(1) Notwithstanding anything in this Schedule,—

(a) every autonomous region existing immediately before the prescribed date in the Union territory of Mizoram shall, on and from that date, be an autonomous district in that Union territory (hereafter referred to as the corresponding new district) and the Administrator thereof may, by one or more orders, direct that such consequential amendments as are necessary to give effect to the provisions of this clause shall be made in paragraph 20 of this Schedule (including Part III of the table appended to that paragraph) and thereupon the said paragraph and the said Part III shall be deemed to have been amended accordingly;

(b) every Regional Council of an autonomous region in the Union territory of Mizoram existing immediately before the prescribed date (hereafter referred to as the existing Regional Council) shall, on and from that date and until a District

Council is duly constituted for the corresponding new district, be deemed to be the District Council of that district (hereafter referred to as the corresponding new District Council).

(2) Every member whether elected or nominated of an existing Regional Council shall be deemed to have been elected or, as the case may be, nominated to the corresponding new District Council and shall hold office until a District Council is duly constituted for the corresponding new district under this Schedule.

(3) Until rules are made under sub-paragraph (7) of paragraph 2 and sub-paragraph (4) of paragraph 4 of this Schedule by the corresponding new District Council, the rules made under the said provisions by the existing Regional Council and in force immediately before the prescribed date shall have effect in relation to the corresponding new District Council subject to such adaptations and modifications as may be made therein by the Administrator of the Union territory of Mizoram.

(4) The Administrator of the Union territory of Mizoram may, by one or more orders, provide for all or any of the following matters, namely:

(a) the transfer in whole or in part of the assets, rights and liabilities of the existing Regional Council (including the rights and liabilities under any contract made by it) to the corresponding new District Council;

(b) the substitution of the corresponding new District Council for the existing Regional Council as a party to the legal proceedings to which the existing Regional Council is a party;

(c) the transfer or re-employment of any employees of the existing Regional Council to or by the corresponding new District Council, the terms and conditions of service applicable to such employees after such transfer or re-employment;

(d) the continuance of any laws made by the existing Regional Council and in force immediately before the prescribed date, subject to such adaptations and modifications, whether by way of repeal or amendment, as the Administrator may make in this behalf until such laws are altered, repealed or amended by a competent Legislature or other competent authority;

(e) such incidental, consequential and supplementary matters as the Administrator considers necessary.

20C. Interpretation.—Subject to any provision made in this behalf, the provisions of this Schedule shall, in their application to the Union territory of Mizoram, have effect—

(1) as if references to the Governor and Government of the State were references to the Administrator of the Union territory appointed under article 239, references to State (except in the expression "Government of the State") were references to the Union territory of Mizoram and references to the State Legislature were references to the Legislative Assembly of the Union territory of Mizoram;

(2) as if—

(a) in sub-paragraph (5) of paragraph 4, the provision for consultation with the Government of the State concerned had been omitted;

(b) in sub-paragraph (2) of paragraph 6, for the words "to which the executive power of the State extends", the words "with respect to which the Legislative Assembly of the Union territory of Mizoram has power to make laws" had been substituted;

(c) in paragraph 13, the words and figures "under article 202" had been omitted.]]

21. Amendment of the Schedule—

(1) Parliament may from time to time by law amend by way of addition, variation or repeal any of the provisions of this Schedule and, when the Schedule is so amended, any reference to this Schedule in this Constitution shall be construed as a reference to such Schedule as so amended.

(2) No such law as is mentioned in sub-paragraph (1) of this paragraph shall be deemed to be an amendment of this Constitution for the purposes of Article 368.

(*Source:* www.constitution.org/cons/india /shed06.htm)

It was in 1952 that the district councils were elected in the United Khasi-Jaintia Hills District, the Garo Hills District, the Lushai (Mizo) Hills District, the Mikir Hills District and the North Cachar District. The working of the Sixth Schedule came under fire quite early. In 1960, a committee was appointed by the Governor of Assam to examine the financial conditions and working of each district and regional councils. The committee after examining the various district and regional councils reported that the financial conditions of most of the District Councils and of the Regional Council is not satisfactory (Chaube, 1999: 105). The Committee also reported that the councils suffered from an excess of clerical staff and even spent government subsidy meant for development purposes (*ibid.*). Similarly, again in 1966, the Pataskar Commission found the performance of the councils generally unsatisfactory.

Critical Aspects in the Sixth Schedule

The Sixth Schedule provides that state governors play a very special and protective role in the areas under Sixth Schedule. The Governor has the power to make regulations prohibiting or restricting the transfer of land to tribals to non-tribals. He has also very important role in preventing exploitation of tribal communities. Moreover, the Governor can modify/divide the boundaries of the scheduled areas by notification. Thus, the Governor has been given wide range of power over the autonomous districts and councils of North Eastern region. However, the Governor acts as per the aid and advice of the State Council of Ministers. Moreover, there is an allegation about the role of Governors in India that he acts as an agent of the Central Government, since he is appointed by the President on the recommendation of the Central Government. This makes many a times, the autonomous councils irrelevant as far as power to legislate is concerned.

Moreover, in the initial time, the laws passed by the parliament or by the state legislatures do not automatically apply to the autonomous councils since they enjoy autonomy protected by the Constitution. But, after the creation of Meghalaya in 1972, the Sixth Schedule was amended *vide* the North Eastern (Reorganization) Act. In accordance with the amendment, Article 12(A) was added to the Sixth Schedule. This addition to the Sixth Schedule, particularly, gives supremacy to the laws passed by the parliament or state legislature over those passed by the district autonomous council. Thus, addition of Article 12 (A), in a sense, diluted the powers of the district councils.

Thus, frequent clash or conflict of power between the District Councils and State Legislatures is always in issue in the states having scheduled areas. Most evident example is the state of Meghalaya where despite the formation of the state, the whole state continues to be under the Sixth Schedule causing frequent conflict between the District Councils and the State.

It has also been criticized that whether the district autonomous councils have any further role within a state which is ruled by a tribal majority. No one can deny that one of the prime reasons behind the adoption of Sixth Schedule was to satisfy the political aspiration of *Nagas*. But, Naga leaders believed that the Sixth Schedule offered too little accordingly rejected it at the initial period. Similarly, Mizoram only retained the councils to govern four ethnic groups. Moreover, it has been alleged that in Meghalaya, the councils have failed in their primary duty. The councils failed in protecting the tribal interest in trade and commerce as well as in terms land ownership. In case of Assam also, where councils like Bodoland Territorial Council (BTC) has been given enormous financial and legislative powers, but even after that nothing remarkable is seen in the way of development.

Another allegation against the district councils created by the Sixth Schedule is that they failed to utilize their socio-economic potentialitics and their concentration is diverted to politics and the pretentions of mini-states. Some of the legislations passed by them is challenged by the Guwahati High Court, e.g. the Trading by Non-Tribals Act passed by the Mizo District council was turned down on grounds of violation of the right to equality (Chaube, 1999: 111). In 1968, the High Court turned down the main section (Section 3) of the United Khasi-Jainitia (Transfer of Land) Act of 1953, which restricted the sale of lands to non-tribals (*ibid.*).

It is also blamed that these autonomous councils have become power centres where a tribal elite is elected to positions of power and authority. They exercise considerable financial power but have failed to deliver basic governance.

Demand for Autonomous State

Since independence, Assam has been experiencing several movements; peaceful, violent and combination of both and as a result of these movements, Assam has experienced reorganization several times (Hussain, 1987: 1329). Hence, demand for autonomy has remained a common and frequent trend in the politics of NER states and this is particularly true in case of Assam. The advantage provided by the Sixth Schedule may be regarded as an important factor for the rising demands for the autonomous status along with other factors such as underdevelopment and continuous neglect by the Union Government for a long duration, which continued until the recent past. Moreover, identity politics is another factor that inspires almost each and every ethnic minority community in the region to preserve and revive their culture and identity. For achieving such goals the ethnic communities usually make use of the available constitutional arrangements like that of the Sixth Schedule.

The communities in the interest of achieving the autonomous status claimed themselves as indigenous tribes or people. But the question arises who in the NER is indigenous? It is to be mentioned that no community in the country is officially declared as indigenous but at the same time some tribes or communities of the region is given special protection under the Constitution of India, e.g. included in the Scheduled Tribe (ST) category. The Constitution has special provisions for the STs in respect to their education, employment, political position etc. Here, it should not be misunderstood that the tribes having ST status is officially recognized as indigenous community. But due to the existence of Sixth Schedule, every tribe in NER used to claim them as indigenous or as aboriginals etc. only for the interest of getting autonomy and to preserve their identity as well. Even some non-tribal communities have started to raise such type of claim.

These demands for autonomy also can back to the colonial and pre-colonial period which was mentioned earlier also. Historically speaking the hill tribals of NER were neither a part of India nor of Assam prior to the British colonization of this region (*ibid.*). The major tribes such as the Nagas, Mizos, Jaintias, Garos, Karbis, Dimasa Kacharis etc. had their own kingdom. Most of the tribes of this region are held to be remnants of ancient Mongolian overflow to this region, still some of them belong to Austro-Asiatic and Tibeto Burman races (*ibid.*). They were different from the plain inhabitant of the Brahmaputra valley and the geographically isolated from the plain people as well. Due to these reasons of geographical isolation, inaccessibility etc. they are able to develop and maintain their own small but distinctive socio-political system. Besides, the hill tribes there were the plain tribes, viz. the Bodos, Sonowal-Kacharis, Mishings, Rabhas, Koch Rajbongshis etc. which are also able to maintain their distinctive socio-political features to a large extent although reside amidst the non-tribal plain communities.

The British rulers always wanted to create a division between the hill and the plains in similar way like that they tried to divide Hindu and the Muslims in the country. The basic motive may be to divide and rule. But at the same time they admitted the distinctiveness of the hill as well as tribal people of the NER. Under the Government of India Act, 1919 the Governor General-in-Council had declared certain areas of Assam as Backward Tracts. The 'Backward Tracks' was changed to 'Excluded Area' by the Government of India Act, 1935. Excluded Area means backward most tribal areas which were under the direct rule of the Governors and districts which were categorized as excluded area had no representation in the provincial legislature. Whereas, districts which were categorized as partially excluded area were under the provincial government and they had representative in the provincial legislature. However, law enacted by the provincial government could not be enforced in the partially excluded area without the approval of the Governor. Moreover, the Governor could use his discretionary power without consulting the provincial government in the partially excluded area.

These two categories of 'Excluded Area' and 'Partially Excluded Area' were the creation of Government of India Act, 1935. Excluded Areas were the Lushai (Mizo) Hills and North Cachar; and the Partially Excluded Areas were United Khasi Jaintia Hills district with partial exception of the Shillong town which was also the capital of Assam at that time, the Garo Hills, Naga Hills and Mikir (Karbi) Hills. So, the incentive to demand for autonomy was already there in the history of Assam. The inclusion of Sixth Schedule in the Constitution and the movement or leadership for inclusion of the same in the Constitution was enough to demonstrate the enthusiasm of tribal people of NER for autonomy.

There is no doubt that Assam has been witnessing these autonomy movements largely among the NER states and most probably than any other state in the country. One of such example is that of creation of Meghalaya. Before becoming a full-fledged state in 1972, Meghalaya was being granted the status of autonomous state within Assam under Art. 244(A) of the Constitution of India in 1971. At recent time, a number of tribal as well as ethnic communities are demanding for autonomous status. However, the movement of autonomy of the Karbis and the Bodos are seemed to be more vibrant.

The hill people of Karbi Anglong have been demanding an autonomous state within Assam is also rooted in the aforesaid history of Assam. The Karbi Anglong is one of the two hill districts of present Assam, the other being the Dima Hasao (formerly N C Hills district). At the beginning, i.e. in 1951, when the districts were carved out both these hill districts were known under the same nomenclature, i.e. the United Mikir and North Cachar Hills. In 1952, both the Karbis and Dimasas were granted autonomy in the form of separate District Councils under the Sixth Schedule (Choudhury, 2014: 207). The present Karbi Anglong by then had a sub-division viz. the Mikir Hills, and this was further renamed as Mikir Hills district, in 1971 by separating NC Hills district from it. In 1976, the old name of the district, i.e. Karbi Anglong was revived. Again, in the year 1995, the Union government by granting more powers to the Autonomous District Council upgraded it to Karbi Anglong Autonomous Council (KAAC) (*ibid.*).

The movement for autonomy by the Karbis is largely determined by their passion to preserve their identity. They believed that autonomy was/is the only way to preserve and promote their identity in such a highly diverse region of NER. The reflection of the same was evident even in the pre-independence period. A section of educated Karbis formed the *Karbi Adarbar*, the first national organization of the Karbis in 1946 to put forward the demand for the creation of a separate district for the ethnic group (*ibid.*).

In this regard, Semson Sing Ingti, the second graduate of the community, who was then serving as a sub-inspector of schools in the then Mikir Hills tract and Khorsing Terong, first MLA (elected to the Assam Legislative Assembly from the Mikir Hills Tract in 1937) from the tribe led the movement for securing autonomy. It may be mentioned here that the Government of India Act, 1935, Karbis were given representation to the legislature for the first time. The prime motto of the *Karbi Adarbar* was to unite the hitherto scattered Karbi inhabited areas into a single political entity to preserve the separate ethnic identity (cultural, linguistic and political) of the tribe (*ibid.*) and for that single political entity achieving political autonomy gradually became their priority. In the post-independence period, the movement for autonomy gained remarkable momentum. It is already mentioned that the Karbis achieved a district of their own in 1950s and a district council in 1952 due to the organized movement led by the *Kari Adarbar*. It was during the 1960s that the demand for autonomy/statehood formally surfaced in the politics of the hill areas the then Assam including in Karbi Anglong district, although such a demand was occasionally raised by the hill leaders ever since the formation of State Reorganization Commission in December, 1953 (*ibid.*).

The Bodos secured their autonomous council, viz. Bodo Territorial Council (BTC) in 2003. BTC came into existence immediately after the surrender of Bodo Liberation Tiger (BLT). The area under jurisdiction of BTC is called the Bodoland Territorial Area District (BTAD) consisting of four districts—Kokrajhar, Baksa, Udalguri and Chirang. However, the formation of BTC is the result of their long organized struggle with a view to maintain their distinct language, culture and identity. Especially, after the setback of the Assam Agitation and when the Asom Gana Parishad (AGP) formed the government in Assam, the Bodos along with other tribal communities were not properly represented in that government. Though Bodo people also struggled hard in the Assam agitation, yet they were neglected later by other upper caste fellows when they came into power. As a result the Bodo people started to demand creation of an autonomous state on the northern banks of the Brahmaputra valley to be known as 'Udayachal' and autonomy for the tribals living on the southern bank of Brahmaputra (Hussain, 1987: 1329).

Demand for Separate State

In the 1950s, NER essentially means Assam, Manipur and Tripura (Madhab, 1999: 320). But it was our colonial history that contributed a number concepts and basis for the people of NER to demand for the creation of new states. The colonial power introduced a number of administrative concepts like excluded areas, partially excluded areas, tribal areas, frontier tracts, North East Frontier Agency etc. to govern the hill areas of the North East (*ibid.*). Out of the erstwhile Assam, partly to rationalize these concepts and partly to give vent to ethnic aspirations, the Government of India (GOI) had created four more states, viz. Nagaland

(1963), Meghalaya (1972), Arunachal Pradesh and Mizoram (1987), which are already mentioned in the previous unit. These reorganizations of the state of Assam for several times have led to the drastic reduction of its size.

However, it is imperative to understand the problem of the tribes as well as of non-tribal communities in Assam *vis-à-vis* the movement for an autonomous state. The plain tribes like the Bodo are demanding separate state, viz. the *Bodoland* even after receiving the autonomous status. The other tribe that in spite of having an autonomous council is demanding for a separate state is the Karbi tribe of Assam and had demonstrated frequent violent and non-violent movement in the past and also in recent time. In such movements ethnicity again plays a greater role.

The demand of the Bodos as well as the Karbis for separate state out of the state of Assam is rooted in the long history of similar movements in NER which led first to the separate state of Nagaland, then Mizoram and later the constitutional experiment with an autonomous tribal state which became Meghalaya.

The separatist movement of the Nagas can be traced back to 1918, with the founding of Naga Club in Kohima by a group of erudite Nagas. However, the separatist movement of the Nagas is different from other separatist movements because they, from the beginning, have been demanding for creation of a separate independent country for themselves. The Naga club tendered a memorandum before the Simon Commission which demanded for exclusion of Nagas from the proposed constitutional reform in British Administration in India. Although their plea was unsuccessful, the nature of gripes took a drastic change with the emerging of Angami Zapu Phizo who was considered as one of the most vibrant leaders of Naga separatist movement. During India's struggle for independence, Phizo had fought on the side of Indian National Army led by Subhas Chandra Bose for Japan against the Allies.

In 1946, the Naga Club was renamed as Naga National Council (NNC). The NNC then, demanded for a separate political geography comprising Naga inhabited areas of Nagaland, Assam, Arunachal Pradesh and Myanmar (Burma), thus marking the beginning of political conflict between Nagas and the GOI. The most important event was taken place on 14th August, 1947, when NNC under the leadership of Phizo declared independence of Naga region, thereby resulting in his arrest in 1948 on the charges of instigating a rebellion. But, he was released in 1950 and became the president of NNC. In 1952, he met the then Prime Minister and pleaded for Naga Independence, which was rejected. Disappointed with this, he turned to Arm Rebellion to sway the Indian Government. However, the Indian Army quash the rebellion, while Phizo escaped to East Pakistan

(Bangladesh) and then to London, where he remained and persisted to support the secessionist movement in Nagaland, until his death in 1990.

The separatist struggle of Naga people came to taste their first achievement at the meeting of the Naga People's Convention in the year 1960, where it was finally decided that Nagaland will be considered a full-fledged state of India and finally in the year 1963, Nagaland was declared a separate state. However, their demand for an independent country, comprising Naga inhabitated territories of Assam, Arunachal Pradesh and Meghalaya as well as Naga inhabited areas of Myanmar, is still continues.

In 1975, an agreement known as Shillong Accord was signed between the NNC and the GOI. But some of the NNC hardcore militants were disappointed with the pact, leading to breakage among the arm cadets. This led to the formation of the Nationalist Socialist Council of Nagaland (NSCN) on January 31, 1980 by Isak Chisi Swu, Thuingaleng Muivah and SS Khaplang. Lamentably, differences shelled out within the outfit later, and on April 30, 1988 the group split into two fractions—the NSCN (IM), led by Isak Chisi Swu and Thuingaleng Muivah; and the NSCN (K) led by SS Khaplang. Although their philosophy differ, their goals remain the same the establishment of independent 'Greater Nagaland' comprising all Naga inhabited areas within India and Myanmar. However, the present GOI on August 3, 2015 signed a historic peace accord with the NSCN (IM) to establish peace in the region.

In case of Meghalaya, it can be mentioned that the movement for a separate hill state began in 1960. As a result of that movement the Assam Reorganization (Meghalaya) Act of 1969 accorded an autonomous status to the state of Meghalaya. The Act came into effect on 2nd April, 1970 and an autonomous state of Meghalaya was born out of Assam. In 1971, the parliament passed the North-Eastern Areas (Re-organization) Act, 1971 which confers full statehood on the autonomous state of Meghalaya. Meghalaya attained statehood on 21st January, 1972, with a legislative assembly of its own.

On the other hand, the creation of separate state of Mizoram was also the result of desires and political aspirations of tribal people for autonomy. These political aspirations had their roots in the colonial period too. Mizo hills were formally declared as part of British India as well as of British Assam by a proclamation in 1895. North and South hills were united into Lushai Hill District in 1898 with Aizawl as its headquarters. In 1919, Lushai Hills along with some other hill districts was declared as Backward Tract under the Government of India Act, 1919. Again under Government of India Act, 1935 tribal districts of Assam including Lushai Hills were declared Excluded Area in 1935. The political awakening among the Mizos in Lushai Hills started taking shape during the British regime, when the first political party, viz. the Mizo Common People's Union was formed on 9th April, 1946. The party was later renamed as Mizo Union. The Mizo Union supported autonomous status for Mizo inhabited areas in front of the Bordoloi Sub-Committee. On the other hand, another party named, the United Mizo Freedom wanted Lushai Hills to join Burma after independence.

However, a certain amount of autonomy was granted to the Lushai Hills following the suggestions of the Bordoloi Sub-Committee and the Lushai Hills Autonomous District Council came into being in 1952. The autonomy, however, met the aspirations of the Mizos only partially which result in the representatives of the District Council and the Mizo Union pleaded with the State Re-organization Commission (SRC) for integrating the Mizo dominated areas of Tripura and Manipur with their district council in Assam. The tribal leaders in the North East were laboriously unhappy with the SRC recommendation. They met in Aizawl in 1955 and formed a new political party, viz. Eastern India Union (EITU) and raised demand for a separate state comprising all the hill districts of Assam. The Mizo Union split and one fraction of Mizo Union joined EITU. By that time, although the Chaliha Ministry understood the problem of hill people, the demand for a separate Hill State by EITU was kept in abeyance.

Another major event in demanding separate state for the Mizos was the formation of a political organization, viz. Mizo National Front (MNF) in 1961. A period of protests and arm insurgency followed in 1960s, with MNF seeking independence from India. After long period of struggle the government agreed to convert the Mizo Hills into a Union Territory in 1971, which came into being Mizoram in 1972. Following the Mizoram Peace Accord, 1986 between the Government of India and MNF, Mizoram was declared a full-fledged state of India in 1987.

The fact that the state of Assam has experienced drastic reduction of size for several times is evident from the above discussion. Once again, the threat of the further reduction of the size and re-organization has sharpened in the wake of new movements launched by various tribal groups both in the plains and the hills especially after the Asom Gana Parishad had come to power (Hussain, 1987: 1329). In recent period, four statehood demands are gaining momentum. These are the demands of creation of Bodoland by the Bodos, a separate state for the Karbis, the Koch Rajbongshis for the creation of Kamatapur, and the Dimasa tribe for a separate state of their own. Generally, the separatist movements in Assam are justified on the following grounds, which are debatable:

(*a*) *Lack of Development and Exploitation by Forward Communities*:

The leaders or the organizations demanding a separate state generally cited this reason. It may or may not be true. Hence, this kind of issue should be probed by a third party with proper investigation.

(*b*) *Assamese Chauvinism in Language Agitation in 1972 and Illegal Migration in 1979-1985:* It is believed by many that these two incidence had induced fear in tribal about losing their culture and language by majority Assamese speakers. The fear of losing their culture and language increased due to illegal immigration of Bengali speaking people from Bangladesh also. So, almost all tribes had formed their student organization in line with AASU during that period. So, to halt the process of assimilation of tribal people with mainstream Assamese people and also with huge number illegally immigrated Bengali speaking people, the tribal leaders demanded separate state for their own to preserve their culture and language and many achieved it also.

(*c*) *Sense of Alienation by Mainstream Forward Society*: Though discrimination of tribal on the basis of caste was not almost non-existent in North East India, but with more education among tribal had made them aware how they have fallen behind other communities which may have forced them to be suspicious about other communities. Lack of proper implementation of 'Tribal Belt and Block' system had also fuelled the fear. {It may be noted that in 1939 the Congress-coalition government of Assam headed by Gopinath Bordoloi came out for the first time with the conception of Tribal Belt and Block system. But it was not finalized then. Again in 1945, the government came out with Tribal Belts and Blocks system, according to which the villages in which the percentages of tribal classes of people exceed 50 per cent over the total population should be marked on the map and tribal belts and blocks may be constituted in that area. This regulation was amended through Assam Land and Revenue Regulation (Amendment) Act, 1964, 1981 and 1990 (Nuntham, 2006: 88-90).}

(*d*) *Separatism by Historical Reason*: Many tribes had a history where they were quite independent and self-reliant in their own small geographical confinement and used to live isolated. Thus demand for a separate state for themselves is being guided by the motive of reviving their earlier kingdom to protect and promote their culture.

(*e*) *Past precedence of creating Separate States*: In order to quell armed separatist movements as well as ease of deploying laws like AFSPA (Armed Force Special Power Act, 1958) may have forced

GOI to create separate states in Assam in 1960s. But this has, on the contrary, created precedence and many tribes now think it is quite achievable to get separate state.

Some recent incidences prove the above reasons of separatist movement. For instance the decision of the UPA Government to create Telangana has brought out more agitation and violation in Assam. As different ethnic groups following or as a result of the decision of the Government demanded for separate states by demonstrating both violent and non-violent agitations and activities, the law and order situation deteriorated terribly. Particularly massive violence was seen in the district of Karbi Anglong, protesters had ablaze Government Offices, Congress Offices etc in the different parts of the hill district, forcing the Government to issue shoot-at-sight order.

At the conclusion of this unit, it is to be cited that the present NER has borrowed a lot from the colonial period. Mention must be made about the concepts or policies of 'excluded areas', inner-line system etc. particularly in this unit. In the post-independence period, these policies has their visible impact as they created conditions of ethnic conflict in the region and in course of time, it led to the formulation of the demand of autonomy and separate homeland.

MODEL QUESTIONS

A. Very Objective Type Questions (1 mark for each)

1. One factor of Regionalism.
2. Name the Hill Districts of Assam.
3. Who was the member from Assam in the drafting committee of the Constituent Assembly?

B. Short Type Questions (4/5 marks for each)

1. Mention four factors responsible for the growth of regionalism in Assam.
2. Highlight any four factors that led to autonomy movement in Assam.
3. Write shortly about the future of regionalism in Assam.
4. Short Notes:
   (a) Autonomous council.
   (b) State and Tribal politics.
   (c) Politics of Hill Tribes.
   (d) State and Tribal politics.

C. Long Type Questions (10-12 marks for each)

1. Define regionalism. Discuss the causes of regionalism in Assam.
2. Discuss composition powers and functions of the District Council.
3. Discuss the nature and future of Regionalism in Assam.
4. Write a note on the Sixth Schedule of Indian Constitution.
5. Explain the factors responsible for the demand for greater state autonomy. Do you think that granting of none autonomy would solve their problems?
6. Write a note on the demand for separate State in Assam.
7. Elaborate the reasons for which New states are created out of some districts of Assam.
8. Discuss the autonomy movement launched by the Bodos in Assam.
9. Elaborate the functioning of the District councils in Assam.

Unit-III
Politics of Ethnicity in Assam

At present, the whole North East, and most particularly Assam is in a state of turmoil due to different ethnic movements. Ethnic insurgency, question of nationality and demand for regional autonomy become the order of the day in North East. The histories of last one hundred years bear testimony to the emergence of a dozen of ethnicity based autonomy movements and conflicts in this region. The autonomy movements of Karbi-Dimasa the Garos, Khasi-Jayantias, the Tiwa, Deuri, Missing began around 1960 and the Bodos demanded separate state in the second half of 1980. At the same time movements for separate state began in Nagaland, Manipur, Mizoram and Arunachal Pradesh which resulted in vivisection of the state of Assam.

Ethnicity or ethnic identity is a sort of community level consciousness necessary for developing group solidarity. Ethnic identity is a tool in the hands of man to ensure an expected response on comforting another human being. It is considered as a process and as an idiom through which distinctiveness is articulated in a contest of cultural heterogeneity and in terms of which political interest defended or advanced. The identity consciousness of a group of people tends to be valuable to any kind of exigency and it leads to communalism and regionalism. This issues and problems, which a nation, state and government had to face, are referred to as ethnic. Ethnic consciousness or ethnic identity as a political force is gaining its ground in North East since the colonial period. The anxiety of the smaller ethnic groups particularly of the tribal of North East has been associated with the identity crisis which they have been facing due to various factors—economic, socio-cultural and political.

What is Ethnicity?

Ethnicity is the socio-cultural group or groups that people identify with or feel they belong to. A number of scholars have defined ethnicity from their own point of view.

According to Berghe: "Ethnic groups are defined commodities both by the objective cultural of their behaviour and by their subjective views of themselves and each other."

Weber defines: "The belief in tribal kinship, regardless of whether it has any objective foundation, can have important consequences especially for the formation of a political community. Those human groups that entertain a subjective belief in their common descant—because of similarities of physical type or of and migration in such a way that this belief is important for the continuation of non-kinship commercial relationship, we shall call 'ethnic groups' regardless whether an objective blood relationship exist or not.'"

According to Issacs: "Ethinicity is making up of what a person is boon with or acquires at birth."

According to Wallman: "Ethinicity is a process by which their difference is used to enhance the sense of us for the purpose of organisation or identification."

According to Phadnis: "Ethincity is a device as much a focus of group mobilisation by the leadership of ethnic groups through select use of ethnic symbols for socio-cultural and politic economic purpose."

Glozer and Moynihan: says, "there is a some legitimacy to finding that forms of identification based on social relations of different, as religion, languages and national origin all have something in common, such that a new term is coined to refer to all of them—'ethnicity'. What they have in comn on is that they have all become effective group mobilization for concreate political ends challanging for primary, such mobilization of close on our hand and nation on other."

Ethnicity is the socio-cultural group or groups that people identify with or feel they belong to the ethnic group is a group whose members have some or all of the following characteristics:

(1) Share a sense of common origins,
(2) Claim a common and distinctive history and destiny,
(3) Possess one or more dimensions of collective cultural individuality, and
(4) Feel a sense of unique collective solidarity.

Ethnicity is self-perceived and people can belong to more than one ethnic group and may change their ethnicities over time or in different social contexts. Ethnicity is not the same as ancestry or race. For example, people of European ethnicity have an older age structure than people of Asian ethnicity and have different social and cultural needs.

As a matter of fact words like "ethnic groups", "ethnicity" and "ethnic conflict" have become quite common terms in the English language, and they keep cropping up in the press, in TV news, in political programmes and in casual conversations. The same can be said for "nation" and "nationalism", and many of us have to admit that the meaning of these terms frequently seems ambiguous and vague. Ethnicity emerges and is made relevant through ongoing social situations and encounters, and through people's ways of coping with the demands and challenges of life.

An important reason for the current academic interest in ethnicity and nationalism is the fact that such phenomena have become so visible in many societies that it has become impossible to ignore them. In the early twentieth century, many social theorists held that ethnicity and nationalism would decrease in importance and eventually vanish as a result of modernization, industrialization and individualism. This never came about. On the contrary, ethnicity and nationalism have grown in political importance in the world, particularly since the Second World War.

Emergence of Ethnicity or Ethnic Consciousness

Ethnicity emerges and is made relevant through ongoing social situations and encounters, and through people's ways of coping with the demands and challenges of life. Stanley Tambiah of Harvard University says, that there are two models of nationalism that are in interaction and contention in many Parts of the world. One of these is "ethnonationalism" and the other is "Nationalism of the Nation State". Ethnonationalism refers to the phenomenon of political movements launched on the basis of ethnic identity. Tambiah helpfully delineates the political history of the Third World countries into three phases. The first phase is the 'decolonization' period, and the second phase which began in the 1950s and lasted, up to 1960s, is "the phase of optimistic nation-building". In this phase the stress on nation-building down played internal diversity and cleavages in favour of the primacy of nation states. The optimism and suppressive characters of nation building in the second phase came to be challenged and even reversed by the eruption of ethnic conflicts in the third and the present phase of 'ethno nationalism'. The phase of ethnonationalism is characterised by regional or subnational reactions and resistances to what is seen as an over centralised and hegemonic State.

The multi-ethnic and multi-cultural setting of India and India's struggle to define its nationhood since the nationalist movement provided a fertile soil for the development of ethnonationalism and other forms of identify-quest among the different ethnic groups. Because, it has not settled the notion of its identity in a manner convincing to all the people groups within

India as a nation. While the dominant India culture at the centre continues its quest for self-identity on the basis of its religions and cultural identity, those in the periphery react to such potentially hegemonic and oppressive movement. In the case of Nagas, Mizos and the others in the North-East, the vary notion as well as movement of ethnonationalism clearly reflects a crisis of identity.

Ethnic consciousness grew up in Assam in the early decades of the 20th century. Due to the heterogenous physiography, Assam became the homeland of various races and tribes. There are as many as 23 Government recognized tribes within Assam living both in plains and hills. Though a process of detribalization and assimilation started in the Brahmaputra valley since prehistoric period and continued till the arrival of the British, it was not completed, rather British separated the hill people from the plains by introducing Inner Line regulation etc. Therefore, tribal elements remain both in the hills and plains in the North-East. Though, all the tribes belong to Mongoloid race they had no political and racial unity among them. Meanwhile under the British rule an elite class though small in numbers emerged among all societies in the North East. Those were the elite classes who sowed the seeds of ethnic consciousness among their own societies and thus ethnicity grew up in Assam. In 1929 an elite group of Bodo community submitted a memorandum before Simon Commission seeking reservation of seats in Local Board as well as in Legislative Council. In the same time the educated middle class of the other ethnic groups also joined hand in the process for which all the Tribal Groups assembled under the umbrella of Tribal League in 1933. Under the pressure of Tribal League the Assam Government compelled to reserved 4 seats in Legislative Assembly and nomination of I seat in Legislative Council for Tribal. Moreover, 33 Tribal belts and blocks were created to safeguard the Tribal Culture and Identity.

In the post-independent period, in Assam the issues of ethnic consciousness took a serious turn due to the Assamese hegemonic and oppressive attitude. After independence the Assamese middle class captured political power of Assam. They followed a policy of Assamisation and tried to impose Assamese language and culture upon all ethnic groups. Fearing the loss of their own culture and racial identity they have raised the demand for autonomy in different times.

Causes of Ethnic Conflict

Most of the ethnic conflicts in the North East are around land for jobs or for the protection of their culture and identity all of which they feel attack. The dams uses an enormous amount of land but will not create jobs even for those who displace, leave alone for the backlog. It can add to conflicts and further marginalize the people of the region.

Again imposition of culture through different media, replacement of regional language and literature by the dominating language, declining right over land penetration of market economy resulting in increased poverty among the ethnic people are some of the factors of ethnic unrest.

The search for one of the major reasons behind the tribal tribulence that has rocked Assam today draws us back to the British famous policy "Divide and Rule". The British with their Machiavellian shrewdness, knew well that a colony can be best ruled if its people remain divided. With this principle in view they started discouraging further Sanskritization and pursued instead a policy of segregation. On recommendation from the Simon Commission they divided the tribal dominated areas of Assam into excluded areas and partially excluded areas.

The greatest endogenous factor is the strong urge of the people to preserve their cultural, linguistic and ethnic identity. To meet their ethnic aspiration preserve their cultural identity and develope their social and economic life, new states, i.e. Bodoland in Assam, were created. In this context, it may be mentioned that in recent years, the All Bodo Students Union in a booklet gave vent to their grievances, thus—"One of the most responsible factors as to why the tribals have become alienated from the mainstream of Assam is the attitude of the Assamese people. The Assamese people have never accepted the tribals as part and parcel of the Assamese community and society in a real sense, though they give a motivated slogan of greater Assamese nationality. As for instance a Goswami Brahmin family will never allow to give its daughter for a social marriage with tribal youth. Even a man like Bishnuprasad Rabha who has been widely acclaimed as the epitome of Assamese culture expressed resentment as the casteist attitude of the Hindus towards the tribals. In his novel 'Missing Koneng,' he made the hero speak thus. The Hindus are Assamese and the Miris are non-Assamese, in spite of they being the natives of Assam. That is why it is generally heard from the Hindus—'This is an Assamese village and that is a Miri village'—i.e. all are victimized by the superior's egotism."

Again, in the 1980s when the movement to expel foreigners from the state of Assam was launched by AASU the tribals unhesitatingly joined it. But when, as a result of the movement the AGP Ministry was formed, the then AASU leaders bloated with vanity, paid little attention to their former colleagues in the ABSU. In consequence, they under the leadership of late Upen Brahma left AGP and rocked Assam by launching a vigorous movement for a separate Bodoland.

The economic neglect by the government and the exploitation by landowners and the trading community, though undeniable may not, however, be called the major reasons for the rise of the ethnic unrest. The core of the problem lies, in the mind, feeling of humiliation, and the apprehension for the loss of identity in the hands of Assamese. In the days of yore, assimilation through Sanskritization had not been an imposed process, but a natural one. But when the Assamese middle class started making high handed attempts to get the tribals absorbed in their cultural and linguistic milieu they got sacred of losing their own identity. The conscious attempt at assimilation thus ended in unhoped for alienation.

Sometimes, identity consciousness does not end at wearing his native dress and eating his style of food but his sensitivity is sharpened to such an extent that the group as a whole becomes vulnerable to any kind of exigencies and is not always able to cope up with the emerging situations. This gives rise to his making concerted efforts to retain his identity markers, resulting into communalism, regionalism, linguism and casteism. The consequences of these schisros are extremely lethal, specially for the maintenance of balance and equilibrium of multigrouped conglomerates of towns and cities. These issues and problems which a nation state and government had to face were referred to as ethnic.

Moreover, The vast socio-cultural change taking place all over the world gave rise to multiplicity of ethnic problem.

The presence and persistence of ethnicity in plural societies were felt mainly due to intense struggle of the inhabitants for the meagre and common resources like employment house, education and political. A person has to secure a job, a house, education for the children. This is an universal truth. Similarly the fulfilment of economic needs and channelling of maximum national resources for a group is largely interpreted in the political terms. Since at the state and national levels the political corporates utilize the eeonomic provisions provided to the groups to ensure their popularity, existence and support. Thus, the very essentials of life are politicized. Once it is politicized the conflict situation existing between several ethnic groups results into ethnic clash and violence. These situations which are violent in nature greatly hampers normal social situation and has a significant death toll.

In certain cases, the government itself was responsible for the economic degradation of the tribals. Tribal belts and block in Assam came into being in 1947 with an aim to separate the tribal people. But the government paid little attention to danger posed before them because of the unrestricted flow of non-tribal people, particularly the Bangladesh his come to the restricted areas.

Moreover, when an industry was set up in a tribal area, they were evicted and their land requisitioned, but little effort to rehabilitate them. For example, in 1932 more than a thousand tribal in Udalguri (Assam) were evacuated in order to establish Dhansiri Irrigation Project. According to a survey organized by the Tribal Research Institute "A large number of villagers that they have neither received any compensation nor any alternative land lost due to acquisition."

Another factor leading towards the ethnic clashes is the role of Christian Missionaries in nourshing the seed of separation in the mind of the tribals, living particularly in the hilly regions. In Assam the cast Hindus with their long and strong religious tradition thwarted the Christian Mission effort at proselytization but the simple minded tribal community felt and easy prey to it. While the Christian Missionary lured the tribal to Western culture, the businessmen smoothed his way to privation and thus set in the cultural, moral and economic degradation of tribal life.

Impact on Present Society

The present society in which we are living today is knowledge and information based society. In this fourth wave, what will be engagement of man is to create the responsive society and will develop holistic and comprehensive view about life and ecology. But the region is an exception in this regard due to varied factors.

The region has abundant natural resources but still backward in industrialization and other economic development. After 60 years of independence, there was no rail link with the state capitals of the region except Guwahati. Though the average literacy rate of NER is almost equal to the average of Indian literacy rate, the living condition of most of the people are low as compared to other parts of India. Even today nearly 12,000 villages and 45 lakh households have not seen electricity. In Manipur 57 remote villages out of 1000 villages have no access to Doordarshan Channels as these villages are yet to be electrified? The development of this region largely depends on human resources through various amenities. But, HRD in North East faced with several problems like low priority, lack of man-power planning, regional imbalance, brain drain etc. A survey made in 192 counties showed that development depends 20 per cent on natural resources, 16 per cent on infrastructure and 64 per cent on human resources and social factors. But not much has been done for growth of 'knowledge' which today has become a major contributory factor.

Under the above mentioned circumstances it will be more relevant to see how far loss of ethnic violence is visible in our society. No body can deny the fact that ethnic violence affects all aspects of life, create deep divisions within society, leading to mutual hatred between groups, tribes, communities and hamper development activities for which the society remain backward for a long time.

North-east India is the gateway to South-East Asia. Centre's 'Look East' policy can reinforce among its people the feeling that Mongoloid Communities are an appendix meant to be a link between maintained. India and South-East Asia. But the region can not be a full partner of 'Look East' policy among these conflicts.

To take advantage of this policy what is immediately required is to match higher education standards prevailing in other parts of India so that the students can complete on equal terms with others. But, the regrettable matter is that in every year, almost 10,000 students of North East are flying off to other states for higher education. So brain drain is one of the factor that will surely affect the development process as well as leading towards responsive society. Conflicts, violence, war affect all aspects of life and have a profound impact on everything we do. Education which is an intellectual activity, requires an environment of peace and calm. It is important that one of the most essential prerequisite for quality education is a stable law and order situation. But unstable situation prevails due to ethnic clashes. Due to ongoing violence no multinational company come forward to set up big industries in this area for which employment problem rises tremendously and hamper the development activities.

In addition to this Dhansiri Irrigation Project is one of the largest projects in Udalguri area (Assam) started to way back in 1975-76 but still today the project has not completed due to varied problems though centre allotted Rs. 200 crore to complete it by 2008. Moreover, reasons like Bodoland movement and Assam agitation has also fuelled the project to remain incomplete for which the farmer community have been deprived of sufficient water of Dhansiri river required for the cultivation purpose.

Again though agriculture is the main occupation but gradually developed a tendency to get them engaged in non agricultural sector after selling their agricultural land to the non-tribals especially in urban areas. This reflects of gradual decline in the relative of agriculture on primary occupation and change in the nature of economic participation among them. Being exposed to various forces of modernization the tribal peoples have witnessed a gradual loss of their tradition bound socio-economic practices. So, all these aspects indicate that the tribal society is in a midway between tradition and modernity. The vast socio-economic change taking place rapidly which gave rise to the multiplicity of ethnic problem and hamper the society.

To overcome the situation, various ethnic groups must, come forward with high knowledge and information skills, along with high esteem through proper education since the present society is full of confusions and tensions; tension between global and local, tradition and modernity, spiritual and material etc.

For this, life long learning is indispensable for social stability. If there is no social stability there can never be a good life. No state or nation can think of peace. Again, present environment of violence gripping the North East has led the conscious people to believe that country's integration has come under threat. In the North East context emotional integration with the rest of India has been strongly felt.

Now it can easily be assumed that only giving autonomy, reservation, legislation cannot solve the problem or serve the purpose unless they are imparted complete education (to educate others and those who have been improvised) are empowered. For this education in general and higher education in particular are fundamental to the construction of knowledge based economy and knowledge linked society.

Critical Observation

From the above discussion, we find that though India believes in ethnic and cultural pluralism in a social order based on democracy yet there were unrest, agitation etc. In spite of having a series of laws, regulation, policies for the constitutional protection and safeguards of ethnic communities, both the centre and state governments have failed in its execution.

Aggressive regionalism has gravely undermined the feeling that the whole of India is the home of all her inhabitants. In the North East context, all ethnic groups, and tribes must avoid aggressive thinking. Otherwise it will be a great difficulty to bring all sections of people under one umbrella. To live peacefully with one another, a spirit of fraternity needs to be developed. However, the present study reveals that, 'Learning to live together' is the need of hour. For this Central and State governments along with intellectuals must come forward to tackle the problems peacefully. Today, no nation can live in isolation. Even countries under endemic conflict with their neighbours are revising their History and Geography to learn to live together. Truly speaking, creation of learning society embracing all indigenous tribes has been a great challenge for us.

Though, it is difficult to eliminate war, violence and conflict entirely yet through 'Education' we can succeed in reducing their frequency and their destructive effect.

Suggestions

In view of the problems relating to the ethnic conflict in NEI the following suggestions can be projected:

(i) A mere plan of economic development would be utterly inadequate. Among with economic planning, their should be social and political planning in an integrated manner.

(ii) Emphasis should be laid on overall socio-cultural development and not merely on material progress. Development planning should be worked out taking into account the customary traditions of the tribal people.

(iii) Formulation and implementation of development scheme in agricultural and industrial sector, should be carried out in such a way that available scope open up to the unemployed youth for earning their livelihood.

(iv) An environment of natural understanding and compromise should be created to solve the problems of tribal ethnicity through discussions. Everybody should realize that only peaceful measures would bring all-round development to the tribal as well as to the state. Peace would bring prosperity to the nation at the present age of Globalization.

(v) Intellectuals of each ethnic group should take the initiative to create a suitable environment for discussion on democratic line to solve the whole problem.

(vi) Literary organization of different groups of Assam like Bodo Sahitya Sabha, Mishing Sahitya Sabha, Tiwa Sahiyta Sabha, Karbi Sahitya Sabha and not the least Asom Sahitya Sabha should adopt plans and endeavour to wash away the age old misery and resentment of the tribals, so that they again join hands in the mainstream of the country.

(vii) Extreme Nationalism should be avoided.

Politics of Migration

Migration is a burning problem of North East India. In the North East region of India, it is new phenomenon. It persisted much before independence. This region for ages had been the destination of various Sperm of Migrants from different parts of the Subcontinent. There was a huge migration of tea garden labourers in the 1870s followed by the neat Sperm of Muslim peasent immigrants from the East Bengal. This process of migration continued until 1940s. The Sperm of immigration gathered momentum during the first half of 1941-1951 decade and specially during the Muslim League Ministry. Prior to 1937, the Muslim League had no influence in the politics of Assam. But after the 1937 election, the United Muslim Party Government followed a policy of patronizing Muslim immigrants in Assam.

In the post-independence period Assam had provided shelter to a large number of immigrants. With the resource available at the time of independence the state was not in a position to welcome further immigration. But the partition of the Country compelled a large number of Hindus to migrate to Assam and other neighbouring states. Even a considerable number of Muslim farm labourers came to Assam after partition. The people that migrated to Assam may be broadly classified into two categories—1. Foreigners and 2. Indian. These two may again be grouped into five classes, namely (1) Land hungry peasants, (2) Nepali as live stock farmer, (3) Refugees from Bangladesh, (4) Traders from Indian communities specially from Bengal and Rajasthan, and (5) Tea garden labourers mainly from Orissa and Bihar. Besides these there are labourers from states like Uttar Pradesh, Madhya Pradesh, Coastal Andhra Pradesh, artisan from Punjab and white collared Job seekers from all over Indian Subcontinent. It is also a fact that the Assamese Caste tradition did not look upon with favour at the low-graded professions such as barbers, washermen, shoe-makers etc. Assamese capacity for accommodation of these elements from outside was, however, not unlimited. One of the most difficult problems which arose out of this migration was that, with little exception, other Assamese communities to remain separate and aloof. In a sense, a certain distance continued to exist between the Assamese and the Non-Assamese.

Thus, it is clearly conceivable that the size of immigration is large and has worked a deep concern in this region. The continuous influx of foreigners from neighbouring countries has endangered the political sovereignty of the people of the state and threatened the security of this part of Nation. The continuous influx of people first from undivided Bengal, then from erstwhile east Pakistan and now from Bangladesh, not only the Assam alone, but to state in the North East has been noticed by us. The process of social polarization on the basis of change demographic character has already started in Assam. The survival against this demographic aggression has become a intricate problem for the indegenous people today. The Muslim infiltration into Assam has been a serious concern for a strategic border with an Islamic countries. Assam had already been accommodated with several lakhs of Muslim immigrants before partition who were brought to Assam by the then state government led by Sir

Mohammed Sadullah. The then Premier of Assam, in 1939 on the pretext of 'Grow More Food'.

Migration and its Impact

Migration has considerable impact on the social geography of the state, new areas are brought under cultivation, Agricultural and agro-industrial production has come into existence, new crops and new method of cultivation are introduced. The influx of migration is also responsible for urbanization in the state though large areas of Assam still remain rural and agricultural in character. Another important impart of migration in ethnic consolidation burred on language. This has turned to ethnic and linguistic conflicts and the best example are the areas inhabited by the Bengali speaking communities on the one hand and the Assamese speaking Community on the other. This, in fact is one of the most important factor which has ignited the Sovereign Issue in recent time. Migration is also responsible for the exploitation of the local people by the unscrupulous migrants—the money lenders, the businessmen and the land grobbers. Due to Poverty the indegeneous people are force to surrender their land to money lander. Wherever the Migrant settled down permanently, there were social tension and fear. The sources of such tension to mention but a few are linguistic, religious and political.

In 1873 Assamese was recognized as the Court language and made the medium of instruction in school. Though Assamese become the language of the Court and also the medium of instruction in school. It did not become the state official language. Later, the Assam Sahitya Sabha demanded that Assamese should be made the State Language. The Government could not make up its mind and its stance is one of the vacillation. Language Politics began to emerge and riot out in the Assam valley. The riot resulted in loss of life and property and relation between the two communities were strained. Later with a heavy price the government declared Assamese as the State Language. This declaration naturally was attained and welcomed by the Assamese but was resented by the Bengalis and the Tribes for example, demanded the separation of tribal areas from Assam. Language riots broke out in 1970s on the issue of medium of instruction and examination at the College and University levels. Bengali continued to be the medium of instruction and examinations in school. In areas where Bengalis were pre-dominent in view of this fact we can assamese that the problems become acute due to two main reason—Socio-economic and cultural. Economically, the business of Assam was controlled by the Marwaris. The Bengalis largely captured the Petty trades, clerical and other jobs and professions like medicines, teaching, law etc. It is interesting to note that although the

Marwaris exploited the Assamese people economically, the Assamese middle class did not feel dominance in the same way as they felt in the case of Bengali. In the cultural field also the Bengali remained orthodoxed and did not accept the Assamese language and culture on the other hand, they propagated their own culture. This has been a constant and continuous fear among the Assamese people even since the British occupation of Assam. The partition of country further accentuated the problem of migration in Assam. After Partition speam of Hindu refugee follow into Assam from east Pakistan now Bangladesh. The 1951 Census report showed the number of refugees in Assam as 2,74,455 of these 272,075 came from East Pakistan, 647 from West Pakistan and 17,333 from other specified areas. Because of their proximity to East Pakistan, the Cachar district sheltered 93,177 refugees and Goalpara 44,967, kamrup 42,87 Durrong 18,833, Lakhimpur 13,965, Sibsagar 7,514, Khasi Hills 5,072. This inflow of refugees evoked a lot of recruitment in the United Assamese elite.

The Assamese elite had been in constant fear and anxiety of being gradually dominated by groups from outside the province. Amongst the States of India, Assam has got the largest proportion of migrant population. Besides, continuous flow of refugees from Bangladesh and migration of people from the rest of the country greatly affected the population composition of Assam and aggravated further the tension of the society. Today not only the people of Assam are afraid of economic in security but also cultural and political insecurity. The Assam movement of foreign national issue was the reflation of such apprehessions. The political orientation of the student community largely centred round the implementation of Assam Accord in letter and spirit and preparation of a correct voter list.

Political Implication of Migration

The course of politics is determined by the quantum of population in a democratic system. What shapes politics in a country or any region prescribly acquires, depands largely on the size of population there. In a state or a country whether there has been on abnormal increases in population at a particular ethnic or religious group is too clear from the number of scales their leader win in either Parliamentary or Assembly elections. Greater is the size of their population the larger the number of their elected representatives.

Since the introduction at electoral politics in Assam, during the British rule, the issue of immigration has been in the centre of political controversies.

Political parties like Muslim league and Congress in the pre-independence period and the various other parties in the post-independence period have been addressing themselves to the issues. Since the 1970s the North East has been troubled by agitation, mostly led by the students against illegal immigrants from Bangladesh. Over the year this has become a major political issue with different national and regional political groups vying with each other in taking advantages of the solution.

Due to the negligence of government and the connivance of self-seeking politicians, a large number of foreign national have already been fraudulently enrolled on the electoral rolls. Further, there is a possibility of a certain section of the immigrant population consolidating themselves on the basis of language and religion. At the time of 1951 Census, mainly immigrant settling declared his language to be Assamese, thereby occulting the principle of Assimilation with the majority community. But, not it appears that they are being with the majority community. But, now it appears that they are being persecuted to reaffirm their original language for political reasons.

The socio-economic condition of east Bangalee cultivators were deplorable. They occupied the hitherto uninhabited char lands, where order the ravages of pestilence and insecure riverine settlements they manage to eke out a precarious consistence for survival. They were driven out of their homeland in quest of the basis necessities for survival—food, clothing and shelter and were ready to brave against all adds in a province which at least guaranteed them a living space. Latter, when they converged beyond the char to encroach upon indigenous settlement, a section of Assamese land holder welcomed then.

The Second World War opened another wave to unplanned and unwarranted influx of migrants into Assam. Most of the migrants came from famine stricken Bengal.

In the euphoria of independence, thereafter, the issue seems to be forgotten. Thereafter, Assam again became a safe sanctuary for immigrants from the East Pakistan and later Bangladesh. Whether it was the Bangalee Hindus feeling from religious Persecution or Bangladeshi Muslims (past-1971) vying for a living spare, the fast remaining that they are found on equally receptive government awaiting them. Then, it was the Congress government who reversed its earlier stand of opposing immigration to one of actively encouraging it finding a fruitful Vote Bank that would consolidate and guarantee its political existence.

Most of these immigrants have moved out of their hearth and have in search of better means of living, which the sparsely populated north-eastern states, seemed to offer. These uneducated and unskilled immigrants sought to be absorbed in agriculture and related sector. These sectors being of the informed in nature, they were not very visible until in growing mass started having an impact on the polity of the NE states. The extreme example of this phenomenon has been seen in Tripura—a state that saw illegal immigrant population marginalized the local inhabitants in power sharing.

Continuously steady and occasionally heavy influx of people into this NE region has resoled in drastic change in demographic land-scape and will inevitable till the balance of political power in favour of migrates. An examination made by the Union Home Ministry revealed that Legal migrants from Bangladesh constitute majority of the voters in as many as 36 Assembly constituencies in Assam.

Of late, the issue has turned into a major one in the North-eastern states of the country. In the political scenario of this region, the fundamentalists have intensified their activities through the infiltration of Bangladeshi nationals into the region, getting a fear psychosis among the indigeneous people of losing their self-identity in a democratic society and encroachment of their land, political right and loss of identity.

Though migration is a natural course in human behaviour and it is initially encouraged by consideration, the migration into this was ever since independence has not always been economic or natural but has been engineered or motivated. The every source of Muslim militant organizations cited and funded by Pakistan and Bangladesh and these disclosed objective of establishing an independent Islamic Republic does indeed signify national disaster.

If the detection and deportation of foreigners are not taken up speedily, the issue of foreign national would pose a major threat to the security of Assam as well as the North East very soon.

Tragically, all political parties seen to be training a blind age to this problem. The reason is not for to seek. It has all along been done to create a block of voter which would enable them to keep winning election without caring for legitimate electoral rolls.

Suggestion for Solving the Problem of Migration

In order to solve the long standing complex critical of migration, the following suggestions can be projected—

A. As immigration is an international problem it can be solved only through international understanding and mutual co-operation between the country which pulls them (India).

B. So long as there is large variation in the population and the economy, it is natural that the flow of population will continue from the country of higher destiny—low level economy (Bangladesh) to that of the low higher density—high level economy. Assam in India in respect of immigration from Bangladesh to Assam and West Bengal, the Government of India should help the Bangladesh Government for developing its economic condition so that further immigration is naturally stopped and some of the immigrants weight return to the motherland to take the opportunity of economic development.

C. In spite of economic measure as mentioned above for the solution of the immigration problem there must be immediate political solution, which cannot be avoided by the sovereign nation in order to protect the national interest. There are evidently two means of political solution. The first is to seal the Border between Bangladesh and NE India and West Bengal in order to stop further immigrating by completely erecting border fencing and military patrolling in both land and water boundaries. To stop immigrants from a foreign country is the constitutional obligation of the Indian Government the second one is to identify and deport the post-1971 immigrants as per the Assam Award with the help of the Foreigner's Act, 1946 and National Registration Certificate (NRC), 1951 or the voters list of 1952 where the NRC is missing. The controversial IMDT Act, 1983 is discriminatory as it is applicable only in Assam according to which the once of proving a migrant as illegal who accorded the border after 1971 lies with the complainant by depositing a fee of Rs. 10 and to be within a radius of 3 km. from the suspected foreigners place of residence. So this Act should be Scrapped and the infiltrators should be dented and deported under Foreigner Act, 1946 and (MRC) or the voters list of 1952 and 2001.

D. The lasting solution of immigrant problem is to develop work culture among the indigenous people who have been hitherto lethargic and averse to do hard labour particularly in agriculture and other kinds of activities where canual labour is necessary. The immigrant have been incessantly coming to Assam to take the opportunities of earning their livelihood easily by engaging themselves in agriculture and all of physical labour for which they find Assam a Virgin land because of indifference and apathy of the indigenous people towards these activities. There is still enough scope for the latter group to occupy lady for agriculture and earn livelihood engaging themselves in various kind of physical labour which have been now mostly done by the immigrants. If the vast wastelands in Assam were not left vacant ouring the last several decades, but occupied by the indigenous people for agricultural or other purposes then the immigrants would not get the opportunity of coming to Assam and occupy the vacant areas for settlement and agriculture. The reburied network of the indigenous people is the root cause of pulling the migrants to Assam. Thus, it is seen that work culture is the best panacea the stop further inflow of immigrants and also to stop further land alienation from the indigenous people to the immigrant which is threatening to uproot the indigenous people from their own homeland and to marginalize them politico-culturally.

E. The problem should be dearly understood and a realistic solution should sought. All political parties and groups cutting cross their political leaning should agree to concentrate to genuinely protect the right of indigenous population. They should not encourage migration and not a patronize the migrant population for the narrow political gain.

F. Complete uprooting of the vast immigrant population is not feasible as the student leaders of Assam movement realized while in power for almost two learn of five years each. Therefore, the problem of immigration should be bifurcated between the existing stock and future flow.

   The existing stock arising a cutoff date may be giver the economic migrants status. This status would entitle than to their living but not to land acquisition and political Rights.

   On the other hand, a concrete and careful strategy to arrest the flow of the illegal migrants with a longer time perspective needs to be adopted.

G. There exists an element of schizophrenic attitude among local inhabitants in the NE states. In private they prefer cheap and pliant immigrants as labour while in public they discard them. This makes the problem more critical. Therefore, long term strategy should aim at alluring the objective conditions.

H. Reservation of seats in Assam Assembly and the Parliament for the indigenous people is an extreme necessity.

I. All Indian nationals should be issued photo identity card, based on the process started during the tenure of T.N. Seshan as Chief Election Commissioner. This system should be mandatory.

J. Local police who know the areas better than a National force like BSF be given Greater responsibility for detection and blocking border crossings.

Identity Movement

Identity Politics: 'Identity claim' and 'Identity recognition' as the basis of the political movements have became the hallmark of the contemporary discourses. It consists of innumerable defining characteristics that make up the whole of who we are in any given movements. This fragments of self-include ours sexuality, gender and sense of belonging to a particular culture nation and religions, family, or some other groups. Current form of Social Communication process, particularly mainstream media, advertising, television and film, along with family, friend teachers, political agenda. Religion society's rules our perception, perspectives, interpretations and assumption and those of others all play a part in creating identity. In North-East India, "Ethno-culture Identity" says A.C. Bhagabati has been an important source for mobilizing the people in Social political spheres. In fact, identity movement may be viewed as a part of overall Process of Social change and modernization of tribesmen in North East India.

Identity formation is a Complex process. It is historical process the character of which is determined by fine and space.

Identification of oneself with a particular group or an organization is a global human phenomenon. It is determined by certain symbols which are variant from period to period and area to area. Such identifications with district symbols or identities are aimed mostly for the cause of material benefits and psychological satisfaction. Identity, however, does not fix on a particular value or symbol. Permanently however, it can safely be stated that an individual or group of individuals may have more than one identity, e.g. multiple identity and each strength depends on the interest with which the individuals identifies himself with the values concern. However, these multiple identity and loyalty can be explained with the model shown below:

Identity Formation

From the above model it is revealed that human collectivity is organized on the basis of certain human values for the cause of fulfilling this aspirations. However, it is important here to note that nation-state is the supreme legitimate political Institution for fulfilment of the aspirations of the human collectivities in the society. Therefore, firstly each and every individual in a nation-state owes his/her loyalty in the Nation. But, when the nation states by human collectivities not in a position to solve the problem, then the individuals through an organized groups trial to project their demands for fulfilling the aspirations. In this regard they made their effort under a common banners such as, religion, language, culture, region, community and so on. Such kind of categorization of human collectivity can be better understood in terms of "ethnic group".

As such the whole development process of society is nothing but the resultant of interaction between the state and diverse Ethnic Groups. However, in the process of interaction the diverse ethnic groups fulfils their socio-economic and political demands and in return they transform the intensity of the identity both in terms of nations and ethnicity. Thus, an ethnic group may transit their identity in order to fulfil each aspirations. As such each and every ethnic group is very much loyal towards the nation with varying degrees despite having loyality towards own group identity. However, here an attempt has been made to understand the identity politics by keeping in mind the present model of multiple loyalty in the context of North East in general and Assam in particular.

The tribal movements in North East stand in a category by themselves because of its unique geopolitical situation and historical background. Many tribes live on international boundaries and share ethnic and cultural affinities with other tribes across the frontier. The hilly areas of North East India were not completely integrated with the politico-eco system of colonial period and the Inner Line system further isolated the tribal region of North East from the rest of the country. Tribals in the region except in Tripura never felt relly threatened of their identity because of their overwhelming majority in the tribal region. Christianity has emerged as a strong factor of modernisation, and has given the tribals a sense of identity. Political processes in the hills became active on the eve of transfer of power. New states were created to accommodate tribal aspirations. The Sixth Schedule in the process became outdated.

The spread of British administration in the North East India helped in developing a sense of identity and alliences between different tribal groups. The growth of administration and administrative centres and marketing centres, the spread of education and christianity offered opportunities for inter-tribal integrations. The establishment of modern social associations and political organisations have played a significant role.

On the eve of independence the situation in North East India was very fluid. The impact of Second World War, the policy of colonial administration, the national movement and communal riots, a growing sense of ethnic identity among different communities in North East all these factors combined together contributed to the growth of enthno-political movements in North East India.

The most important factors in any analysis in tribal identity are the class nature of the present day tribal society, the. under-development of tribal economy and scarcity of resources. The under-development of the economy resulted in an uneven development of the economy of tribal societies and this uneven growth brought the problems of tribal identity in the limelight. The reason for tribal movement lies in the conflict for controlling of political power and economic resources by the elite of tribal societies and neighbouring society. The tribal insurgency is a militant assertion for a share of limited economic resources. The rising tribal aspirations are expressed through movement on cultural identity crisis, the basis of which is economic. As aspirations rise and economic development is painfully slow and uneven, millitancy is bound to grow. The rising middle class and petty bourgeoise in tribal society are bound to take up arms against their counterparts in other societies.

The political movement in the hills surfaced with the transfer of power. The tribal movement, though apparently political in character, agrarian issues and economic aspirations give a new dimensions to the movement. Industrialisation in the hills is non-existent. Agriculture is primitive, unable to cater the minimum needs of the hill people. The problem of land alienation is acute. The communal ownership of land is notional. The rich in the tribal society have concerned all social wealth in the form of forest and agricultural land all over North-East India. The un-planned exploitation of mineral resources has created a class of neorich alianated from traditional tribal society. The poverty is the relief map of the hills in the North-East India. The agrarian issues are bound to dominate in tribal identity movement.

Absentee landlordism is reality in the hills. National social equality is on its way out. The new owning class in tribal society need political instrument to consolidate its hold on economy of the under-developed tribal society. The political instrument is in the hands of new elite alienated from traditional society with the distinct class affiliation, cutting across inter-tribal distinctions. Identity crisis is an urban phenomenon rooted among the rising petty bourgeoise and middle class with a definite class solidarity all over North-East India.

The Sixth Schedule to the Constitution of India gave legal sanction to identity movement by providing a political mechanism in the hands of rising middle class in the hills. The Sixth Schedule was chosen as a means of quieting the potential opposition of the emerging middle class in the hills by proliferation of offices of profit. The Khasis, the Garos, and the Mizos took advantage of this new political institution in the form of District Councils. The emerging middle class consolidated its initiative in economic field in the hills areas. The middle class leadership of Tripura tribals saw in it the class advantage and went to use it to consolidate class rule in the autonomous tribal district.

The middle class moderate leadership in a broad spectrum of matriliny was content with the autonomous state. The radical wing of hill leadership with roots in rural area demanded a full-fleged statehood in the form of Meghalaya within Indian Union. The autonomous state blossmed in a full-statehood and the middle class hill leadership got a strong political foot-hold in the Khasi, Jaintia and Garo hills. The elite class is urbane and took the constitutional way to achieve their political goal of identity. The Naga experience is not much different. The influence of Church shaped the social and political outlook of the middle class leadership of the hills. The Baptist Church in Naga hills and in the former Lushai hills attracted the radical rural leadership. Christianity is the North East India in the cultural dimension of the political process. It became a symbol of tribal identity and produced organised middle class leadership in tribal society. Church spread education in tribal society of the North-East and helped the birth of elite dominant class in the hiIl urban centres. The dependent rural people remain in utter poverty under semi-feudal social set up in all the hills of North-East India. The towns have become fortified centres of wealth and middle class solidarity.

The soliderity movement started in the Jaintia Hills, with the establishment of the Jaintia Durbar as a socio-cultural organisation in 1900. Politics came in the wake of the Montford Reforms inseparably with social movements. In 1923 J.J.M. Nichols Roy took the initiative of establishing the Khasi National Durbar and becoming its founder secretary. The Durbar consisted of the Siems and other aristocrats. In 1923 it codified some of the Khasi customary land-laws. In 1927 Nichols Roy became a minister in the Assam Government, and gave up the secretaryship of the Durbar in favour of a personal follower, Joab Solomon.

In 1928, with the appointment of the Indian Statutory Commission and the Indian States Commission, full-scale political activity started in the

Khasi Hills. On 9 March, 1928, the Durbar headed by the Siems decided not to submit any memorandum to the Statutory (Simon) Commission as the proper authority to receive any representation from the Khasi states was the States Commission which was not visiting the Khasi hills.

But, Joab Solomon, along with two other Khasi gentlemen, made a representation to the Simon Commission in which Solomon signed as the secretary, Khasi National Durbar. The memorandum complained against the system of issuing *sanads* since 1859, which had put the Siems under complete subjection to the authority of the Deputy Commissioner enabled the local government to grab the land of the Khasi and entitled a chief to make profit out of the lease, sale or other disposal of the minerals of the Khasi Hills. The memorandum suggested that the Khasi National Durbar "which is now in its formative stage may be legalised and made representative as much as possible". It also carried a draft constitution for the Durbar, which was to consist of the chiefs and other elected and nominated members, and would have the power: *(a)* to make laws which shall be subject to the assent of the Governor of Assam, *(b)* to levy taxes for the improvement of the states, and *(c)* to frame rules for the conduct of its own meetings and the meeting of the Executive Council. But the representative character of Solomon's memorandum was denounced by an another memorandum submitted by Babu Sib Charan Roy and others. It said that the Khasi National Durbar 'as at present composed' was too young and 'still far from being a representative body'. The difference. thus centred on the question whether democracy would mean, in Khasi society, the creation of a centralised organisation like the Durbar where the followers of Nichols Roy—were in considerable strength, or maintenance of the islands autonomy that were the Siemships.

Another aspect to the reforms controversy was the conflict in attitudes towards the Judicial system. The Traditionalists in the hills had long been complaining about the officials' lack of understanding of their customery laws. As late as 1939, Jobang D. Marak, a Garo MLA, potested that some Deputy Commissioners disdain some of their customs on account of which some innocent persons suffered extremely severe punishments. The second memorandum submitted with the Siems' blessings, therefore, demanded the appellate jurisdiction of the High Court of Calcutta stressing that while the Khasi may not at present need any reform in respect of self-determination, they stand in real need of a reform of the British Courts here. After the report of the Indian States Commission attempts were made by the Khasi states to set up a Khasi States Federation. In 1933, the Association of Khasi states presented a memorandum to Viceroy Willingdon demanding representation of the Khasi states in the proposed Indian federal legislature.

Willingdon assured them of representation after the Khasi states had united. The federation came to being early 1934 decided to send its representative to the Chamber of Princes and demanded the curtailment of powers of the Deputy Commissioners.

The other hill districts where political activity in the form of a social movement was recorded in the second decade of the last century was the Naga district. In 1918, a Naga club set up at Kohima with officials and a few village headmen. The Simon Commission recorded that beyond Dimapur they had met representatives of the North East Frontier people including the Naga. The Naga hills demanded the Simon Commission exclusion from the reform scheme.

Around 1930, several mushroom 'tribal' organisations of small groups were born sometimes with official backing. Mae Donald KharKongor reportedly tried to unify them into a kind of Hills Union, but failed.

In the Mizo Hills some 'commoners' raised a demand for representation to the Provincial Assembly of 1937. But the movement was suppressed.

The new- phase of the movement had started first in the Khasi hills. To early 1946, a Khasi-Jaintia Political Association was set up at Shillong, mainly with the backing of the Siems. In March 1946 it submitted a 'memorial', to the Secretary of State for India and the Cabinet Mission, and to this Excellency the Governor of Assam and the Deputy Commissioner of the Khasi and Jaintia Hills. The 'memorial' stressed that the Khasis belong to a race quite distinctly individual from any other race in India living in democratic communes, and have preserved their characteristic independence and ancient democratic institutions from time immemorial. They did owe a deep gratitude to the British Crown for preserving this individuality and showed apprehension for the future change, as the last election in January 1946, in which Nichols Roy had been returned on a Congress ticket and accompanied by a Congress woman, Bonelly Khongman (Khasi), had shown that a mixed electorate would deprive the indegenous people of real representation. The memorial called for a federation of the Khasi areas within a 'Sovereign Assam' with adequate culture and political autonomy.

In the Naga Hills, in April 1945, the Deputy Commissioner of the Naga Hills district, C.R. Pawsey, had established the Nage District Tribal Council as a forum of the various Naga groups in the district. In February 1946 this body was reorganised as a political platform called the Naga National Council (NNC) under the leadership of Aliba Imti Ao. When the report of the Cabinet Mission was published, the NNC in June 1946 passed a resolution at Wokha demanding autonomy within Assam. Towards the end of February 1947, the NNC passed a resolution in which they called for the establishment of 'an interim Government' of Nagas with financial provisions for a period of ten years, at the end of which the Naga people should be left to choose any form of government. The Bordoloi Sub-Committee claimed to have met the substance of the claims made by the Nagas, namely to maintain their customery laws and courts, management of their land with its resources, the continuance of the regulations by which entry and residence in the hills could be controlled and a review of the whole position after ten years.

In case of Lushai Hills (now Mizoram), the then Superintendent McCall, perturbed by the diminution of the chiefs authority and drafted a scheme for a District Chiefs Durbar to advise the administration on the regulation of the social life of the people. His sucessor, MacDonald, convened a District Conference in 1946 with 20 representatives each from the chiefs and the commoners chosen separately. By October 1946, the conference practically disintegrated.

The Conference was revived shortly before the visit of the sub-committee to the district. This time representatives were jointly elected by the chiefs and commoners. The Bordoloi Sub-Committee found that in the Lushai Hills there were responsible sections of the population who were concerned mainly with the protection of their lands, social customs and interests. In Arunachal Pradesh village councils were evolved as an administrative mechanism for fulfilling local needs. The village council is known by different names in different tribes. They were Mongjom among the Monpas, Jumba among the Sherdukpens, Melley among the Akas, Nele among the Nishis, Buliang among the Apatanis, Abala among the Idu Mishmis, Mokchup among the Khamtis, Ngothun among the Noctes and Kebang among the Adis. The village councils differs considerably because of differences in social outlook and psychology among the tribes.

The indegenous and traditional village councils govern and administer the life of the people. Among the Village Councils the Kebang of the Adis is considered to be highly participatory and democratic. Among the three tiers of the Kebang-Dolung Kebang, Banggo Kebang and Bogum Bokang Kebang, the third tier, i.e Bongum Bokang Kebang is the supreme Kebang. It acts almost like an "Adi Parliament".

Thus, it can be said that in the Assam hills, political awareness grew first in the Khasi hills, In the other hills political participation really began with the reforms of 1937. In the 1930s the Congress was born in the Tripura and Manipur states. But except in Tripura and that too chiefly among the plains people the Congress could never with a substantial following. Almost all the hill people remained uninterested in the party. Working in Assam from 1942, the Communist Party failed to enrol any hill person as member, but at the end of the Second World War, the student wing of the party began to be active in Shillong. In 1945 an Assam Hill Students' Association was formed in Calcutta. Again in 1946 there was an All-Assam Students Conference in Shillong in which even some Naga and Lushai students took part.

But in spite of various efforts it was not possible to establish a common political platform for all the hill people.

Introduction of the modern democratic institutions, particularly the Panchayati Raj in the NEI in general and hills in particular was great venture towards bringing the people of the hills in the mainstream of democratic life of the country. The basic objective of Panchayati Raj System was for rural development and to give it a distinct political identity, thereby to develop a new political culture, involving the participation of the people in a truely democratic manner, by integrating the different community into the larger national life. It was aimed at decentralized form of administration, giving opportunities to rural folk to study their problems and to find solutions by themselves.

Though, the Panchayati Raj System was introduced with the objective to speed up the developmental activities with the peoples' participation and to generate conditions favourable to a uniform growth of political development of different tribal groups but its introduction had a far reaching impact on traditional political institutions of the tribes. It has upset the age old political equilibrium and the political system of the village. However, it will be difficult to say that the traditional institutions completely declined or eroded altogether. Still some of the institutions are popular among the tribal society although it has no longer enjoys the same legitimacy as it had enjoyed in the traditional society.

Language Movements

Language Politics in India

The general perception about language is that it a means of communication through which one can express his or her feelings, likes, dislikes etc. Apparently, therefore, it seems that language has nothing to do with politics and it is apolitical. However, this perception about language cannot be a universally acceptable perception. This is because; sometimes language develops its nexus with politics. Political dimension of language may either be unifying or be divisive. It is unifying, if it serves as the basis of political unity among the people speaking common language. It is divisive, if it creates contradiction around linguistic identity in a multi-lingual society. Because of these political dimensions of language that study of linguistic politics always has been a focal point in the study of a political system.

India is not free from linguistic politics. Linguistic politics, in fact, was one of the challenging issues that India had to face immediately after the achievement of Independence. Emergence of successive language movements, in different parts of the country, formation of political parties around linguistic identity, re-organization of state, adoption of Uri-lingual policy etc. are some examples which indicate political dimension of language or linguistic politics in India. Although language was emerged as a dominant issue in the post-Independent period yet linguistic controversy was there even in the pre-Independent India. Such linguistic contradiction was basically between Urdu and Hindi and of Devnagri and Persian script. Partition of the country, however, put an end to the Urdu-Hindi conflict and a new question arose, whether English should be allowed to continue as official language, or not? And if not, then what language should be recognized as official language in place of English. Continuity of English as official language, as Paul Brass (1990: 160) observes, "raised both practical and an emotional question". Practically, continuity of English was justified because English serves as the means of "international communication and transmission through the educational system of modern science and technology" as because "none of Indian language was fully prepared either in vocabulary or in the availability of translated text'. Such a practical consideration was reflected in Mr. Naziruddin Ahmed's speech in Constituent Assembly Debate when Mr. Ahmed said:

> "...English should continue as the official language of India for all purposes for which it was being used, till a time when an All India Language is evolved, which will be capable of expressing the thought and ideas on various subjects, scientific, mathematical, literary, historical, philosophical, political". Mr. Ahmed also repudiated the emotional consideration of the language question by saying—"I submit that the British have gone; British domination was a thing worth removing. But what about their language? Is the English language is a British language? I submit it is a world language that is why I submit that English should be compulsory."

However, despite of having such practical consideration, the emotional consideration got precedence over the practical one. Accordingly, effort was made to find out a language, which could have given the status of national language. Because of the numerical strength of Hindi speakers that Hindi was recognized as national language. Recognization of Hindi as national language accelerated the linguistic problem in India, instead of bringing any lasting solution to the language problem. This was because the so-called majority of Hindi was relative majority and therefore, in the areas where

Hindi's status was minority the movement was started against the recognition of Hindi as national language.

Language Politics in Assam

Assam was one of those states where linguistic issue has emerged as dominant issue in the post-Independent period. The two successive language movements indicate that how dominant was the language issue in Assam. The first language movement started in 1960s, demanding Assamese as official Language and the second was in 1970s, which demanded Assamese as a medium of instruction upto university level.

The language issue of Assam was, however, somewhat different that of the other parts of the country. Following are some aspects, which distinguish the language problem of Assam from that of other parts of the country.

Firstly, unlike the language movements of other parts of the country the language movement of Assam did not demand for reorganization of states on the basis of language. Rather the demand of language movement of Assam concentrated only for the recognition Assamese as official language and as medium of instruction.

Secondly, the language movement of Assam was a reaction against Bengali chauvinism, whereas the language movements of other parts of the country were the reaction against Hindi chauvinism. They were basically the product of recognition of Hindi as national language. Contrary to that the language movement of Assam was less concerned with the status of Hindi as national language.

Thirdly, most of the language movements of other parts of the country ended with the formation of political party Tamil Nadu and Andhra Pradesh are the best examples where the language based political parties came into existence because of their history of language movement. But in Assam the language movement did not lead to the emergence of any such language base political party although some organizations played vital role in the language movement.

The language movement of Assam started in the post-Independent period. However, it has got its momentum in April 1959, when the Assam Sahitya Sabha set the year 1960 as deadline to implement their demands. Meanwhile, incidents and counter incidents of violence began to take place between the Assamese and Bengali at the different parts of the state. Under such a situation the then Chief Minister of Assam, Bimal Prasad Chaliha felt it necessary to introduce the Official Language Bill in the State Legislature.

Accordingly the Assam Official Language Act (*see* Appendix-A) was introduced and Mr. Chaliha said as—

> "During the last few years several states in India have decided upon their respective official language and therefore, this question naturally has assumed some urgency and importance in Assam also Meanwhile public opinion grew in intensity and volume and the matter was again raised in all seriousness in the last Budget Session of the Assembly (therefore) in the situation prevailing in the state today it no longer desirable to postpone a decision on this question. Emotions have been raised and sentiments played up and the state has passed through some unfortunate and tragic happenings" (Assam Legislative Assembly Debate: 1960: 233).

Thus, for Mr. Chaliha, it was imperative to introduce Official Language Bill keeping in mind the developments of other parts of the country and also the 'emotions' of Assamese people.

However, while providing the justification to the introduction of Language Bill, Mr. Chaliha kept in mind only about the sentiments and emotions of the Assamese speaking people and not about the discontent of other linguistic minorities which was almost equally significant. As a result a statewide reaction was noticed, particularly by the Bengali community. As a protest against the Assam Official Language Act the Nikhil Assam Banga Bhasha Samiti had submitted a memorandum to tle President demanding recognization of Bengali for all official purposes throughout the state. The Bengali speaking people were so dissented that they started a movement, particularly under the guidance of Sangram Parishad and Bhasa Andolan Samiti. As the situation was deteriorating, the Central level leader of the Congress Party had to intervene on the issue. As a result, the then Prime Minister Lal Bahadur Shastri came out with a formula which was popularly known as "Shastri Formula". The basic objective of Shastri Formula was to find out the solution to the linguistic conflict in Assam by making the Official Language Act some will be flexible and by giving opportunity to the linguistic minorities.

Assam had to witness another language movement in 1970s, which was known as movement for Medium of Instruction. It did take place, when, in early 1970s, Gauhati University decided to introduce Assamese as the medium of instruction in all colleges under jurisdiction with some exception. This decision was come into effect from the academic year 1972-73. Decision of Gauhati University to introduce English and Assamese as a medium of instruction, created discontent among the Bengalis and hence, demands were made to declare Bengali also as a medium of instruction. Keeping in mind the increasing demands of the Bengali speaking people, the Academic Council of Gauhati University came out with a 'Circular' according to which —

(i) English was to be retained as the medium of instruction for a period of time, and
(ii) Students would be permitted to answer their examination questions in Assamese, English and Bengali.

The decision of the Academic Council to permit the students to answer in Bengali had provoked the Assamese speaking people and started agitation. Under such an agitational pressure the Academic Council had to review its decrision. Accordingly the Academic Council came out with its revised decision on 12 June, 1972, which included following aspects—

(i) Assamese shall be the medium of instruction in all colleges under the jurisdiction of Gauhati University.
(ii) English will continue as an alternative medium of instruction till such time not exceeding ten years as may be considered necessary by the Academic Council.
(iii) Students shall have the option to answer either in Assamese or in English in University Examination.
(iv) The above decision shall come into force with effect from the session 1972-73 in respect of two years, pre-university course from the session 1974-75 in respect of two-year degree course.

The revised circular, again, created discontent among the Bengali speaking people and the government had to establish separate university for the people of Barak valley.

The above mentioned points distinguish the language movement of Assam to that of the language movements of other parts of the country. But in spite of having all these differences the language movement of Assam could be able to put tremendous effect both in the politics of Assam and India as well.

Causes of Language Movement

As already has been mentioned the language politics of Assam was somewhat a different to that of other parts of the country. This distinctiveness, ostensively suggested the causes of the language movement would be different to that of the other parts of the country. In following discussion, therefore, an attempt is being made to explore the distinct causes of language movement of Assam.

(i) Independence and Partition: India got her Independence on August 15, 1947. But, it was independence at the cost of partition. Partition of the country led to certain geographical changes. What contributed towards the language movement of Assam was that the annexation of Sylihet with East Bengal (present Bangladesh). Annexation of Sylihet had made the Bengali speaking people relatively smaller in size and the Assamese speaking people emerged as relatively larger one. Following table shows how the population of Bengali speaking people was declined and Assamese speaking people was increasing.

Distribution of population language-wise

Language	*1911*	*1921*	*1931*	*1941*	*1951*
Assamese	35.3	33.43	32.32	56.29	57.14
Bengali	26.9	27.60	27.56	19.64	17.36

Source: Language Politics of Assam (1997), Sandhya Goswami, p.42

Increase of Assamese speaking people had provided the numerical logic to demand for recognition of Assamese as difficult language. The strength of various linguistic groups in Assam is given as below:

Major Language groups in Assam, 1971

Language	*No. of speakers*	*Percentage of Population*
Assamese	8,904,917	60.89
Bengali	2,882,039	19.71
Hindi	792,481	5.42
Bodo	533,713	3.65
Nepali	349,116	2.38
Mikir	191,354	1.31
Miri/Mishing	177,226	1.21
Oriya	150,196	1.03
Manipuri/Meitie	87,167	0.60
Santhali	86,086	0.59

Source: Census of India, 1971, Assam part.

The Above table shows that the Assamese is the major language group having 60.89 percentage of total population. However, it should here be mentioned that some of the plain's tribes also identify themselves as Assamese speaker and therefore, the percentage of Assamese speaking people was raised. Whatever may be the cause, the fact was that the Assamese speaking people emerged as dominant language group and with this language group they started their movement.

(2) Historical Factor: To state the historical factor of language movement it can be traced back from the colonial period when Bengali language was introduced by the colonial ruler as court language.

Introduction of Bengali as court language created discontent among the Assamese people. Anandaram Dhekial Phukan and Moniram Dewan were prominent among those who also submitted petition to the colonial ruler by protesting the introduction of Bengali as court language. Then onwards, the Assainese educated class developed their consciousness to promote their language. The Calcutta educated figures like Lakhminath Bezbarua, Chandra Kumar Agarwala, Hemchandra Barua, Gunabhiram Barua etc. greatly contributed towards the promotion of Assamese language. The organization like Asomiya Bhasa Unnati Sadhini Sobha, Asom Sahitya Sobha also played vital role in this regard. In fact, the national consciousness of early 20th century was developed around the linguistic identity and the language movements of post-Independent period were the reflection or legacy of such linguistic consciousness.

(3) Role of Press: Role of Press is always omnipotent and omnipresent in any social movement. The language movement was not an exception to that. The press, both the Assamese and Bengali medium, has played significant role in motivating, in articulating the language issue and also in agitating the people of respective languages. As Dr. Sandhya Goswami observes:

> The press had played a significant role in creating, encouraging and sustaining the language riots in Assam. The Press both, Assamese and Bengali, were active in spreading canards among the two communities. Not only was the display of needs provocative, there was, in addition editorials as well as letters to the editors emphasizing these points. However, it observes to be mentioned that the newspapers of Assam being limited in their circulation, do not reach as large as leadership as the Calcutta based newspapers do.

Dr. Goswami's observation clearly indicates that the Press was one of the motivating factors behind language movement of Assam.

(4) Role of Various Organizations: Various organizitions both Assamese and Bengali also contributed towards the language movement of Assam. Asom Sahitya Sobha, Asom Jatiyatabadi Mahasabha, All Assam Student's Union (AASU) were the prominent among such Assamese organisations. Whereas the Nikhil Assam Banga Bhasa Samiti, Sangram Parishad, Bhasa Andolan Samitti etc. were the prominent Bengali organisations. All these organizations through petition and counter-petition, demonstration and counter-demonstration, processions and memorandum etc. had made the language movement a vivid one.

(5) Political Situation: The political situation of Assam in post-

Independent period was instable and insecure. Reasons were different—the ongoing tribal movements, the influx of Muslims from East Bengal and Hindu refugees, transfer of Sylhet etc. created a sense of insecurity among the Assamese people about their identity and about their language. Therefore, an instable and insecure political situation also can be held responsible for the language movement.

(6) Economic Factor: Economic factor always continued to exist in any movement either in hidden or in manifested form. Though the economic issue was not a prominent issue of the language movement yet, economic insecurity also was responsible for the language movement. Compared to the advance regions, Assam did not witnessed with any noticeable economic development in spite of having vast natural resources. The state did not witnessed with any mega projects or big industrialization. Communication was not much developed. Employment situation showed not much of progress. The major sectors of state economy, i.e. agriculture did not pass through any revolutionary progress. After the entire economic situation failed to bring a ray of expectation among the Assamese people. Such economic insecurity brokedown the mental set up of the Assamese people and reflected through language movement.

The discussion on the causes of language movement makes it clear that the language movement was not the product of a single factor. Number of causes were there which, less or more degree, contributed towards the language movement. It was not like that the Assamese people developed an apprehension about their linguistic identity but also at the same time they were facing with a situation of insecurity both economic and political. Therefore, the language movement was the product of sets of factors than that of a single factor.

Implications of Language Movement

As a result of language movement Assamese was recognized as an official language and Assamese was recognized as Medium of Instruction in all colleges under the two universities of Assam. Declaration of Assamese as official language and medium of instructions created discontent among other linguistic minorities. As Mohan Das from Cachar said:

> "You may pass the language bill today by a majority but do not think for a moment that the problem is solved by it. For haven's sake do not do anything which would embitter our feeling more and make disintegration of the state a settled fact."

The apprehensions of Mr. Das come into practice when the Bengalis started protest against the action of the government and academic Council of Gauhati University. To satisfy the Bengalis the 'Shastri Formula' was adopted and 'Assam University' was established.

The Tribals, particularly the hill tribes also expressed their discontent over the action of the government. This was reflected from the speech of hill tribe leader Captain Williamson Sangma. While debating on official language Bill Sangma said:

> "It is already known to the people of the entire state that we, hill people, are vehemently opposed to the introduction of the Bill. We are opposed to declaring Assamese as the Official Language of the State. Our stand is considered to be not justified. As you personally know Sir, ever since 1918 when the move for declaring Assamese as the state language the Hill leaders including myself expressed our strong opposition to the proposal. Even since that time the Hill leaders made it very clear that they were not prepared to accept Assamese as the state language of Assam. It was not because we disliked Assamese or we had ill feeling against our Assamese brothers and sisters. But we are considered that by accepting Assamese as the official language we shall be handicapped: Regarding the Negotiating committee Sangma said that "the Negotiating committee was nothing but a mere show", and the committee had already "determined to dominate" the tribals. He also mentioned that the Official Language Bill has destroyed all the endeavours of the leaders to build a united Assam by bringing the people of the Hills and the plains into closer relationship and understanding. It was, basically, because of the linguistic chauvinism that the tribes started their separatist tendency.

Apart from above mentioned implications, one most lasting severe implication of the language movement was that it created a sense of stiff-ness and hatredness between Assamese and other linguistic groups, out of them the Assamese-Bengali rift still continues to exist.

Foreign National Movement

After the partition of the country, heavy influx of Hindu refugees took place. In Assam the ruling Congress government allowed the illegal immigrants to settle down in Assam. For their self-interests, i.e. so that they become vote bank of the Congress Party in future. The government also opened the land and gave ample opportunity for their settlement. Thus, the illegal immigrants created the language and cultural problems. Besides there were problems of economic disparity. Assamese elites were very much concerned about the economic backwardness of Assam. They felt that economic disparity was the root cause of the economic underdevelopment of the state. It appeared to the Assamese elite that they are being deprived of the benefits of mineral resources and other materials, such as tea, jute, coal etc. To assert their disatisfaction, the Assamese people, launched the oil refinary movement in 1958 and 1968, official language movement in 1960, and medium movement in 1972. The feeling of apprehension of threatening of the Assamese identity both, politically and culturally, reappeared when it was found that a large number of foreign nationals were enlisted in the voters list of the Mangaldoi Lok Sabha Constituency in 1979. The vital and sensitive issue, i.e. foreign nationals was taken up by the dominent Assamese elite for launching the movement, under the leadership of the All Assam Students Union (AASU), All Assam Gana Sangram Parishad (AAGSP), which came to be known as 'foreign national movement'. Thus, heavy influx of illegal immigrants to the state also generated a sense of regionalism in the minds of the Assamese.

The issue of foreign nationals gradually became a headache in almost all quarters of Assam. To fight this problem the All Assam Gana Sangram Parishad (AAGSP) constituted a coordinating body consisting of the representatives of Asom Jatiyatabadi Dal (AJD), Purbanchaliya Loka Parishad (PLP), Asom Jatiyatabadi Juba Chatra Parishad (AJYCP) and Asom Sahitya Sabha (ASS) on 27 August, 1979. The leaders of the foreign national movement had initially taken care to keep the movement secular and peaceful but certain interested sections made use of linguism and communalism to spark a sectarian riots in different pockets. The movement leaders asserted that the all India political parties were not relevant to Assam to tackle its prorblems. Therefore, workers and supporters of all India parties were victims of assult and murder in the hands of movement porters. In the midst of movement, however, the 'politics of discussion' started between AASU-AASGSP and Central Government (February 2, 1990), but no solution to the problem was found. Agitation continued vigorously and in the course of maintaining law and order situation, 697 agitationists were killed which added fuel to the fire and turned it more violent. In the meantime, elections to the Assam Legislative Assembly (1983) was conducted with the assistance of security forces despite strong opposition from the agitationists. The election was boycotted by the agitationists which resulted in killing of about 4000 people at Neli, Gohpur, Silapather, Goreswar, Laharighat and Dhula attack. The AASU and AAGSP charàcterised the newly constituted Legislative Assambly as 'unconstitutional' and demanded its immediate dissolution. But Hiteswar Saikia by that time able to gain the support of diverse sections of people. Thus the policy of Saikia had crippled the agitation and normalcy was restored in the state. Under the circumstances, the agitationists were compelled to look for an amicable settlement of the vexed problem. It appeared that they were even prepared to come down from their earlier stand regarding the cut off year of the detection and deportation of the foreigners. It may be reiterated that at the peak of the movement the agitationists struck to the 1951 as the cut off year. Although Indira Gandhi, the then Prime Minister of India proposed the 1971 as the cut off year for its viable solution, in no way the movement leaders were prepared to come down from 1951. But, when it was found that the mass base of the movement was gradually eroded, they had no alternative except to adopt a face saving device to meet the objective reality of the situation. Thus the agitationists confined on to the one point programme, i.e. removal of Saikia Government to pave the way for installation of a new government led by the leaders of the movement. Keeping in view this inherent intention, they started making several rounds of talks with Rajib Gandhi, who became the Prime Minister of India on 31 October, 1984 after the assassination of his mother. Ultimately after 27 rounds of talks the historic 'Assam Accord' was signed between AASU, AAGSP and Central Government on 15 August, 1985. This accord brought an end the six year old foreign national movement. As per understanding, the Assam Legislative Assembly was dissolved and the mid-term poll was ordered. In the event of this, under- the leadership of AASU, a convention was organised at Golaghat on 12-14 October, 1985 to form a political party with the movement leaders to capture political power of the state through election. Thus the regional aspiration of the Assamese people culminated in the formation of 'Asom Gana Parishad' as a common political plateform of the Assamese to fight the election of 1985.

The 'Asom Gana Parishad' fought the election with the issue of 'Assam Accord'. The main election pledges of the AGP were:

1. The AGP would take effective steps for the permanent solution of the foreign national problem and establish peace and amity among all the communities of the state.
2. Unity, peace and progress.
3. Implementation of Assam Accord.
4. Security to every citizen of India.
5. To bring about an end all kinds of suppression and to strengthen democracy etc.

The AGP contested the elections in 105 seats out of the total of 106 Assembly Constituencies in the Brahmaputra valley and won 65 seats and formed its government in the state.

Insurgency and Secessionist Movement

At the time of Independence the entire region was known as Assam comprising the province of Assam and the native states of Manipur and Tripura, the Governor of Assam having special responsibilities towards the native states. The province of Assam had many normal and some scheduled districts. Assam as an independent province was constituted in 1874. Administration in the British portion, i.e. excluding territories under the native states was run through normal legislators (Central and Provincial) in the districts and through special legislations called Regulations in the Scheduled Districts. Governors General-in-Council had the power to declare 'backward tracts'. Scheduled districts were a part of such 'backward tracts'. 'Backward tracts' were of two kinds—one, which the governor administered as agent of the Governor General and the other, which he administered without interference from his Ministers even in relation to Transferred Subjects. The system was fully formalized and made quite explicit after the Government of India Act, 1935 and the Government of India (Excluded and Partially Excluded Areas) Order, 1936 came into force. The North East Frontier Tract, The Naga Hills, The Lushai Hills and The North Cachar Hills (a subdivision of Cachar district) were designated as Excluded Areas while the Garo Hills. The Mikir Hills and the British portion of Khasi and Jaintia Hills district excluding the Shillong municipality and the cantonment were designated as Partially Excluded Areas. The Governor of Assam was the exclusive administrator of the Excluded Areas; Even Indian citizens were not permitted to enter there areas without the permission were the local authorities. Partially Excluded Areas were within the Jurisdiction of the Ministry, but central and provincial legislations were applicable only after the Governor had so approved with whatever modification he deemed suitable. Soon after Independence Lushai Hills was named as Mizo district.

The Excluded and, to some extent, Partially Excluded Areas (earlier Backward sacts) had been kept isolated by the British administration. The tribal inhabitants of the areas were encouraged to manage their interval and local affairs through their traditional institutions. The interest of the district administration was to ensure that peace and tranquillity prevailed in the area.

Taking into account the comparative isolation of the hills people, the way they had managed their internal affairs under the British rule, and recognising their fierce will to preserve their individual identities within the Indian Union and inherently democratic way that their social and traditional institutions functioned, a certain measure of autonomy to manage their affairs was decided to be provided in the Constitution through the Sixth Schedule.

This Schedule mandated that autonomous district councils with administrative, legislative, judicial and taxation powers would be set up in the areas of Khasi and Jaintia Hills, Garo Hills, Mikir and North Cachar Hills, Mizo Hills and Naga Hills to enable the indegenous people to manage their internal affairs in a democratic way. These institutions came into being in the early 1950s in all these districts of Assam excepting the Naga Hills, where the Naga leadership did not accept this offer and continued with their demand ofa Sovereign Greater Nagaland. Gopinath Bardoloi and Rev. J.J.M. Nichols Roy were the architects of the Sixth Schedule, and were strongly supported by Dr. Ambedkar and Prof. Jaipal Singh in getting this provision approved in the Constituent Assembly against very vehement opposition launched by Kuladhar Chaliha, Lakshyadhar Choudhury and Brajeshwar Prasad.

In a bid to contain the turmoil through which Naga Hills was undergoing, an agreement was arrived at with the leaders of Naga People's Convention in early 1960, and a separate state of Nagaland was created within the Union of India comprising the area of Naga Hills district of Assam and Tuensang Division of NEFA by the State of Nagaland Act, 1962.

Relations between the District Councils and the Government of Assam had not been free from tensions, and the tribals residing in the autonomous districts had misgivings about the intentions of the Assamese people. When the Assam Legislature passed the Official Language Bill in 1960 making Assamese the official language of the state, the people in the hills felt that their individual identities were under threat, and they launched a successful non-violent mass movement for the creation of a separate state for themselves. Initially, an autonomous state of Moghalaya was created comprising the districts of Garo Hills United Khasi and Jaintia Hills (the people of Mikir Hills and North Cachar Hills having decided to continue with Assam).

Meanwhile, in the 1960s trouble had broken out in Mizo Hills, Manipur and Tripura. In order to give strength to the administrative actions which were being taken to contain these problems, it was felt that some political accomodation was also called for. As a result, in 1972 the region was reorganised by setting up the states of Meghalaya, Manipur and Tripura and the Union territories of Arunachal Pradesh and Mizoram besides the existing states of Assam and Nagaland. The North-Eastern Council was also set up to pursue a coordinated approach to development and security of the region. Nagaland did not initially join the Council because of a feeling that membership of the Council would detract its status as a full-fledged state. In 1985-86 Mizoram and Arunachal Pradesh were also elevated to full statehood.

At present the region has eight states: Assam, Arunachal Pradesh, Manipur, Meghalaya, Mizoram, Nagaland, Tripura and Sikkim.

Since 1947, the North-East has remained in a state of turmoil. Intrinsic problems of this region, a legacy of the British policy to keep the peripheral areas of this region aloof from the rest of the country and to divide and rule and the nefarious role played by some British officials just before the country became Independent, initially highlighted by the violent Naga underground movement, are yet to be successfully tackled to the full satisfaction of all the concerned people. Meanwhile, many new problems have surfaced in different segments of the area adding to the volatile character of the entire region. Besides the sections of Nagas living in Nagaland or in other States, sections among the Meiteis in Manipur, the tribals of Tripura, the Kukis, the Bodos and even the Assameese have been engaged in movements which are far from peaceful. Mizos had also started a violent uprising in 1966, which fortunately has been tackled.

The Naga movement for independence, the Mizo rebellion, the tribal insurgency in Tripura, the anti-foreigners agitation in Assam, and the clamour for greater autonomy by Bodos in areas where they generally live but are not in majority have been fuelled by the same core cause: the strong desire of small but distinct communities, which have different ways of life and have managed their affairs in their own ways for long, to preserve their cultural identities and their perceptions that these are under great threat. Of course, during the British rule it was their differences with others that were only emphasised which only accentuated their feelings of separateness.

The Naga insurgency, initially backed by certain external forces, began almost immediately after India became Independent, and has continued with varying degrees of intensity. The creation of the state of Nagaland in 1962 anl the Shillong Accord of 1975 had only provided short-term resites. The main reason of the movement has been to have a Greater Nagaland as a Sovereign State comprising all the areas where Nagas traditionally lived. This covers parts of other states and also parts of Myanmar. After the Government of India Act, 1935, when Burma was separated from India as another country, this problem had emerged, and the Nagas made their first demand in 1937 before the Governor-General.

After Independence, the Nagas became more adamant in their demands and launched a violent underground movement in early 1950s, not being satisfied with the district council set up envisaged in the Constitution to confer autonomy on the hill people. Overtly violent activities had abated to some extent when the state of Nagaland was formed in 1962 as a sequel to the agreement with the Naga People's Convention, but even then sporadic acts of sabotage and sniping had continued which only increased in volume with the passage of time. Mediation efforts by leaders like Shri Jai Prakash Narayan and Shri Bimal Prasad Chaliha did not yield any worthwhile result. Subsequently, an Accord was reached in Shillong in 1975 between the Governor and the leaders of the underground movement and violence was suspended for a few years. In late 1970s the movement revived once again under a new organisation called the National Socialist Council of Nagaland (NSCN). This group included militant elements of earlier Naga bands who had received training in China and forged new alliance with the Kachin Independent Army inside Myanmar and with some sections in Thailand and Bangladesh. They were also successful in establishing a pipeline for their supplies of arms, ammunition and other materials, and gained hideouts for their safe sanctuaries and bases.

In the 1980s NSCN split into two major factions of almost comparable strength—NSCN (Khaplang) and NSCN (Muivah Isaac Swu). The former is composed substantially of Burmeese Naga and is well entrenched on that side of the border. It is gratifying to note that talks are being held with the leaders of NSCN (IM) to find a solution to this issue.

Most other militant movements of this region owe their inspiration to the Naga underground movement and have also received support from them from time to time.

A Mizo insurgency launched in 1966 by the Mizo National Front had its origin in widely perceived apathetic attitude of the Assam government towards the Mizos manifested by the mismanagement of relief operations in the wake of *Mautam* (the great famine) of 1959-60 and continued inaction in checking exploitation of Mizos by the traders of neighbouring Silchar of Cachar district of Assam. To an extent, a very slow pace of development in the district and the state government's distrust of the district council also played a role in making the insurgency a possibility. The insurgency was tackled with energy and with some innovative measures like grouping of villages. With gradual dimunition in foreign inspiration and support to the movement, it was possible to reach a negotiated settlement with the insurgents by the middle of the 1980s, and the Mizo National Front was absorbed in the national mainstream. This was a matter of significant satisfaction.

In Tripura the problem boiled over due to a drastic change in the demographic composition of the State over a period time. The position of tribal majority in the state had become reversed following a large scale influx of the people from East Bengal, and after Partition, from East

Pakistan. The tribals of the state had been asking for a larger measure of autonomy within a defined area (the extent of this area was also a matter of confrontation). Consistent denial of this demand led to sustained and vicious insurgent movement led by Tripura National Volunteers. The insurgency was brought to an end by an agreement in 1988, when an accord was reached with TNV in which their basic demands were accommodated. But the failure to fulfil the commitments of the accord in full measure may lead to difficulties in future.

In Manipur the situation is somewhat more complex. NSCN had been operating in the state in which 10 per cent of the area, which is the valley land, has about 70 per cent of the population while 90 per cent of the area, which is hilly has only 30 per cent of the population, most of whom are tribals. The local indigenous people of the valley, who are called Meiteis, had earlier demanded that they should also be considered a Scheduled Tribe. These are talented people and incidence of education is quite high. Employment opportunities being very limited the Meiteis feel deprived of their rightful dues when the opportunities go to the tribals not due to any merit but because of various schemes of reservations in favour of the tribals. This led some youth groups to take to the path of insurgency after getting their initial training in China. The total picture of general turmoil becomes complete only when to the violent activities orchestrated by the Meitei insurgent groups and NSCN, the frequent clashes between the Nagas and the Kukis and incidences of inter tribal conflicts are added.

The problems in Assam had started when 'anti-foreigners agitation' was launched in 1978-79. The Assamese have always feared becoming a minority in their own state due to a regular influx of the people from the south since the beginning of the twentieth century and more particularly 1920s. The fertile low-lying river banks were generally left fallow by the Assamese cultivators. These lured landless peasants from East Bengal (later East Pakistan) in very large numbers. Initially, this influx of hardy cultivators using marshy and uncultivable lands were welcomed by the Assamese landowners. Later, after Partition. from time to time large numbers of Hindus from East Pakistan had to flee their homes and take shelter in Assam and other parts of the North-East as refugees. After Independence, the Assamese noted with some concern the growing number of, what they consider, to be non-indigenous Assamese, being elected to the Assam legislative assembly. The proportion of the Assamese-speaking people in the state also started declining in the census returns. The movement leaders, therefore, wanted "detection, deletion, and deportation" of all foreigners in Assam. Though there was a negotiated settlement with the leaders of the agitation in 1985, violence and militant activities by

ULFA, which had all along wanted a sovereign and independent Assam, has continued. ULFA has created safe sanctuaries in Bangladesh, has developed links with KIA inside Myanmar and has links with NSCN and PLA (a Meitei insurgent group). It also had at one stage designs for well coordinated insurgencies in the region.

Bodos are, what is called, plains tribals in Assam. They are thinly spread along the north bank of the Brahmaputra. The areas inhabited by the Bodes straddle both the main road and the railway links of the region with the rest of the country. This single factor has bestowed enormous importance upon the Bode insurgency. During the Assam agitation, the All Assam Bodo Student Union (AABSU) was with AASU. Even when the Prafulla Mahanta Ministry had taken office, the Bodo students were allies of the ruling party. At that time, they had asked for certain administrative safeguards to protect their legitimate interests, particularly in lands and forests. Getting no response they parted company with AASU, added political demands to their list, and started a voilent and militant agitation in support. Though an agreement has been reached with a section of the Bodo leadership for the creation of an Autonomous Bodo Council, it is doubtful if this would be able to contain the movement.

So far this chapter has given the political dimensions of the insurgencies, which are more visible and comparatively easily comprehensible. It is also true that in tackling insurgencies, military or police action has to be followed by political action to reach a political agreement for cessation of such a movement. But to establish sustained tranquility it is necessary to understand the underlying causes and to seek their removal.

The North-East was a poorly developed region even during the British rule. Till 1960 there was not a single bridge on the river Brahmaputra. The railroad was designed to serve only the commercial interests of the empire. The Partition had created a further setback to the people in economic terms. The commercial markets, which were available to the hill people along their foothills, became too distant. Traffic through the water-ways also ceased to operate. The link with other parts of the country was only through a narrow corridor. The People of the region being very poor and the backlog of even normal development activities like roads, bridges, irrigation facilities being very high, whatever scarce resources were available could neither satisfy individual aspirations nor meet the backlog in any significant measure. Structural and systemetic difficulties for development in the region were tended to be glossed over. All these factors have resulted in stagnation in the North-East.

Even if today is gloomy, a person can look forward to a brighter tomorrow if he has a hope. What does a youth in the North-East hope for in the future? The employment opportunities are highly limited. State government and public institutions, which to an extent, had served as employment agencies in the past (In the NER, state government have inorbinately high work force) are already overstaffed. They have few skills and are not very keen to go out of the state, much less the region. In such a situation, even if all the autonomy is conferred upon the communities, grievances of the people will persist.

On the other hand, it is ironic to note that the region has very high potential for development. The area is endowed with very large reserves of minerals including coal and limestone; has enormous potential for generation of hydel power has rich fertile plain land and an extremely favourable climate for crop plantation in the hills has an excellent climate for sericulture, pisciculture, animal husbandry, poultry, dairy and for growing mushrooms, orchids and other items of horticulture. Regeneration of forests with valuable timber can also be an economic enterprise.

Besides funds, which can also be available through financial institutions if the requisite conditions are created, there are two major constraints to rapid economic developments.

Most of the mineral deposits and likely sites for hydel generation are either in the reserve forests or near them. Some viable and practical solutions have to be found so that the designated development activities are not allowed to languish on environmental factors in the given legal setting of today; at the same time environmental concerns are also to be handled by creation of new forest areas with adequate protection. In fact, if only the hill farmers can be successfully weaned away from jhooming or shifting cultivation, it will lead to a large-scale regeneration of forest land.

Secondly, most of these agricultural enterprises, like crop plantation, are highly capital intensive. Institutional funds can become available only when collateral security of land is possible. In all the hill areas not only legally is this not possible. there is a vehement popular opposition to it. While alienation of land should rightly be resisted if that is for exploitation purposes, yet if security of land is needed to make available funds to a tribal member of the same community for his enterprise, some ways are to be found to make it possible. It may be opined that given the right information the inherent genius of the tribal mind and their robust traditional institutions should be able to find viable solutions.

Vigorous participatory economic activities in which the local people, their traditional institutions and the state governments, are equal partners, the creation of visible productive infrastructural assets is the only answer to contain fissiparous tendencies which generate violent insurgencies.

Counter-Insurgency Operations

The Government of India has adopted a tough stand on the issue of talks with the militant outfits and decided to intensic operations against the militant groups, which have not shown any willingness to come forward for talks. After the change of stand of the Government, there is every possibility of intensification of the operations against the militant groups in the North-east region, where a number of outfits including the hardline faction of the United Liberation Front of Asom (ULFA) and the breakaway faction of the Ranjan Daimary faction of the National Democratic Front of Bodoland (NDFB) are still adopting a tough stand on the issue of talks with the Government for political solution of their problems. Earlier, the Government had adopted an open door policy on the issue of talks with the militant groups and whichever outfit expressed it willingness to come for talks was allowed to do so. But, the policy also had its drawbacks as there have been instances where breakaway factions of militant groups created problems and indulged in lawlessness even after the main bodies came overground to solve problems through political dialogues. The Joint Secretary (North-East) of the Ministry of Home Affairs, Sambhu Singh recently commented that any group having grievances should try to solve their problems democratically instead of taking up arms and indulge in activities like killings and extortions. He is, of course, correct as the open door policy of the Government on the issue of talks had, in fact, encouraged some people to take up arms.

Singh also pointed out that the process of talks with the militant outfits, which have already expressed their desire to find political solution to the problems, would continue. The Government should expedite the process of talks with the militant groups, which have already come forward for political solution of the problems as slow progress of peace process often leads to complications and division in the ranks of the outfits. The talks with the NSCN (IM) are going on since 1997 and till date, the Government and the outfit have not reached any agreement, which is unfortunate. The Government should make it clear what it can offer the militant outfit at the time of starting the process of talks as unnecessarily dragging the process will not serve any purpose. The process of talks with the pro-talk faction of the ULFA should also bd expedited as this may encourage members of the hardline faction to join the peace process. The Government has also decided to start formal talks with the Ranjan Daimary Faction of the NDFB and the process should start soon as such a move will definitely encourage least some members of the breakaway faction to join the peace process.

Secessionist Movement

Secessionism is not a new phenomenon. It has existed in all ages in one form or the other. In Indian scenario the problem of sessionism has been experienced since Independence. At present a huge number of sessionist organisations are active in North East India. They are such as the National Socialist Council of Nagaland (NSCN), Tripura National Volunteers Force (TNVF), Tripura Tiger Force (TTF), Mizo National Front (MNF), People Liberation Army (PLA), People's Revolutionary Party of Kangleipak (PREPAK), United Liberation Front (ULF), and the Red Army in Manipur, the United Liberation Front of Assam (ULFA), National Democratic Front of Bodoland (NDFB), Bodo Liberation Tigers (BLT) in Assam etc. These secessionist/extremist organisations in many cases have been armed and aided by foreign countries such as Pakistan, China, Bangladesh on the one hand, and by the upsurge of religious fundamentalism, aggressive cultural resurgence, particularly among communities Sikhs, Muslims and Christians on the other.

Their members have developed a close nexus with the law enforcement agencies, politicians and bureaucrats also. The Assam Accord, Mizoram Accord, Punjab Accord and Darjeeling Accord have further their imagination to have similar settlements on their own terms and conditions, hence they are indulging in large-scale violence.

National Socialist Council of Nagaland (NSCN)

Soon after independence, the Naga National Council (NNC) under the leadership of Phizo declared Nagaland as an independent state. The extremist group of NNC had carried out a poll boycott in 1952 in support of their demand for an independent Naga nation. The total boycott of the 1956 general elections in the Naga Hills district of Assam marked the beginning, of a long and protracted struggle by the Naga National Council. Since 1954 the extremist group of NNC started armed rebellion. In the meantime the NNC went for a plebiscite in which thousands of Nagas have expressed their willingness to lead a separate independent existence. While calling for the boycott of elections, the NNC maintained that the Nagas had a separate "Constitution" of their own which provided for a Parliament called the Tatar Hobo and an Upper House called Kimhao to which any Naga who has completed thirty years of age could seek election. The NNC constitution worked out in details the powers of the legislature, the executive and the judiciary and those of the Regional, Sub-regional and Village Councils.

As the time passed, with that the whole movement became violent. In order to counter their activities, the Government of India took necessary counter-measures and deployed army to control the situation.

Meanwhile there were some leaders among the Nagas, who did not follow this policy or approve Phizo line of action. They demanded that the Nagas should be united and brought under one single administration. Prime Minister Nehru was willing to meet such a demand provided the Nagas restored peace and agreed to settle every problem within the framework of the Constitution of India. To satisfy the Naga people the government decided to provide a separate state and for this on 21st August, 1962, Constitution 13th Amendment Act was introduced and was passed on 4th September, 1962.

But, this arrangement did not satisfy extremist Nagas under the leadership of Phizo. Then Phizo and his hard core supporters turned to China and Pakistan and they received good support from these countries including arms and ammunition. Even they received financial support. However, in November 1975 an agreement was signed in Shillong, known as Shillong Accord. But, the extremist group did not prepare to accept the accord and as such the Issack Swu group broke away from the federal group and formed the National Socialist Council of Nagaland. Emerging basically from the disatisfaction arising out of the Shillong Accord the NSCN could build up a militant profile in North East India in recent times. But the NSCN failed to remain united and ultimately came to be divided into two factions—one lead by Khaplang and the other by Muiva. The NSCN was formed in January 1980 and it immediately dubbed the NNC and Phizo as betrayers of the Naga cause and opportunist Indian agents.

Mizo National Front

Mizo National Front was formed in 1960 under the leadership Laldenga. It raised the demand of sovereign independent greater Mizoram and started sending volunteers to China and East Pakistan (now Bangladesh) for military training. Laldenga was arrested in 1963 but released in 1964. After his release he established the Mizo National Army and intensified the activities recruiting volunteers for forceful collection of funds and set up guerilla training camps. To satisfy the Mizos the Union Government raised the status of the Mizo district to that of a Union Territory in 1972.

But, there were many extremists and hard core Mizos headed Laldenga who were not satisfied with this arrangement. They wanted that a separate state outsides the Union of India could satisfy them. They continued their guerilla activities. In 1975 they killed Inspector General of Police, Deputy Inspector General of Police and Superintendent Police of Mizoram and thus created an unbearable situation. In order to bring the situation under control

Government deployed armed forces. In 1976, an agreement was signed between the Government of India and Laldenga by which it was decided that all disputes and problems between Mizos and the Central Government will be solved without the use violent means. But in March 1977, this agreement was violated when Laldenga launched a massive drive to enrol his followers and again began to follow extremist means.

In March 1981 Laldenga submitted a proposal to the Prime Minister for solving Mizo problem. He suggested greater Mizoram Containing some part of Tripura, Manipur and Assam. In 1982, the Centre banned MNF. In 1984 Laldenga was called to India and prolonged discussions followed. In 1986 Mizoram Accord was signed between the Prime Minister and Laldenga under which the latter was appointed as a Chief Minister which thus ended an era of extremist activities in Mizoram.

In Manipur as mentioned earlier, there are many extremist groups such as 'Peoples Liberation Army', the 'Red Army', 'People Revolutionary Party of Kongleipak', 'The Meite National Front', 'Pan Manipuri Youth League' and 'National United Liberation Front'. All these groups are indulging in extremist activities in order to fulfil their demands. It is to be said that they are not satisfied with their present status because they are not treated at Par with tribals who have embraced christianity, and secondly their demand that Minipuri should be included in the Eighth Schedule has not been accepted. These extremist organisations are trying to organise the Pan Mongoloid Movement of the Nagas and Mizos also. They have indulged in large scale violence against non Manipuries, forcing them to leave Manipur.

United Liberation Front of Assam

United Liberation Front of Assam was organised by a few Assamese youth at the premises of Rangghar, Sibsagar with the objective of liberating Assam from the colonial clutches of Indian nationalism. Gradually this organisation expanded in size when a sizeable number of unemployed youth were attracted to it and by 1990 this organisation turned to a extremist organisation.

Assam is rich in natural resources. But, these resources have been exploited by people and agencies from outside the region. Thus due to the intrusion of outsiders and the control of the state's economy by the migrant business communities. Assam still remains economically underdeveloped in comparison to other states of India. The employment potentialities of the state not encouraging due to industrial backwardness, whatever employment opportunities are there in the Central Government and industrial sectors Assamese speaking people are outnumbered by non-Assamese. The

Assamese middle class finds itself locked in an unequal and unfair competition in the field of business, professions and to some extent in the state government jobs also.

All these factors are responsible for the growth of a feeling of discontentment and frustrusion and thus a process of alienation started to grow in the minds of the people of Assam. This all led a section of youth to adopt extremist methods to solve their sensitive problems and this way ULFA was born with a demand for secession from the Indian Union. Although a section of the militants responded to the Government's appeal to surrender arms and renounce extremist activities and come back to the mainstream yet the problem did not end. ULFA is still a force to be reckoned with.

The Bodo Movement in Assam was started in 1967 and this movement turned to a extremist movement in 1988. During this period the Bodo People's Action Committee (BPAC), Bodo Security Force (BSF) and Bodo Students Volunteer Force were formed to materialise the demand for the creation of a separate homeland for the Bodos. The Bodo militants started extremist activities by involving themselves in senseless killings of non-Bodos.

Bodo Accord was signed on February 20, 1993 to provide an Autonomous District Council to the Bodos. As a result of this accord a large number of Bodo extermists surrendered their arms. But soon the Bodos began to realise that they were deceived by the state government. The reason for this is that the state government failed to spell out a clear cut boundary of the Bodo land. Lately another agreement was signed between the government and the Bodo by which the Bodo Territorial Council has been provided to Bodos. But the problem of extremism still remains.

MODEL QUESTIONS

Very Objective Type Questions (1 mark for each)

1. From which word the term ethnic derived?
2. Can you nomenclate tribal movement as a kind of Identity Movement?
3. Define Ethnicity.

Short Type Questions (4/5 marks for each)

4. Write short notes on:
   (a) Assam Movement
   (b) Politics of Migration
   (c) Insurgency in Assam
   (d) IMDT Act.

Long Type Questions (10/12 marks for each)

1. Discuss critically the Language Movement of Assam. Do you think that Language Movement of Assam had given birth the Tribal Politics?
2. Discuss the factors responsible for the State Language Movement in Assam.
3. What is the response of the Government towards fulfilment of the demands of Bodo Community? Discuss.
4. What do you mean by Identity Politics? Explain the Nature of Identity Movements in the context of North East India.

Unit IV
Electoral Politics

Electoral Politics has become a major field of study in contemporary social sciences. Though India's north eastern states have been keenly observed by journalists, scholars and policy makers because the politics of these states seem to challenge some of the major theories of Indian democratic politics yet serious efforts at electoral analysis of the region have rather been limited. Electoral politics of contemporary North East have been dominated by the issues of ethnic identity. This part of the book closely examines electoral politics in North East India.

Elections in India, the world's second-most populous country, evoke descriptions like 'spectacle' or 'carnival,' in part due to the overwhelming numbers that participate in the process. In this country of over a billion people, 714 million voters will decide who rules the world's largest democracy for the next five years. In the 2004 elections, over 5,400 candidates from 230 political parties participated. Nearly the same number of candidates will compete for seats in Parliament in 2009. Electoral candidates vie for votes by promising reforms, such as better governance, greater socio-economic equity, and bolstered efforts at poverty alleviation. However, corrupt politicians with criminal records, caste and religion-based politics, and allegations of vote-buying continue to mar the democratic process. Meanwhile, the coalition politics of the last two decades, while more inclusive, have resulted in giving power to small parties that have used it to further their short-term agenda.

India's parliamentary system is based on the Westminster model of constitutional democracy, a legacy of British colonial rule. The Parliament is comprised a bicameral legislature: the Rajya Sabha, the 250-member upper house, where members are elected by state legislative assemblies (12 members are nominated by the President), and the Lok Sabha, the 543-member lower house directly elected by the people (with two additional seats reserved for Anglo Indians nominated by the President). In the Lok

Sabha, voters elect candidates based on the electoral system where the person securing the largest number of votes in each district wins.

India has an asymmetric federal government, with elected officials at the federal, state and local levels. At the national level, the head of government, Prime Minister, is elected by the members of Lok Sabha, lower house of the Parliament of India. All members of Lok Sabha except two, who can be nominated by President of India, are directly elected through general elections which take place every five years, in normal circumstances, by universal adult suffrage. Members of Rajya Sabha, upper house of Indian Parliament, are elected by elected members of the legislative assemblies of states and Electoral College for Union Territories of India.

Election Commission

Elections in North East are conducted by the Election Commission of India, there is also provision of State Election Commission, the authority created under the Constitution. It is a well established convention that once the election process commences; no court intervenes until the results are declared by the Election Commission. During the elections, vast powers are assigned to the Election Commission to the extent that it can function as a civil court, if needed.

Electoral Process

Electoral Process in India takes at least a month for state assembly elections with the duration increasing further for the General Elections. Publishing of electoral rolls is a key process that happens before the elections and is vital for the conduct of elections in India. The Constitution of India sets the eligibility of an individual for voting. Any person who is a citizen of India and above 18 years of age is eligible to enroll as a voter in the electoral rolls. It is the responsibility of the eligible voters to enroll their names. Normally, voter registrations are allowed latest one week prior to the last date for nomination of candidates.

Pre-Elections

At first before the elections the dates of nomination, polling and counting takes place. The model code of conduct comes in force from the day the dates are announced. No party is allowed to use the government resources for campaigning. The code of conduct stipulates that campaigning be stopped 48 hours prior to polling day.

Voting Day

Government schools and colleges are chosen as polling stations. The Collector of each district is in charge of polling stations. Government employees are employed to many of the polling stations. Electronic Voting Machines (EVMs) are being increasingly used instead of ballot boxes to prevent election fraud *via* booth capturing, which is heavily prevalent in certain parts of India. An indelible ink is applied usually on the left index finger of the voter as an indicator that the voter has cast his vote. This practice has been followed since the 1962 General Elections to prevent bogus voting.

"None of the above" Voting Option

"None of the above" is a proposed voting option in India that would allow voters who support none of the candidates available to them to register an official vote of "none of the above", which is not currently allowed under India Election Regulation. The Election Commission of India told the Supreme Court in 2009 that it wished to offer the voter a None of the above button on voting machines; the government, however, has generally opposed this option.

Post-Elections

After the Election Day, the EVMs are stored in a strong room under heavy security. After different phases of the elections are complete, a day is set to count the votes. The votes are tallied typically, the verdict is known within hours. The candidate who has mustered the most votes is declared the winner of the constituency.

The party or coalition that has won the most seats is invited by the President to form the new government. The coalition or party must prove its majority in the floor of the house (Lok Sabha) in a vote of confidence by obtaining a simple majority (minimum 50%) of the votes in the house.

Voter Registration

For few cities in India, the voter registration forms can be generated online and submitted to the nearest electoral office.

Absentee Voting

As of now, India does not have an absentee ballot system. Section 19 of the Representation of the People Act (RPA) 1950 allows a person to register to vote if he or she is above 18 years of age and is an 'ordinary resident' of the residing constituency, i.e. living at the current address for 6 months or longer. Section 20 of the above Act disqualifies a non-resident Indian (NRI) from getting his/her name registered in the electoral rolls. Consequently, it also prevents a NRI from casting his/her vote in elections to the Parliament and to the State Legislatures.

In August 2010, Representation of the People (Amendment) Bill, 2010 which allows voting rights to NRIs was passed in both Lok Sabha with subsequent gazette notifications on November 24, 2010. With this NRIs will now be able to vote in Indian elections but have to be physically present at the time of voting. Several civic society organizations have urged the government to amend the RPA Act to allow NRIs and people on the move to cast their vote through absentee ballot system.

Formation of North Eastern States

During the entire British colonial period in India, North East India was ruled as a part of Bengal Province. The state of Assam came into existence in 1874. After India's Independence from the British Rule in 1947, the Northeastern region of British India consisted of Assam and the princely states of Manipur and Tripura. But, later on, Nagaland, Meghalaya, Arunachal Pradesh and Mizoram were carved out from Assam in 1963, 1972, 1975, 1987 respectively. Manipur and Tripura remained as Union Territories of India between 1956 until 1972 when they attained full-fledged statehood. Sikkim was integrated as the eighth North Eastern Council state in 2002.

The city of Shillong acted as the capital of the Assam province created during the British Rule. It remained as the capital of undivided Assam until formation of the state of Meghalaya in 1972. The capital of Assam was then shifted to Dispur, a part of Guwahati, and Shillong became the capital of Meghalaya.

The North East region can be physiographically categorized into the Eastern Himalayas, Northeast Hills (Patkai-Naga Hills and Lushai Hills) and the Brahmaputra and the Barak Valley Plains. North East India (at the confluence of Indo-Malayan, Indo-Chinese, and Indian biogeographical realms) has a predominantly humid sub-tropical climate with hot, humid summers, severe monsoons and mild winters. Along with the west coast of India, this region has some of the Indian subcontinent's last remaining rain forests which support diverse flora and fauna and several crop species. Similarly, reserves of petroleum and natural gas in the region constitute a fifth of India's total potential. The region is covered by the mighty Brahmaputra-Barak river systems and their tributaries. Geographically, apart from the Brahmaputra, Barak and Imphal valleys and some flat lands in between the hills of Meghalaya and Tripura, the remaining two-thirds of the area is hilly terrain interspersed with valleys and plains; the altitude varies from almost sea-level to over 7000 metres above MSL. The region's high rainfall averaging around 10000 millimetres and above creates problems of eco system, high seismic activity and floods. The states of Arunachal Pradesh and Sikkim have a montanic climate with cold, snowy winters and mild summers.

North East India is a slightly sliced region between eastern region in India and Purvanchal Range—an eastward extension of the Himalayas in the northern belt of India that primarily consists of all the regions that have been carved out of the original Province of Assam of British India that consists the present day Assam or Assam Valley and rest of the contiguous states—Arunachal Pradesh, Meghalaya, Mizoram, Nagaland and former Princely States of Manipur and Tripura. Apart from these, more recently as a part of greater North East India, state of Sikkim and parts of North Bengal (districts of Darjeeling, Jalpaiguri, and Koch Bihar) can also be collectively referred as North East India. Sikkim was recognized as a part of North East states in the 1990s.

Linguistically the whole region can widely be distinctly differentiated into two portions: one region is characterised by speakers of Asamiya or Assamese which is written and spoken in Assam Valley and other parts and indeed one of the most recognised and established language systems that dates back to 900c and traces its origin from Charyapada; the other region which essentially includes the rest of the states with preponderance of Tibeto-Burman languages, however, to this exception could be Tripura where Bengali is spoken due to the heavy influx of immigrants from Bangladesh who have now marginalized the indigenous tribal population. The states are officially recognized under North Eastern Council (NEC) constituted in 1971 as the acting agency for the development of the eight states. The North Eastern Development Finance Corporation Ltd. (NEDFC) was incorporated on August 9, 1995 and the Ministry of Development of North Eastern Region (DoNER) was set up in September 2001.

The Siliguri Corridor in West Bengal, with an average width of 21 km to 40 km, connects the North Eastern region with the mainland Indian sub-continent. The region shares more than 4500 kilometres of international border (about 90 per cent of its entire border area) with China (South Tibet) in the north, Mayanmar in the east, Bangladesh in the south-west, and Bhutan to the north-west.

Electoral Politics in Assam

Looking beyond the upcoming elections, the 2016 Assam Assembly may have the most interesting composition of legislators. The Congress, AGP,

BJP, NCP, TMC etc. will be sitting on one flank of the house while the other flank is occupied by leaders and cadres of at least eight terror groups now engaged in talks or are almost ready for talks with the Government of India. Two such groups are already represented in the State Assembly. The political formation of what was Bodo Liberation Tigers (BLT) and a few Independent legislators with terror profiles are already part of the government. The BLT used to be the most violent of the armed groups; having blown up passenger trains and causing heavy human casualties. It is not only part of the coalition government but it governs an autonomous council with little accountability. The Assam Police may not have any definite records about the violent activities of BLT members, but a few hundred killings can easily be attributed to this group. Amongst the Independent MLAs, there are also surrendered cadres. The 2011 Assam Assembly may lose out on some of the big names who have just descended on the scene and will take a while before settling down, but it will have its own share of celebrity legislators.

Few terror groups in the region which sustained itself for thirty one years without a split, is now a divided house. But an evaluation of its terrorist activities has not been carried out. The police do not have sufficient records and the documentation of conflict rests heavily on orally recounted stories. One such incident during the early nineties was the killing of a doctor; he was crucified on a tree in the Upper Assam town of Lakhimpur. During the same time, in the same town, a student leader was buried alive simply because he refused to join the group. Numerous instances of stories similar to these are available with several families. The mastermind or possibly even the perpetrator of each of these crimes allegedly was extremist leader, who is now an aspirant for a seat in the Assembly. And a national political party has nominated them as its candidate.

Nowhere, except in India's North East, would one find so blatant a policy of granting amnesty and legitimacy to people or groups of people who have used the most abhorrent forms of violence against civilians, women and children. The law allows every individual to contest for elections even it is from the jail. If election is a participatory process, then surely elections in Assam are well participated in (even by once self-styled 'underground' commanders who still carry guns but engage in 'overground' extortionist methods).

Mizoram perhaps set the trend with former guerillas taking over the office of the Chief Minister. That office has been virtually reserved for former rebels. But the Mizo insurgency was different in nature from the others. Some of the biggest underground leaders are waiting their turn in the Nagaland and Manipur assemblies, though their *de facto* control over the political establishment is well known. In Assam too, the influence of the underground rebels and the alleged nexus of politicians and parties with various groups is not only a media speculation but a matter of current investigation.

Emergence of Assamese Middle Class and their Role in Politics

The Emergence of the Assamese middle class in the second half of the nineteenth century was the permanent and positive legacy of British rule. Unlike other social classes such as the priests, the peasants and the pensioners of the old nobility, the middle class had no inseparable link with the past. They had no nobiliary pride in them. In a sense, they marked a rupture with the past.

Though the emergence of the middle class in every state of India as a formidable social force is directly related to British rule, their social roots varied from state to state. Let us consider their position in two vibrant regions of British India. In Assam, as a social category, the middle class was at the top of the social hierarchy. But in nineteenth century Bengal, according to the social historian S.N. Mukherjee, the middle class really belonged to the middle rung. At the peak was the *abhijata bhadralok* class was comprised big *zamindars*, merchants and top administrators and who controlled land and capital market. Below them were the *grihastha bhadralok* or the *madhyabitto srenie* (middle class) and it "accepted the leadership of the *abhijata* and imitated their life-style".

Obviously the term "Middle Class" covers a broad spectrum of social and economic categories possibly with antagonistic interests within itself. Compared to Bengal and Punjab, the Assamese middle class had a narrower social base and it had to follow an uncommon trajectory. By bringing in the examples of Bengal and Punjab we are trying to emphasize the distinctiveness of the Assamese middle class.

Among the scholars, Manorama Sharma tried to pinpoint the social roots of the Assamese middle class. She says:

> One line of social roots of the Assamese middle class can, therefore, be traced back to early British revenue officers, the most important of whom were the Mauzadars because of their numerical strength, their affluence and social importance. The other line of these roots must be looked for in the other important social institution of the time—the Vaishnava Satras.

But we are unable to reason it out as to how these two institutions could provide grounds for the emergence of a new social class. On the face of it, they were less fertile than other areas. Emergence of the middle class was primarily an urban phenomenon. In nine cases out of ten the chiefs of *satras* and the *mauzadars* lived out their lives in the villages. They were not brought up on urban bread, though they were obliged to maintain close links with the district or sub-divisional towns. Towns attracted them a little later.

What was the real situation of the two institutions? The British established their control over Lower Assam before the Treaty of Yandaboo (1826). Upper Assam came under their control after the treaty. By 1853, the British Government in Assam was fully settled with a uniform system of general administration for all districts of the Brahmaputra valley. On revenue matters, so far as the Lower Assam was concerned, the government showed some flexibility and allowed the old system to continue, which meant the rule of the *zamindars* in Goalpara and those of the *choudhuries* in Kamrup. In upper Assam the Government introduced the *ryotwari* system which created the *mauzadars* almost in a parallel situation with the *choudhuries* though their legal incidents were not the same. Leaving aside their tale of fluctuating fortunes, the *choudhuries* and *mauzadars* were the men of consequence, of wealth, power and prestige in the villages. Form 1872 the *choudhuries* came to be known as mauzadars.

The *mauzadars* were the necessary adjuncts of the *ryotwari* system. As commission-agents they were under the control of a hierarchy of revenue officers. They could not take their privileges for granted. Manorama Sharma herself suggested from a contemporary description that by 1886, "the *Mauzadars* were no longer given the importance and respect which was given to the early *Mauzadars*". IT is difficult to locate who the 'early *mauzadars*' were and what was the quantum of their 'importance and respect'. Maniram Dewan's petition submitted to A.J.M. Mills, 33 years earlier, did not give any favourable account of them. Padmanath Gohain Barua, in one of his successful plays, *Gaonburha* (The Village Headman) defied a true picture of the rural society in the early phase of the British Rule. One *mauzadar*, a familiar character of the village had a strong presence in it. As then everyone knew, most of all himself, as son of a resourceful *mauzadar*, what it meant to be a *mauzadar* in those days. The *mauzadar* did command little respect and loyalty, he often evokes pity. His peace of mind, nay, every moment of existence is haunted by fear of the inspecting *sahib*. His fortune's wheel might turn any moment from bad to worse. At best he lived a life of dazzling uncertainty.

It is Marx who seems to have first referred to the expression 'middle class' in his "contribution to the Critique of Hegel's Philosophy of Right in 1844, of course, without precisely defining it. Thereafter, in the Manifesto of the Communist Party", Marx categorically identified small traders, shopkeepers, retired tradesman, handicraftsmen, the peasant and small manufacturer as constituents of the lower middle class. On the basis of Marx's specific identification of the constituents of the lower middle class Dandekar defines the middle class in the following terms, "Judging by whom he includes in the lower strata of the middle class, it is not difficult to see the implied scheme of classification course, between the bourgeoise and the proletariat those who own the means of production, do not themselves work but employ wage-labour, and those who not own any means of production and must work as wage-labour. In between the two lies the middle class." Middle class, therefore, is a group of people whose existence in society is in between the bourgeoise and the proletariat. In another writing, Marx refers to the middle class as those "who stand between the workmen on the one hand and the capitalist and landlord on the other."

British administration and the material foundation laid by it resulted in the destruction of the old feudal classes and in the rise and growth of new social classes, in Assam as elsewhere. Of all the social classes thus emerged, the middle class was the most prominent and it helped in social regeneration, and besides being the colonial collaborator, this class was the only social buttress of the alien regime.

The connotation of the middle class has kept on changing from time to time. During the British colonial rule in Assam it took several years for the emergence and development of the middle class. Being predominantly an agricultural country based on natural economy the people had strong roots in the feudal attitude to life and property and moorings in social relations and behaviour. Therefore, the middle class that emerged during the British rule in Assam, appeared to be docile, loyal, compromising and subservient to the ruling class, i.e. the British bourgeoise. The group of men whom we can cover by the term (Assamese) middle class during the colonial rule in Assam was the government officials and job holders, both in the civil and judicial branches, revenue officials such as *choudhuris*, *mauzadars*, *tahshildars* and *mandals*, school teachers, tea planters, clerk in the tea-gardens called '*babus*', advocates and *mukhters*, traders and contractors, *mahajans*, shopkeepers and moneylenders, big landholders and rich peasants (who used to lend money, grains and seed to the tenants and cultivators), who received rents and a share of the produce from the share-croppers and cultivators.

With this conceptual framework of the middle class, it is make an attempt to briefly outline the history of the rise and growth of the Assamese middle class during the British colonial regime in Assam. As has been mentioned earlier, it was Dr. Hiren Gohain who had first initiated a discourse on the rise and growth of the Assamese middle class in early seventies of the twentieth century through his path-breaking documented essay captioned '*Asomiya Madhyabitta Samajar Etihsa*'. This was followed by his essay in English under the caption of the 'Origin of the Assamese Middle Class' in 'Social Scientist'. As he said, this was the English rendering, in brief, of the '*Asomiya Madhyabitta Samajar Etihsa*'.

The Assamese middle class had four distinct roots of growth and stages of development, and they are trade and commerce, government jobs, land and the tea plantation industry. The pattern of growth and development of the Assamese middle class was similar to that of the middle classes in other provinces of British India during the same period.

The material foundation laid by the British colonial regime in Assam, as elsewhere in India, contributed towards the emergency of a new middle class as distinct and different from the surviving feudal aristocracy or the group of traditional elites. Among the factors responsible for the rise, growth and development of the Assamese middle class where the increasing trade and commerce, the paraphernalia of bureaucratic administration and law courts, a new system of education based on Western ideals of civil liberty, social ethics, legal procedure, notions of state and political theories and concept and organization, the creation of private property in land in absolute terms with the right of transfer, sale and mortgage, and the introduction of institutional devices for the collection of land revenue, and the opening up of modern system of transport, roads and communication, the railways and the tea industry.

The trading and commercial classes that had emerged from amongst a section of the Assamese people in Kamrup and Goalpara with direct contact with the European and English traders, merchants and interlopers with their trading centres and outposts at Jogighopa, Rangamati and Goalpara formed the nucleus of an emerging middle class in the quatter of the eighteenth century and several years before the occupation of Assam by the English East India Company. And the process continued thereafter. Barpeta, Sualkuchi, Sarthebari and Guwahati became busy commercial hubs which were linked up with those of jogighopa, Rangamati and Goalpara and these centres helped much to create a class of trading people who, under direct British colonial rule, later emerged as members of the Assamese Middle class. While studying the emergence of the middle classes in Britain, Lewis and Maude observed—"The historical origin of the middle classes is to be found mainly in trade, but not in trade alone. Middle class activity was concerned from the first with the exchange of goods and services, and therefore with the use and abuse of money." And invariably, therefore, in Assam the middle class began to emerge with the beginning of the Assam-Bengal trade with distinct connection with the European traders, merchants and interlopers almost since the middle of the eighteenth century. The European traders, merchant adventure and interlopers had established their trading relations with the Asssamese traders and merchants with Goalpara, Jogighopa and Rangamati as trading centres by the middle of the century.

The members of the Duwariya Baruwa family by virtue of their being the custom-officials at Hadira Chowki or Bangal-Hat, amassed large wealth and riches since the days of Lakshminarayan Brahmacharin, the founder of the family, through "the exchange of goods and services, and therefore, with the use and abuse of money" as had been done by the early British traders in Britain. This Duwariya Baruwa family, to which Anandaram Dhekial Phukan belonged, also had business connection with the house of Jagat Seth of Murshidabad. The Duwariya Baruwa family had established a virtual monopoly on the Assam-Bengal trade by the last two decades of the eighteenth century. The Brahmacharin left huge properties, in terms of several large estates and trading concerns, at the time of his death in 1816, and after his death, Parashuram Baruah, one of his foster sons, enriched the family with enormous properties. The riches and wealth of this family reached such a height that Sitaram, another foster son of the Brahmacharin, filed suit claiming 9.72 lakh as his share from the undivided family at the time of its partition.

Others, like Sibram Sarma Bairagi, also had business transactions with European traders and merchant adventurers in the second half of the century.

The land revenue system of the district of Goalpara by virtue of its being a part of the Bengal suba since 1639 was propitious for the rise and growth of a middle class with various interests in land and its management. This became more so with the introduction of the Permanent Settlement by the Government of Bengal in 1793 including Goalpara which later formed a part of Assam from 1826.

Next, the Mughal revenue system introduced in Kamrup with one *choudhury* on each of the seventeen Purgunahs as the revenue official supported by a hierarchy of subordinate officials such as *Talukdar* and *Thakuria* (*Thakuri*) and *Tarui*, i.e. a *tekala* or messenger. Which the Ahoms also retained, had prepared the ground for the rise and growth of a middle class with interests in land in the wake of the occupation of Assam by the Company. To be precise, the Mughal revenue system introduced in Kamrup which continued to be followed even during most part of Ahom rule in the eighteenth century had also contributed in the growth and development of the middle class later under the British administration. Already under Mughal system, the revenue official of each Purgana called *Choudhury* had amassed large wealth and riches, including landed properties, and this in turn helped in the emergence of a middle class in Kamrup much earlier than in other parts of Assam under the British. Most of the *Choudhuris* of the district of Kamrup under British rule were the offspring of the *Choudhuris* of the erstwhile Purganas.

The institutional devices created by the British for the collection of land revenue and also the measures to give employment to the members from amongst the decadent feudal nobility set in motion a process of creating a middle class so as to work as a social buttress of the alien government. As a matter of fact, the collection of land revenue was entrusted to the native agents, with one or two outsiders here and there like Haribilash Agarwals, known under the denomination of *mauzadars, tahsidars, choudhuri* etc., "...the object in view being to provide employment for the better classes of Assamese." Lieut. Colonel Matthie writes that the revenue administration in Assam "...gives employment to many of the Assamese gentry". In Nowgong, the revenue collectors were selected from amongst the members of the old aristocracy. Some members of the erstwhile feudal nobility were also given employment in the junior adjuncts of the civil and judicial administration of the country. The main qualification for such appointments is government establishments being the good family lineage or 'noble birth'.

The policy of modern education in India, as its author Lord Macaulay had put it emphatically, was to create a class of people who would be "Indian in blood and colour, but English in tastes, in opinions, in morals and intellect". By raising such a class of men in India the British wanted to get their assistance in running the administration and developing the resources of the country "necessary or the payment of the increasing imports of British manufactures". In Assam, in the initial stage, the knowledge of English was not considered necessary by the people for getting government jobs, but in due course, when it became necessary, the members of the feudal nobility had begun to show keen interest in giving their offspring English education.

Anadaram Dhekial Phukan writes, "That the people, especially the higher classes, are still anxious to instruct their children in the knowledge of European science and literature, has been amply proved from the circumstances that several native gentlemen have already sent their youth to the Government Colleges in the Presidency for the express purpose of giving them an English Education." Captain Butler, the Collector of Nowgong, had witten several years before the visit of Mills to Asssam, "The motive which brings the boys to the schools is simply the prospect of getting Government employ."

To encourage Assamese youth to take up employment in the petty clerkship in the administrative establishments, the government created stipendiary posts at an annual expenditure of Rs. 277 against each of them. In the words of Mills, "To each office in the Province are attached some Assamese youth, who receive salary varying from three rupees to seven rupees per mensem, the total expense on this account amounting to 227 rupees per mensem. The object in establishing these class stipendiary aspirants to Government employ was to bring forward Assamese youth and bar the intrusion of Bengallees, but it does not appear to have been gained."

By and large, the Assamese middle class emerged under the direct patronage of the colonial government. Members in the higher echelon of the administration in the valley like Colonel Francis Jenkins, Colonel Matthie and Captain Eden, among others, took keen interest in the education and development of the careers of several luminaries of Assamese middle class, such as Anandaram Dhekial Phukan, and others. Benudhar Sarma writes, "Captain Eden befriended Gangagovinda Phukan much more than Jenkins did Anandaram Dhekial Phukan, David Scott did, Maniram Dewan, Agnew did, Hem Chandra Baruah, and Captain Vetch did Jaduram Dekabaruah." Gangagovinda Phukan had his education under Reverend Higgs at the latter's residence and under Lionel Angel as did Anandaram Dhekial Phukan under Reverend Bland.

Both Anadaram Dhekial Phukan and Gangagovinda Phukan were the most loyal and trusted government officials hailing from amongest the nascent Assamese middle class in the middle of the 19th century. It may be mentioned in passing that while Gangagovinda Phukan was the most trusted and confidential clerk of Captain Holroyd, the Principal Assistant of Sibsagar, and helped the latter by translating the letters written by the freedom fighters of 1857-58 including those of Maniram Dewan, Anandaram Dhekial Phukan was the only source of hope for the British in Nowgong in those trying times.

The Assamese middle class passed through four stages of development, the first stage may be called the period of gestation, stretching from the latter half of the 18th century to about 1820, second, that of rise and growth from 1820 to 1850, third, that of further growth and development from 1850 to 1880, and fourth, that of further development and expansion from 1880 to 1947 and beyond. The rise of the Assamese middle class did not take place as a result of a single historical event and its rise and growth spread over a long period of time under British colonial regime.

The opinions expressed both by Dr. Gohain and Dr. Guha on the growth and development of Assamese middle class are of opposite nature. Dr. Gohain says, "the new middle class was not formed from the ranks of the former nobility. The advantages of British education and the new avenues of employment and trade were concerned by caste Hindus who had served the former rulers as their clerks and bureaucrats what seems to have struck the Ahom feudal nobles a deadly blow was the abolition of chattel slavery and the widespread system of forced labour that supported them."

There is no gain-saying that fact that while the caste Hindus mainly appropriated the 'advantages of new education' and 'the avenues of employment' introduced by the British, the Marwari and Bengali traders and merchants monopolized the trade and commerce with little or no Assamese participation. There was little scope for the rise and growth of middle class from amongst the Ahom ethnic nobility. Apart from this the abolition of slavery (in 1843) equally affected the economy and life style of Ahom feudal nobility as well as the Hindu spiritual leaders, mainly the Brahmins of the country. Apparently, therefore, there was little or no scope for the rise and growth of a viable middle class immediately from amongst the ethnic Ahoms. Being deprived of the royal authority in the wake of the Treaty of Yandaboo (1826) the Ahom royal house and the Ahom nobility as well as the community viewed the British as the usurpers. The British rulers too, because of repeated feudal risings in 1828, 1830, 1857-58, had been suspicious about the intentions of the Ahoms. On one hand the Ahoms could not reconcile to the loss of power and authority in the state and on the other, nor the British could not trust the Ahoms.

It is to be mentioned here that since the middle of the 17th century a good number of caste-Hindu men were being appointed in the higher echelon of the Ahom administration and by this process they certainty became part and parcel of the Ahom feudal nobility. While dealing with this issue, therefore, we must keep in mind the distinction between the Ahom nobility and the enthnic Ahoms, for instance, the ancestors and members of the Bezdoloi Bhandari Baruah family, of Maniram Dewan, of Haliram Dhekial Phukan, of Harakanta Baruah Sadaramin, of Sailadhar Rajkhowa, of Jagannath Baruah, of Nilmoni Phukan, of Hem Chandra Baruah, of Lakshminath Bezbaruah, of Anandaram Baruah, of Kuladhar Chaliha, of Benudhar Rajkhowa, of Gangagovinda Phukan and of Manik Chandra Baruah had served the Ahom administration in various times and capacities. And with the changeover of the administration most of the members of these families were quick enough to change their allegiance to the new rulers. The members of these families, among others, got various responsible appointments under the new administration and this enabled them to rise to the new social status group called the middle class under the British.

As a matter of fact, the Ahoms, as a community, were trailing behind them in this regard and this does not indicate that the Assamese middle class did not arise from amongest the Ahom nobility at all. Rather the new Assamese middle class partially emerged from the Ahom nobility itself. Towards the later part of the Ahom rule there appeared rather a clear disjunction between the ethnic Ahoms who had very clear feudal function like the command of the armed forces, and the non-Ahom elements skilled in various bureaucratic works, necessary for running a complicated state machinery.

Now we shall take up the opinion of Dr. Guha. He says, "the landed gentry" and "also the upper strata of the pleasantry formed the seed-plot of the new Assamese middle class." He further says, the Assamese middle class "emerged largely from the landlord class and, marginally, also from the upper strata of the peasantry." In the early stage of British administration, when the Assamese middle class had its infancy, land did not seem to have actually played a major role, it was rather the government jobs and employment avenues that provided the basis for its growth and eventual development. The partial resumption of lands held by the spiritual and temporal lords under the grants from the former rulers, the gradual expansion of the acreage under tea cultivation, and the settlement of lands with settlers coming from outside the country, like Nepali and ex-tea garden labourers, had left little scope for the growth and development of a middle class with land as the basic economic foundation.

The prevalent land rights in the district of Kamrup, because of its being under the Purgana system of the Mughals, were landlord oriented and were akin to the Zamindary system of Goalpara district, while the general land rights in other districts of the valley were based on peasant proprietorship, and the situation in Kamrup and Goalpara was, to a great extent, conducive to the growth of middle class with land as the basis for economic production, and this actually did happen in these two districts. And, therefore, the opinion of Dr. Guha seems to be partially correct. The families of Anandaram Dhekial Phukan, of Harakanta Sadaramin, of Uttam Chandra Baruah, of Tarun Ram Phukan, of Rajani Kanta Bardoloi, of Madhab Chandra Bardoloi, to name some, were big landholders in the district of Kamrup.

As a matter of fact, government jobs and employment avenues played a major role in the rise and growth of Assamese middle class, and this class from the very beginning was careful enough against encroachment by outside elements, costly from Bengal, because government employment could alone keep up a ready and regular supply of hard cash necessary in the new economic set-up created by the British. This was partially true of the tea gardens which also kept up a regular supply of hard cash in the economy. At that time money was the scarce commodity, and only the government and tea garden employees among the Assamese or some traders had a steady supply of it.

The fear of encroachment on government jobs and employment avenues remained the central point in the politics of the Assamese middle class for a long time down to the present day. In other words, this fear outside the province, more particularly by the Bengali job seekers haunted the minds of the nascent Assamese middle class since the days of Maniram Dewan and the visit of Mills to the province. This was due to the fact that, land was not found to be conducive for the growth and development of a middle class then in Assam.

In view of the Partition of Bengal *vis-à-vis* the reconstitution of the province of Assam with the addition of the districts of Eastern Bengal into a new province called "East Bengal and Assam", the Assamese middle class people became alarmed as to the question of jobs in the new province. Jagannath Baruah and Manik Chandra Baruah, the two leading lights of the Assamese middle class, expressed the need for the preservation of sufficient employment scope for the youth of Assam in the services of the proposed province.

Jagannath Baruah, the President of the Jorhat Sorbojanik Sobha, writes to the Government on 10th February, 1904, among others, "...all inferior appointments in Assam proper should be entirely reserved to the Assamese, and at least 75 per cent of the superior appointments be likewise be reserved to the Assamese. This provision is necessary in the interest of the Assamese, who have, for obvious reasons and lack of facilities, not yet come up to the level of people in advance districts of Bengal and who for the above reasons still require a little paternal care and special treatment." Adverting to a Government Circular on the preference to be given to the Assamese in government services in the new province, Manik Chandra Baruah also writes in the same vein on 17 February, 1904, thus, "The excellent Circular regarding the preference to be given to the Assamese in all appointments in the province, which if carried into effect, will secure to the people almost all they want, has only lately been issued, and it remains to be seen how the several District Officers take up the matter." He further appealed to the government for the reservation of 80 per cent appointments in all branches of the provincial services.

The apprehension of the Assamese that the Bengali people will encroach upon their services and jobs was fully utilized by the British for the realization of their own imperialist designs. Faced as they were by an all-India political movement of a serious nature immediately after the execution of the Partition Plan of Bengal, the administrators left no stone unturned to win over the people by whatever means they could and the issue of government jobs in the newly reconstituted province became very much handy to them. Sir Bamfylde Fuller, the Lieutenant-Governor of Eastern Bengal and Assam, and the Lieutenant-Colonel P.R.T. Gordon, the Commissioner of the Assam Valley, appeared on the stage overnight as the full-throated champions of the cause and interest of the Assamese people. While making an attempt at allaying the feelings of the Assamese people Sir Bamfylde Fuller raised the slogan of "Assam for the Assamese" in 1909, almost in tune with the Bulgrians (of 1886-87) who has said "Bulgaria for the Bulgarians". The sentiment expressed by the officials circles found immediate support and response from the Assamese middle class. Manik Chandra Baruah while delivering his speech on 8 April, 1909 in the Legislative Council of Eastern Bengal and Assam at Dacca, said, "Sri Bamfylde Fuller, in his most laudable desire to improve the condition of the Assamese, had the Assamese Language recognized by the Calcutta University, and this has infused a new life, as it were, into the rising generation of Assam. He further emphasized the Principal of "Assam or the Assamese" by officially recording in unambiguous words the exclusive rights of the children of the soil to the public services of their country."

It may be observed here that if the British administrators had earnestly translated their sweet words into real deeds, much of the problems threatening the Assamese would have been removed for good. There would have been no fear in the Assamese mind of Bengali expansionism at all. But the slogan was simply a ploy. They simply appeared to play the role of an honest broker, without any materials benefits being offered to the people of Assam whatever.

The coming up of the commercial tea plantation industry initially under British finance capital also had opened up new avenues for the eventual rise and growth of the Assamese middle class. A sizeable section of the Assamese youth got employment in the tea-gardens under British planters and thereby rose to the status of the middle class. Such luminaries called '*babus*' were much more numerous and many of them became the acknowledged leaders of the Assamese people in various fields, viz. politics, economy, art, culture and literature. The industry has produced a lot of political leaders besides enriching the literacy and intellectual history of Assam. Imitating the foreign tea planters many of the Assamese people took to tea plantation industry and some of them shone in this field luxuriantly.

The history of the Assamese tea planting class begins with Maniram Dewan when he started two tea gardens, one at Chenimora and the other at Chenlung on a total area of 2000 bighas of land. The success of the European tea planters gradually attracted the attention of a section of the educated Assamese to the industry. Next to Maniram to enter into the industry was Dinanath Bezbaruah (1813-1895) and he opened two tea gardens, Sighaduwar and Rajbari in Sibsagar on a 'grant' from the government. Then came Rosheswar Baruah who opened a dozen tea gardens in the sixties of the nineteenth century. Manik Chandra Baruah (1851-1915) owned some tea gardens such as Sapekhati, Lonmati, Panikhaiti, Woodland and Mitni. Hemadhar Baruah, a government servant, opened a tea garden under the name of Letekujan after retirement from service and his son, Jagannath Baruah (1851-1907), purchased a garden at Jorhat and soon besides developing the Letekujan tea estate, established some other gardens such as Tipomia, Bassabari and Rawraiyah.

Among others who entered and flourished in the industry were Rai Bahadur Bistu Ram Baruah, Sarbananda Barkakati, Rai Bahadur Siba Prasad Baruah, Debicharan Baruah (1864-1926), Malbhog Baruah, Haribilash Agarwala (1842-1916), Maulavi Shah Noor Ali Hazarika, Narayan Chandra Bezbaruah, Kali Prasad Chaliha (1862-1914), Ghanshyam Baruah (1867-1923), Gangagovinda Phukan (1841-1926) and Ganga Ram Sarma. Bistu Ram Baruah purchased Madhupur tea estate from Rosheswar Baruah and started Thengalbarrie with his nephew Sarbananda Barkakati, and thereafter he purchased Rangajan tea estate from a Euripean tea planter and soon "developed these properties into full-fledged the estates fully equipped with factories and machineries". His son Rai Bahadur Siba Parasad Baruah soon joined him and opened and added some new gardens to those already owned, such as Haroocharai, Mezengah, Rajabarrie, Kuhum, Aideunari and Salkathoni and he soon became a 'tea magnate' and 'was considered to be the biggest Indian Tea Planter of his time'.

By the latter half of the nineteenth century many more Assamese joined the tea planting industry. Those of them who came to the limelight as tea planters were Kali Prasad Chaliha with four tea gardens under direct European patronage and his two sons, Jadav Prasad and Bimala Prasad, Ghanashyam Baruah with Dolowjan Tea Estate, Radhakanta Handique (1847-1952) with Tirual and Bartiman Tea Estate. The latter's son Krishna Kanta Handique (1898-1982), the renowed Sanskrit scholar, also was and remained a tea planter almost throughout his life.

Those who came into limelight as tea planters in the early part of the twentieth century were Nilambar Dutta, Someswar Baruah, Padmanath Sarma, Maulavi Taffazal Hussain Hazarika, Mihiram Saikia, Debraj Roy, Kamakhyaram Baruah, Nandeswar Chakraborty, Jadunath Baruah, Rajani Baruah. Prassana Kumar Baruah, Chandradhar baruah etc.

Kamakhyaram Baruah bought a 'grant' from Rai Bahadur Radhakanta Handique and, for the management of the tea garden opened on this grant, he floated a company called the 'Bahadur Tea Company' in 1926 with Dr. Harekrishna Das, Bishnu Ram Medhi, Bishnu Prasad Dutta, Rai Bahadur Kanaklal Baruah, Sarat Chandra Baruah, Golokeswar Goswami as share-holders with Baruah himself acting as the Managing Director. The same Managing Director and the shareholders organised another company under the name of 'Govindapur Tea Company'.

However, due to colonial constraint the tea planting class as the leading force of the Assamese middle class had to follow the policy of co-operation with the colonial regime. On the other hand, the interest of the tea planting class depended much on government support, blessings and encouragement. "The class of Assmese tea planters emerged", remarks Dr. Gohain, "as the appropriators of the leftovers of the imperialist plantation industry (in Assam). In comparison to the general masses of the Assamese people their income was tremendous." He further says, "The Assamese tea planters were the inevitable leaders of the educated Assamese middle class who used to survive through government employment, trade, business etc. as the junior partners in the system of exploitation under imperialism." The Assamese middle class, as a matter of fact, had to play second fiddle from the beginning almost till the coming of the Non-Cooperation Movement.

The tea planters were the richest section from amongst the Assamese middle class, and they with their riches and wealth behind them, monopolized the social, culture and political life and leadership of the entire Assamese society almost throughout the colonial period. During the periods of the peasant movements of 1836-94, the middle class remained with the British Raj. Being itself a cog in the system of colonial exploitation, the social and political leadership of the Assamese middle class then through it prudent not to do anything for ameliorating the grievances of the Assamese peasantry in revolt.

However, towards the beginning of the period of 1914-1918 there started to emerge a dissenting voice against the prevailing line of thinking of the elders amongst the younger sections of the middle class people. As a matter of fact, there emerged a new leadership comprising the youth of the valley and they, with the help of a section of the middle class, mostly lawyers and professionals, organised and led the political movements in Assam against imperialism. In this way the middle class leadership of the tea planting class came to be challenged for the first time for the cause of Swaraj of the country. Though they aligned themselves with the all-India political movements of the time they faced stiff opposition from the section of the middle class having interest in tea.

Manorama Sharma, in her study, while speaking of the Assamese middle class exercising a hegemonic role since 1910 onwards simply ignores the tea planting class as belonging to the middle class. In her words, "Emerging as a class at the end of the nineteenth century, this middle class, by 1910, had ascended to the position and strengthened it by championing some of the interests and ideological practices of the classes below it—practically the peasantry. This hegemonic status of the middle class was so well established that, despite the fact that it was not a ruling class, its value premises came to be accepted as the value premises of a major segment of the Assamese society, especially in the period after 1910." To quote her again, "the middle class, crystallised into a class and began to emerge as a new class only in the last decade of the nineteenth century and in the early twentieth century. The first signs of the formation of a new class can be seen in 1893,.. But by 1893 such a class had begun to emerge,..." She has identified the year 1893 as crucial for the emergence of the Assamese middle class, because in that year this class, she believes, made common cause with the struggling peasantry against the British government. She says, "The Raijmels had their own traditional leadership, but in 1893, when the nascent Assamese middle class took up the cause of the pleasantry against the British, the traditional leaders were gradually pushed into the background, because the middle class leadership introduced a method of agitation—constitutional agitation—which was foreign to the organisation of the Raijmels."

The middle class did not make common cause with the pleasantry in their struggles against the British, rather they remained loyal to the British government. Again her contention that the 'Assam Association which later became the Congress Party' or that 'in 1917 the Assam Association became part of the Indian National Congress' is totally wrong and baseless. Due to stiff opposition from a section of the middle class it became difficult to transform the Assam Association into the Congress, and therefore, the Assam Provincial Congress Committee had to be formed on 5 June, 1921 at a meeting of the Congress minded people held at the residence of Nabin Chandra Bardaloi in Guwahati.

It is pertinent here to see whether the Assamese middle class played a hegemonic role. Manorama Sharma says the Assamese middle class emerged in the year 1893/last decade of the nineteenth century/the early twentieth century, i.e. three different points of time for the emergence of the Assamese middle class ! And this class, as she says, 'by 1910, had ascended to the position of a hegemonic class'. If this has to be accepted, then we must admit that the Assamese middle class emerged as a hegemonic immediately after its birth, secondly, we must admit that there had been tremendous economic development in Assam under British tutelage from the very beginning conductive for the rise and growth of a middle class capable enough of becoming hegemonic immediate after its birth. And, therefore, there should be no argument, as she has done, that economically Assam was under 'a period of stagnation' during 1870-1910. But the ground reality was different from what Ms. Sharma appears to dish out as history. As has been argued earlier, the Assamese middle class had emerged much earlier than she has said.

Again, the historical situation then prevailing in Assam did not allow or rather did not prove congenial for the middle class to establish its hegemony at all. The question of hegemony may arise in a free society. As per economic laws there was constant and unfair competition between the British/European tea planters and the tea planters from amongst the Assamese middle class. In this competition the colonial regime always sided with their compatriots. And if the Government had allowed the Assamese middle class to exercise their hegemonic role then the existence of the colonial government itself would have been in jeopardy. Of course, there is no denying the fact that the Assamese middle class, in comparison to other ethnic groups of people, both in the plains and in the hills, established their leadership only in the social and cultural spheres, albeit, negating the same social and cultural rights and privileges to the various tribes at times. Even if one likes to accept the Assamese middle class exercising a 'hegemonic role' in the social and cultural spheres to a certain degree, doubts still persists as to the scope for performing the 'hegemonic role' by any social class in a dependent country or subject nation. Only the ruling class always exercise the hegemonic role by virtue of its power of controlling the 'state', and the class that survived on the leftovers of the ruling class, in the context of Assam under colonial regime, cannot be expected to have had exercised the hegemonic role at any point of time.

Role of Middle Class in Politics

Middle class is the backbone of modern societies across the globe. The imagination wisdom and enterprising spirit of members of this class determine whether a society is progressive or regressive. In the case of Assam, the onus of forging and preserving the Assamese identity lay with the Ahom rules prior to annexation by the British. Later, the burden shifted to the middle class which had its genesis in that era. This segment displayed a great spirit of Assamese rationalism as well as social cultural enterprise. One of the earliest members of this class, Maniram Dewan, completed with the British by opening out tea gardens. When Bengali replaced Assamese as official members of the middle class such as Anandaram Dhekial Phukan, Hem Chandra Baruah, Gunabhiram Barua, Lakhminath Bezbruah, Hem Chandra Goswami, Chandrakumar Agarwalla etc. fought to restore the language to its due place. The renaissance brought about by individuals like Jyoti Prasad and Bishnu Rabha ushered a 'golden era' in the social cultural sphere.

The struggle in Assam for India's freedom was led by the middle class, which also provided post-Independence political leadership. Various significant movements in the recent past, such as the mass movement against foreign influx, were led by youthful elements of the Assamese middle class. The progress and development of modern Assamese society has been, in fact, inextricably linked to its middle class. The Assamese middle class is the most articulate section of the society. It has been providing leadership in all major socio-economic and political issues of Assam since colonial era till today. Middle class occupies an important place in Assamese society because they voice the demand of the Assamese people in general. Almost all the movements of pre- and post-colonial period of Assam were led by middle class section of the society. Middle class politics took different contours at different situations. While this depends much on the aims and aspirations of the middle class of a given society, the nature and character of the ruling power also determines its course and contents for realisation. The emergence and functioning of the middle class socio-political organizations mostly reflected, as the pages will show, the aims and aspiration of the Assamese middle class, their ideology and attitude to the alien rule as well as to their own countrymen. Three major elements, viz. the loyalty to the alien rule, provincial exclusiveness and the preservation and expansion of the class interest, formed the core of the ideology of the Assamese middle class. As the emergence of this class, as elsewhere in India, was the direct of European contact and British rule, among other things, the existence and survival of this class, therefore, depended much on the continuation of British rule in the province Haliram Dhekial Phukan and Maniram Dewan, among many others, through that the British rule came as a providential boon and the former had genuine hope that this political dispensation would last for ever.

Loyalty to the alien rule and provincial exclusiveness were the two main political planks of the Assamese middle class. "Loyalty to the British was...", says Barpujari, "...their article of faith,...Their immediate objectives were the reform in collection of revenue, administration of civil and criminal justice, lowering of taxes, replacement of Assamese for Bengali in the court and schools, higher education and above all larger representation of the sons of the soil in the public offices. To the attainment of these, they carried on peaceful constitutional agitation through prayers, editions, memorials and associations." As such, the middle class in Assam, as elsewhere, did not appear to be revolutionary, rather their role in the period under review was at times ambivalent, conservative and reactionary. In this regard Marx's analysis of the character of the middle class seems to be correct. Despite this general character of the middle class as pointed out by Marx, a section of the Assamese middle class people came out openly against British imperialism by the end of the First World War. Many of them worked for the anti British mass movements of the period for national independence under the aegis of the all-India bourgeois leadership. By so doing, they played a positive role in the nation-building processes in the country, and this was dictated, among other things, by the needs of their own class too. Basking in the sunshine of British imperialism their earlier genre could not deliver the goods for themselves or for their countrymen at all. As they were under colonial constraints they could not fulfil their aspirations, both social and economic. Economic stagnation coupled with political bondage made them restive, and invariable the political struggle took the form of direct confrontation in place of collaboration. This was crucial as far as the Assamese middle class was concerned. For the first time loyalty gave way to political confrontation which ended only with the attainment of freedom and independence of the country.

The socio-political organization of the Assamese middle class did not take shape before the sixties of the nineteenth century. The year 1867 was marked by the foundation of the Assam Association in Guwahati. Its first session was held at the premises of the Government English School and was attended by the leading citizens of the town including some government officials. There a committee was formed with ex-king Kandarpeswar Singha as permanent President, Kulananda Mukherjee as Vice-President and Gangagovinda Phukan as Secretary. However, the Association soon became defunct most probably due to the unkind attitude of Mr. Angew, the then Officiating Commissioner of Assam. The connection of Kandarpeswar Singh with the rebellion of 1857-58 appeared to be an additional cause of anxiety for the Government. The last session of the Association was held in Sibsagar with Dinanath Bezbaruah on the chair in 1880. Paramananda Bharali was the Secretary then.

Therefore, even without a formal middle class organization in the preceding period the wishes and aspirations of the middle class in particular and those of the Assamese people in general were ventilated through numerous petitions and memorials to the government. In this connection mention may be made of the memoranda submitted by Maniram Dewan and Anandaram Dhekial Phukan to Mr. A.J. Moffatt Mills when he came to Assam on official visit in 1853. Though each of the memoranda was couched in different tune and spirit they bore testimony to the middle interest of the period.

Maniram Dewan (1806-1858) and Anandaram Dhekial Phukan (1829-59) were the two most outstanding elites of the rising Assamese middle class of the period. A very intelligent person though without formal modern education, Dewan was the last of the Ahom feudal aristocrats. The son of an exceptionally wealthy noble, Ramadatta, and afterwards a powerful *mauzadar* of three *mauzas* in Sibasagar, Maniram rose to great height to be reckoned with by the British even during the lifetime of his father. He proved his mettle in the prosecution of the war against the Burmese (1824-26) and in the expansion and consolidation of British rule in the Brahmaputra valley as well as in the neighbouring hill tracts. Situated as he was nearest to the seat of the Ahom administration with all its political vicissitudes of the day, he had learnt all the traits, etiquette and customs of the Ahom nobility and in the wake of British occupation he became the supreme collaborator of the latter. Maniram had a strong feudalistic tinge in his character, due perhaps to the lack of modern Western education combined with a craving for power and pelf. Despite his being the best of the collaborators, he had been let down by the British, on one count after another. This led him to make good his position by the opportunity offered itself by the rebellion of 1857. To be precise, Maniram had an axe to grind in this political whirlpool and he had to pay dearly for it.

Maniram had ventilated the grievances of the upper class people caused by the sequestration of pykes and then the abolition of slavery in 1843. He complained in unequivocal terms to Mills, "The upper and middle classes have been seen those Offices abolished, which were most suitable for them, their Logwas and Licksos taken away, and their male and female slaves set free." He continued, "Those classes who had been exempted from the payment of revenue for 600 years and now brought under the assessment."

Unlike Maniram Dewan, Anandaram Dhekial Phukan had his initiation to modern Western education in the Hindu College (1817), (re-christened as Presidency College later) in Calcutta and became imbued with Western ideas and the principles on bourgeois political economy. He viewed the Company's government in Assam as the prime mover of regeneration and improvement in all directions in Assam on modern lines. His ideas and feelings found clear expression in his memorial to Mills and other writings, particularly in 'Englandar Bibaran'. Drawing a dividing line between the personality of Maniram and Anandaram, Barpujari writes, "While Maniram and his followers felt that the British rule was an evil which must be done away with Anandaram wanted to improve it by effecting liberal reforms." Like Maniram he too criticized the government for its failure effectively to improve the material 'condition of the people and the government of the province' in his representation to Mills in 1853. But, he was a trusted and loyal official of the government with a long history of his academic and service career being built up directly under official patronage. While appreciating the government measure for the preservation of the *Ryotwari* settlement of land revenue in the province, he expressed his sanguine hope that the fiscal officers would be allowed to have 'a lasting interest in their charges,' meaning thereby the *mauzadars*, *chaudhuris* and *bisayas* were to be allowed to hold the fiscal divisions for a long period extending from 20 to 25 years, "on the basis of an assessment to be fixed on an accurate survey and that the farmers be permitted to appropriate to their own use any increase in the revenue which they may be able to affect during the period of their lease...". He was opposed to any enhancement of land revenue 'under the present circumstances of the province' because that 'would be to overburden the people with taxes, which they could but ill-afford to bear'. He argued, "An increase on assessment will inevitably lead to an increase of the unhappiness of the people." Besides this he spoke on many other issues in his memorial. He asked for the improvement of agriculture, irrigation and drainage to facilitate agriculture pursuits, manufactures, education and schools, the abolition of the opium evil, police and law courts and judicial system etc. He expressed his unhappiness at the abolition of the rights and privileges enjoyed by the grantees of the revenue-free estates in Assam by the British.

With these memories and petition Maniram and Anandaram had ushered in an era of politics of petitions and thereby constitutionalism in the history of Assam. This was precisely the same political practice followed by the men of the then middle classes all over India. Once initiated, this practice was even followed by other middle class people of Assam thereafter. Even two Assamese students, Jagannath Baruah and Manik Chandra Baruah, studying in the Presidency College, Calcutta, resorted to submitting a memorial to the victory and Governor-General of India, Lord Northbrook, in 1872. They were assisted by two other Assamese, Radhikaram Dhekial Phukan and Gangagovinda Phukan. Moreover, they had the support and guidance of Bengali middle class men, like Krishnadas Paul of Calcutta. To be precise, Calcutta became the veritable nursery for the Assamese students and youth for the acquisition of liberal Western ideas and etiquette and it provided them with a congenial ground for their practical training in the art of middle class political activities.

In the month of August 1847, a few months after the reconstitution of the Province of Assam into a Chief Commissioner's Province, Lord Northbrook, the Viceroy and Governor-General of India, paid an official visit to Assam. In the course of his visit, besides being welcomed with the erection of monumental arches, one of which still survives as a living memory of his visit in Guwahati, Sukreswar Ghat, the middle class members of the Assamese society presented him with two memorials. In the Welcome Address the signatories from amongst the Assamese middle class expressed their "....sanguine hope that before long Assam will be raised to the same footing as her sister provinces in regard to her material and moral prosperity."

The middle class knew better as to which side of the bread was buttered, and, while they were careful enough to preserve and expand their class interest, they did not ignore the issues of general improvement of the masses as a whole. This is testified by the demand raised by Maniram and Anandaram in their petition to Mills for the eradication of opium evil in Assam, and next by the request to Lord Northbrook for the establishment of a medical school in Guwahati. In the welcome Address to Lord Northbrook at Sibsagar on 22 August, 1847, the middle class expressed their dissatisfaction at the measure for abolishing the distinctions that had existed in the Ahom period between the "...three grades of society, viz. the nobility, the middle class, and the commodities." They deplored that "the Upper Class are now very much reduced and are entirely bereft of their position."

In view of the distress of the Assamese nobility caused by the abolition of slavery, among others, they requested the Viceroy graciously "...to make to the Principal families an adequate assignment of waste land revenue-free for ten years, and subsequently at one-third the usual rate of Government revenue in perpetuity. Such grants will considerably open up the country, and will sustain the dignity and prestige of the ancient houses, and yet will entail no loss on the Government. On the contrary, Government will derive material assistance from this class in the contingency of political trouble, while the proper will have their natural leaders to rally round in such times on behalf of Government."

The English East India Company's Government also viewed, since the days of the introduction of the Permanent Settlement in Bengal, the existence and maintenance of a powerful class of indigenous land owners as a bulwark against revolutionary upheavals. Lord William Bentinck, Governor-General of India, 1828-1835, declared this policy during the course of an official speech, "If security was wanting against extensive popular tumult or revolution, I should say that Permanent Settlement, though a failure in many other respects and in most important essentials, has this great advantage at least, of having created a vast body of rich landed proprietors deeply interested in the continuance of the British Dominion and having complete command over the mass of the people." Thus, there was nothing wrong in the arguments of the Assamese middle class for requesting for the allotment of sufficient wastelands revenue free for their upkeep and maintenance. They further continued, "A class of monied (*sic*) will be created, who being acquainted with the state of the country, will be able to develop fully her latent but unbounded resources. They will also have leisure to study the physical and economical sciences, and will be capable of advising the Government on subjects affecting the welfare of the people."

For the educational advancement of the people they requested the Viceroy "....to make a larger allotment of money", to "form a graded educational service ranging from Rupees 400 to 100 per month", "to create a post of District Inspector of Schools", for each district on a salary of Rs. 300 per month etc. As a necessary bait "to attract good men from Bengal for the headmasterships of the six valley districts of Assam" they wanted the Viceroy to raise the salary of each post to Rupees 200. And soon thereafter they put on record their strong "protest against the employment of Bengalis and other foreigners in the few appointments available in Assam, where most of the gentry have no other vocation except Government services." They further requested the Viceroy to take effective measures for the establishment of a medical school at Sibsagar so as to put a stop to "demonology and astrology which retained the holds of men's mind in the British Isles till very late period are still now held to form in Assam the chief preventives of diseases and death amongst the masses of the people."

The middle class put their faith in unambiguous terms in the good governance of the British and in their justice and fair play. The cup of loyalty was full to the brim. It was their conviction, right from the days of Haliram Dhekial Phukan to Lakshminath Bezbaruah, that the country under British rule made much progress and improvement, and they wanted, therefore, the continuation of the British rule. The thought of freedom and independence did not occur in their minds at all, and this sentiment was also prevalent in other parts of the country, and, as a matter of fact, the middle class men thought alike everywhere, whether they were Assamese or Bengali or Marathi. Haliram, Anandaram, Gunaviram, Lakshminath Bezbaruah of Assam, Raja Rammohun Roy, Iswar Chandra Vidyasagar, Michael Madhusudhan Dutt and others of Bengal and Gopal Krishna Gokhale, Mahadev Govinda Ranade and Dadabhai Naoroji and many more of the period were of the same mould and held the same view. They accepted British rule and wanted its continuation as a providential dispensation. For instance, Raja Rammohau Roy's attitude to British rule as outlined by Bimanbehari Mazumder may be quoted here. He writes, "Rammohun took great pains to prove that the loyalty of the people of India to the British Government was deep and unshakable. As proofs of loyalty he said that the people entrusted Government with their money, while under the previous governments they had buried their riches under the ground, that the landlords improved their lands without fear, that the citizens of Calcutta offered payers for the victory of the British during the third Mahratta and the Nepal wars, that the enlightened people frequently made favourable comments on the fair justice and solicitude shown by the Government for the spread of education and looked upon the English as delivers than as conquerors."

Assam is economically backward in spite of abundant natural resources - minerals, agriculture and forest. The main reason for the economic— backwardness is that most of the raw materials of the state are siphoned off for feeding industries outside the state. Even after independence, Assam was largely neglected in regard to central investments and industrialization. The Assamese middle class has been playing a vital role since colonial period in ventilating the needs and inspirations of the Assamese people in these major problem areas.

Role of Political Parties

Assam, an upcoming industrial hub and the gateway to the North East is also a prime contributor to the agricultural output and economy of the country. Several national parties and three state level political parties dominate the political scenario of the politically active state. Noted national political parties are Bharatiya Janata Party, the Indian National Congress, Nationalist Congress Party (NCP), the Communist Party of India (Marxist) (CPM) and Communist Party of India (CPI). The state parties of Assam include the Asom Gana Parishad (AGP), Asom Gana Parishad (Progressive) (AGPP).

Apart from the national political parties the state parties too have an iron grip on the administration of Assam. In fact, the years spanning from 1985 to 2004 saw the control of the state oscillating between the national level Indian National Congress and the state party, Asom Gana Parishad.

National Political Parties

The Indian National Congress has been ruling the state since the country gained its independence from British dominion in 1947. The party ruled the state till 1978. In 1978, a Janata Party Government took over the control of Assam. Nevertheless, the government had a short stint and the Indian National Congress returned to power once again in 1980. They ruled the state till 1985. In 1985, the Asom Gana Parishad (AGP), a party which backed the Assam Agitation, was elected by the people of the state to rule the state for the next five years. After 1985, the Asom Gana Parishad and the Indian National Congress governed the state alternatively till 2001. Since 2001, the Indian National Congress again came to power and since then the party has been ruling the state in an uninterrupted manner. They became successful in winning the assembly elections held in 2006 and 2011 successively. Tarun Gogoi is the only Chief Minister in the chronicles of the state to be chosen as the CM for the third successive time.

Assam State Assembly Election Results in 2011

The state features a unicameral assembly comprising 126 seats. Assembly election for 126 constituencies in Assam took place in 2011. AIUDF (All India United Democratic Front), which contested the polls just for the second occasion, was successful to get 18 seats in the assembly. All India United Democratic Front is the principal opposition party in the house. Given below is a list of the various parties that contested the assembly polls in 2011:

- Indian National Congress (Congress)—Got 78 seats and came to power
- Asom Gana Parishad (AGP) —10 seats
- All India United Democratic Front (AIUDF) —18 seats (principal opposition in the assembly)
- Bodoland People's Front (BPF)—12 seats
- Bharatiya Janata Party (BJP)—5 seats
- Independent Candidate—2 seats
- Trinamool Congress (TMC) —1 seat

The following parties could not win any seat in the assembly polls 2011:

- Sanmilito Ganashakti Assam (SGA)
- Communist Party of India (CPI)
- Autonomous State Demand Committee (ASDC)
- Purbanchaliya Loka Parishad (PLP)
- Communist Party of India (Marxist) (CPI-M)
- Role of Indian National Congress (INC)

Indian National Congress (INC) is one of the oldest party in India. Its membership base makes it the world's largest political party. It is also known as Congress party. It was founded in 1885 as an organization to lead the independence movement of India. Various Congress leaders in pre-Independence era had played a pivotal role in Indian Independence

Movement. In the history of independent India, Congress party has been the dominant force.

After Independence, INC was established as a major political party and Pandit (Mr.) J.L. Nehru, who was the President of INC, elected as the first Prime Minster of India in 1952 and under his leadership, INC won other two elections in succession (1957 and 1962). After Pt. J.L. Nehru's death in 1964, Mr. Lal Bahadur Shastri took over as the leader of Congress party and after his death, Mrs. Indira Gandhi became the next president of Congress in 1966.

In 1967, INC was split into two parties. One faction of which was led by Mrs. Gandhi and the other was led by Mr. Kamraj. Later the faction led by Mrs. Gandhi was recognized as INC and in 1975 she declared a National Emergency in the face of growing opposition. It curtailed the power of courts and unleashed a police state.

After the emergency was lifted in 1977, more Congress factions were formed and joined hand with other political parties. The faction which remained with Mrs. Indira Gandhi was called Congress (I). In 1977 General Elections, Janata Party won by a substantial margin and formed the government. The Janata Party coalition government could not stay for long due to infighting and next General Elections were held in 1980, in which Congress party won the elections with a huge margin and returned to power. After the assassination of Mrs. Gandhi in 1984, her son, Mr. Rajiv Gandhi took over and led the Congress party to a large victory in 1984. In the next General Election 1989, Congress party was defeated and in 1991 election campaign, Mr. Rajiv Gandhi was also assassinated and Mr. P.V. Narasimha Rao took over as the party president. In the last two decades Congress party (INC) has seen huge up and downs. With Mrs. Sonia Gandhi's acceptance for party leadership, there was another breakup of the INC. The breakaway group called Nationalist Congress Party (NCP). General elections in 1999 saw the Congress tally to an all time low. Since then, Congress party regained itself as one of the major political force in Indian Politics. Currently, INC is leading the UPA government in the Centre.

History of Assam Legislative Assembly

The Assam legislative structure is unicameral and consists of the 126-member Assam Assembly. Members are elected for a period of 5 years. The Assam Assembly is presided over by the Speaker, who is generally a member of the ruling party. Position of different political parties in Assam Legislative Assembly since 1946:

Year	Assembly	Total seats	Government	Seats won	Chief Minister	Opposition
1946-52	Provincial Assembly	105	Indian National Congress	50	Gopinath Bordoloi/ Bishnu Ram Modhi	Muslim League
1952-57	1st Assembly	108	Indian National Congress	76	Bishnu Ram Medhi	Socialist Party
1957-62	2nd Assembly	108	Indian National Congress	71	Bishnu Ram Medhi/Bimala Prasad	Praja Socialist Party
1962-67	3 rd Assembly	105	Indian National Congress	79	Bimala Prasad Chaliha	All Party Hill Leaders Conference
1967-72	4th Assembly	126	Indian National Congress	73	Bimala Prasad Chaliha/Mohendra Mohan Choudhury	All Party Hill Leaders Congress
1972-78	5th Assembly	114	Indian National Congress	95	Sarat Chandra Sinha	Samyukta Socialist Party
1978-79	6th Assembly	126	Janata Party/Communist Party of India/Plains Tribals Council of Assam	53/17/4	Golap Borbora/ Jogendra Nath Hazarika	Indian National Congress
1979-80	—	—	Government of India	—	President Rule	
1980-81	6th Assembly	126	Indian National Congress/Communist Party of Indian/ Independents	51/11/4	Anowara Taimur	Janata Party
1981-82	—	—	Government of India	—	President Rule	—
1982	6th Assembly	126	Indian National Congress/Communist Party of India/ Independents	51/11/4	Kesab Chandra Cogoi	Janata party
1982-83	—	—	Government of India	—	President Rule	—
1983-89	7th Assembly	126	Indian National Congress	91	Hiteswar Sailkia	Plaints Tribals Council of Assam
1989-90	8th Assembly	126	Asom Gana Parishad	89	Parulla Kumar Mahana	Indian National Congress
1990-91	—	—	Government of India	—	President Rule	—
1991-2001	10th Assembly	126	Indian National Congress	66	Hiteswar Saikia/ Bhumidhar Barman	Asom Gana Parishad
2001-06	11th Assembly	126	Indian National Congress	71	Tarun Gogoi	Asom Gana Parishad
2006-11	12th Assembly	126	Indian National Congress/ Bodoland People's Front	53/10	Tarun Gogoi	Asom Gana Parishad
2011	13th Assembly	126	Indian National Congress/ Bodoland People's Front	78/11	Tarun Gogoi	All India United Democratic Front

Role of Regional Political Party in Assam

The role of Regional Political Parties in ALA is insignificant. In Assam the Indian National Congress has been able to maintain its dominance till today. Till the sixth general election to the House of the People Indian National Congress maintained its dominance at Centre as well as in States. In sixth general election when the rest of India particularly in the north the electorate rejected the INC, in Assam it could manage to secure 10 out of 14 seats with 50.6 per cent vote share. The INC dominated the state politics of

Assam by securing absolute majority in all the first five general elections to the ALA and formed the government in the state. Right from the first to the fifth Legislative Assembly the opposition was numerically weak in Assam and were incapable of checking effectively the dominance of the ruling INC.

However, the sixth general election of 1978 marked the beginning of a new era in the history of ALA. It was in this election the Janata Party effectively challenged the dominance of the INC. In 1978 general election to the ALA the ruling INC was forced to sit in the opposition. But the INC legislators in the state were not content to play the role of responsible opposition.

It is found that prior to 1985 general elections the regional political parties had limited success in the state politics. In 1985, for the first time a regional political party, namely Asom Gana Parishad (AGP) formed the Government in the state and in 1996 for the second time they came to power. Thereafter, the Congress party unbeatably comes to power and continuing their rule in the state.

It is clear that regional political parties in ALA failed to play a significant role to provide opportunity to the people for the change of a government. There was an exception of this only in 1985 and 1996 ALA elections. Earlier in 1978 general election the Janata party had been capable of challenging the dominance of the INC by coming to power but unfortunately failed to retain the same. Though there was exception from this generalization, the INC has uninterruptedly been dominating the state politics of Assam since independence.

It is to be admitted that there is a need of strong opposition which would be able to get adequate opportunities to oppose. The opposition while opposing the Government generally resorts to certain tactics such as pressure, criticism and influence over the Government so as to persuade to carry out its activities keeping parity with the public opinion and interest in framing policies and programmes. Government does not mean the rule of one section of people or the expression of will of one section of people.

Democracy is not one man show or for that matter, of any one section of people as such. A government having faith in democracy cannot be unmindful of the presence of the opposition and cannot consider the opposition's suggestions and arguments as mere meaningless. This is because today's opposition is tomorrow's government. In a developing society the needs of the people grow rapidly. The best is never reached and hence there is always opportunity to promise more and more and to do better. Election manifestoes and the propaganda of parties in various elections carry the testimony of such promises and assurances of doing better. It leads to a competition and struggle between the government and opposition for political power. The promises and assurances made by the parties at the time of elections, more often than not, are not fulfilled entirely when they capture power. But it will also be a reverse side of the truth if it be held that they give hollow promises and assurances only. It is clear that whatever welfare has been achieved by the people of different countries was because of having parliamentary democracy.

Asom Gana Parishad, also recognized as the Assam Peoples Association is an eminent state level political party in Assam. The auspicious Assam Accord of 1985 was responsible for the birth of the AGP. Prafulla Kumar Mahanta was elected as Chief Minister of Assam and his claim to fame rested on his being the country's youngest Chief Minister. The Assam government has been under the jurisdiction twice extending from 1985 to 1989 and from 1996 to 2001.

However, the former Chief Minister, Prafulla Kumar Mahanta has broken out of the AGP to form his own offshoot political party, the Asom Gana Parishad (Progressive). This has led to considerable weakening of the party's political stronghold in Assam as evinced by their dismal performance in the 2006 elections where they managed to grab only a single seat. This led to the downfall of the monarch of the State Level Political Parties of Assam followed by the establishment of the able Congress rule.

Given India's social, cultural, and historical diversity, it is only natural that regional parties play an important role in the country's political life. Because of India's federal system, state assembly votes are held in an electoral arena that often enables regional parties to obtain power by espousing issues of regional concern. Simultaneously, the single-member district, first-past-the-post electoral system has given the advantage to national parties, such as the Congress, which possess a realistic chance of gaining or retaining power at the national level and the opportunity to use Central Government resources to reward their supporters. Although regional parties have exercised authority at the state level, collectively they receive only from 5 to 10 per cent of the national vote in parliamentary elections. Only during the governments of the Janata Party (1977-79) and the National Front (1989-90) have they participated in forming the Central Government. However, as India's party system becomes more fragmented with the decline of the Congress (I), the regional parties are likely to play an important role at the national level. Regional parties are parties whose main holds are in one certain state and mostly they participate in the elections only within that state. Most of these regional parties have agenda fitting certain culture dominant within that state. Some of these regional parties also participate in neighboring states, which have constituencies with culture similar to the first state. Different state parties were established at different periods because of different reasons. Some even have origins prior to India's independence.

With the lapse of time and rapid changes in political scenario the illusion of regionalism is waning in Assam and the north eastern parts of the country. During last several years Indian politics reached a chaotic situation throughout the country leading an air of hatred against the national political parties. There was a deep feeling in the people that the national political parties failed to deliver goods and look into the interests of the region. In a vast country like India every region has got different types of problems. Simultaneously, all regions of the country face different types of situations. To safeguard the interest of the region, the necessity of regional political parties was felt for the betterment and welfare the people of the region. In Assam, even though some regional parties existed earlier, their role was negligible. With the launching of movement against the foreign nationals in the state by the All Assam Students' Union (AASU) and Asom Gana Sangram Parishad (AGSP), the people were inspired to struggle and fight against mal-administration, corruption and other evils of the society. The controversy over the voters' list in the state, which arose in the year 1979, is still alive. Due to inclusion of foreigners' name in the lists, for the first time elections had to be stalled. The reports from various parts of the state came that the lists contained the names of foreigners. The delay in the process of identification and deportation of such people led to more complexity of the issue. After continuous President's rule for a long time a 'drama of election' was played by the ruling party at the Centre in 1983. Despite opposition and agitations by majority of organizations, the Congress government at the Centre was firm in its decision to hold the elections and it won the 'so-called' elections too, which was rejected by the people. However, with the signing of the Assam Accord on August 15, 1985, between the state government and the movement leaders, in presence of erstwhile Prime Minister, in New Delhi, peace returned to the state and the political scenario changed.

Ironically, the fresh elections in 1985 were held on the basis of the same electoral rolls, against which the movement was launched. The results of the polls were surprising. The newly formed Asom Gana Parishad (AGP), the staunch advocate of regionalism came to power defeating the mighty Congress. Politically immature the AGP leaders took the reins of the state administration in December 1985. The AGP rose to power in Assam on the crest of Assamese nationalism. Immigration to Assam—primarily by Muslim Bengalis from neighbouring Bangladesh—had aroused concern that the Assamese would become a minority in their own state. By 1979 attention was focused on the controversial issue of determining how many immigrants would be allowed on the state's list of eligible voters. The Congress (I), which gained a substantial share of the immigrants' votes, took a more expansive view of who should be included while the Assamese nationalist organizations demanded a more restrictive position. An attempt to hold state elections in February 1983, and in effect to force the Assamese nationalists to accept the *status quo*, resulted in a breakdown of law and order and the deaths of more than 3,000 people. The subsequent formation of a Congress (I) government led by Hiteshwar Saikia was widely viewed in Assam as illegitimate, and it was dissolved as part of the terms of the Assam Accord that was signed between Rajiv Gandhi and Assamese nationalists on August 15, 1985. The Assam Accord also included a compromise on the voter eligibility issue, settled the issue of the citizenship status of immigrants, and stipulated that new elections were to be held in December. The AGP was formed by Assamese student leaders after the signing of the accord, and the new party won the December 1985 elections with 35 per cent of the votes and sixty-four of 108 seats in the state legislature.

The people of the state kept high hopes on the team in handling the affairs of the state, as its active members were fully aware of the problems of the state and almost all of them were enthusiastic. The new leaders were firm in their opinion that the national parties were 'useless', so far the state's matters were concerned. On public platform they declared that Delhi could not solve the problems of Assam, as it did not try to understand them. The AGP ruled the state once for a full term of five years, but failed to provide any package of relief for the people of the state. The vexed foreign national issue remained unresolved. New problems raised ugly heads. The tribal communities of the state began disassociating and struggling to save their identity and culture. The law and order situation deteriorated. The administration could not detect and deport any foreigner from the state. The victory of the AGP did not end the controversy over Assamese nationalism. The AGP was unable to implement the Accord's provisions for disenfranchising and expelling illegal aliens, in part because Parliament passed legislation making it more difficult to prove illegal alien status. The AGP's failure to implement the Accord along with the general ineffectiveness with which it operated the state government undercut its popular support, and in November 1990 it was dismissed and President's Rule declared. As the AGP floundered, other nationalist groups of agitators flourished. The United Liberation Front of Assam (ULFA) became the primary torchbearer of militant Assamese nationalism while the All Bodo Students' Union (ABSU) and Bodo People's Action Committee (BPAC) led an agitation for a separate homeland for the central plain tribal people of Assam (often called Bodos). The ABSU/BPAC-led mass agitation lasted from March 1987 until February 1993 when the ABSU signed an Accord with the state government that had been under the Congress (I) control since 1991. The Accord provided for the creation of a Bodoland Autonomous Council with jurisdiction over an area of 5,186 square kilometres and 2.1 million people within Assam. Nevertheless, Bodo agitation continued in the mid-1990s as a result of the demands of many Bodo leaders, who insisted that more territory be included under the Bodoland Autonomous Council.

The next election in 1991 was crucial for the regional party and the Congress came to power again. It was a lesson for the AGP, which failed to deliver goods. The Congress also failed to prove its worth during its term. The people were in dilemma having no alternative to decide between these two national and regional parties. In the next elections, electorate gave another chance to AGP to rule over the state, but the party proved complete failure in administration. The state was ruled by the corruption, abduction, killings etc. The AGP has formed government twice from 1985 to 1989 and from 1996 to 2001. The differences in the ruling party came to the surface, which was completely against the wishes of the people. The people have no choice. Illusion of regionalism has taken back seat and the Congress, the national party has made its root strong, despite all odds.

Splits and Mergers of AGP

The AGP in March 1991 underwent a split when party general secretary and former Assam Home Minister Bhrigu Kumar Phukan, former Union Law Minister and MP Dinesh Goswami, former state Education Minister Brindaban Goswami, Assam Legislative Assembly Speaker Pulakesh Barua and others formed the Natun Asom Gana Parishad. This fraction came back to the party fold in 1992. In 2000, Atul Bora moved away and formed Trinamool Gana Parishad.

After the second AGP Government's reign under Prafulla Kumar Mahanta came to an end and Congress regained power, numerous allegations were raised against him related to the corruption during his tenure, government's involvement in secret killings, and Mahanta's overall inactive leadership. These led to his demotion from being President of the party and later he was expelled from the party on July 3, 2005 after being accused of anti-party activities. Mahanta then formed his own party, Asom Gana Parishad (Progressive) i.e. AGP (P).

In 2008, a process started to reconcile the differences among all the breakaway fractions and to bring back everybody under the mother party umbrella to strengthen the regional party movement in Assam. Finally, on

14th October, 2008 all breakaway groups reconciled in one umbrella at the historic town Golaghat. Prafulla Mahanta merged his AGP (P) with it. Atul Bora and Pulakesh Barua merged their TGP with the AGP and farmer leader and former legislator Pabindra Deka, too merged the PLP with it.

Other Regional Parties in the State

The Asom Bharatiya Janata Party is a break-away group of the Bharatiya Janata Party in Assam. Asom BJP was founded by senior BJP leader and former Inspector General of Police, Hiranya Bhattacharya in 2001. Bhattacharya had objected to the decision of BJP to align with the Asom Gana Parishad.

Asom BJP Contested the 2001 State Assembly Polls Unsuccessfully

Asom Gana Parishad (Progressive), or AGP(P), was a regional political party in Assam, India. It was formed by Prafulla Kumar Mahanta after he was expelled in 2005 by the Asom Gana Parishad for anti-party activities. In the 2006 Assembly elections, the party won just one seat, namely that of Prafulla Kumar Mahanta. In 2008, the party merged again with Asom Gana Parishad.

Asom Gana Sangram Parishad (Assam Popular Struggle Association), a political party in the Indian state of Assam. AGSP was launched by the Asom Jatiyatabadi Yuva Chatra Parishad (AJYCP) in 1999. Party president is Jatindra Kumar Borgohain. In the 2001 state legislative assembly polls in the state, AGSP joined the Rashtriya Democratic Alliance led by the Nationalist Congress Party.

Asom Jatiya Sanmilan (Assam National Conference), a political party in the Indian state of Assam. AJS was founded by Asom Gana Parishad dissident Bhrigu Phukan in 1998. In March 2001 the AJS General Secretary Hemanta Barman and many other members joined the Indian National Congress. In the state legislative assembly elections 2001 AJS contested as a part of the Rashtriya Democratic Alliance, on a Nationalist Congress Party symbol.

Autonomous State Demand Committee, originally the Peoples Democratic Front, was set up as a mass organization of the Communist Party of India (Marxist-Leninist) Liberation in order to fight for statehood for the Karbi Anglong region in the Indian state of Assam. Several elections to the Lok Sabha and the District Council were won under ASDC banner. Dr. Jayanta Rongpi represented the area in the Lok Sabha, elected as the ASDC candidate in 1991, 1996 and 1998. Later a split occurred in ASDC, with one section the Autonomous State Demand Committee (United) breaking away from CPI (ML) Liberation and aligning with the Bharatiya Janata Party. The group loyal to CPI (ML) Liberation reorganized themselves as Autonomous State Demand Committee (Progressive). From 1999 election onwards, Autonomous State Demand Committee (Progressive) candidates contest election on the banner of Communist Party of India (Marxist- Leninist) Liberation.

Bodo People's Progressive Front, (BPPF) is a political Party in Assam formed on April 12, 2005 for participation in the Bodoland Territorial Areas District elections.

Split

The party suffered a vertical split into BPPF (R) with Rabiram Narzary and BPPF (H) with Hagrama Mohilary, the then supreme of the dissolved BLT as the Party President respectively.

BPPF(H)

The Hagrama faction aligned with the Indian National Congress in the April 2006 elections for the Assam Assembly and won 11 seats. It became the junior partner in the Assam government. This was a historical occasion since the Bodo's long associated with the Bodoland statehood movement, are now sharing power in Dispur, the capital of Assam.

BPPF(R)

The Rabiram faction, aligned with the Asom Gana Parishad in the April 2006 elections, did not win any seats in the Assam Assembly.

The Bodoland People's Front (BPF) is a state political party in Assam state in northeastern India. In the general election, 2009 its candidate, Sansuma Khunggur Bwiswmuthiary was elected to the 15th Lok Sabha from Kokrajhar constituency. Biswajit Daimary of this party was elected to the Rajya Sabha in May 2008. BPF had 10 members in the 12th Assam Legislative Assembly, and it is a constituent of the current Indian National Congress led ruling coalition in Assam. In the 2011 Assam Assembly election, BPF won 12 seats.

Cachar Congress, was a regional political party in the Barak Valley, Assam, India. CC was formed ahead of the 2001 Assam assembly elections by a group of Indian National Congress dissidents. The founders of CC were dissatisfied with the distribution of tickets for election and the leadership of Santosh Mohan Dev, who is a Veteran leader of the Indian National Congress. The president of CC was Anil Chandra Dey. CC contested the 2001 Bidhan Sabha elections. On November 17, 2004 CC merged with Bharatiya Janata Party. Sources claimed that CC had 520 members at the time of the merger.

Krishak Banuva Panchayat (Assam Peasant and Labour Party) was a political party in Assam, India. It functioned as the open mass front for the Revolutionary Communist Party of India in Assam. It was founded on May 2, 1940 at a convention in Gauhati.

The Marxist Manch is a political party in Assam, India, which emerged as a local splinter group of Communist Party of India (Marxist). The party has some base in the Ratabari assembly constituency, where it has entered into electoral cooperation with Asom Gana Parishad. The party was divided in two factions, but reunited ahead of a 2003 by poll in Ratabari. Abdul Khalik Bangal became president of the party and Chinmoy Choudhury general secretary after reunification.

Marxist Manch took part in the founding of the Confederation of Indian Communists and Democratic Socialists in 2002.

Natun Asom Gana Parishad ('New Assamese People's Association') was a political party in the Indian state of Assam. NAGP was formed through a split of Asom Gana Parishad (AGP). NAGP was led by former Union Law Minister and MP Dinesh Goswami and former Assam Home Minister Bhrigu Kumar Phukan. Goswami and Phukan had been prominent leaders of the Assam Agitation led by All Assam Students Union and All Assam Gana Sangram Parishad in the early 1980s. Other prominent leaders of the party included former Assam Education Minister Brindaban Goswami and former Assam Legislative Assembly speaker Pulakesh Barua.

In 1994 NAGP merged with AGP, with Bhrigu Phukan as the Working President of the Asom Gana Parishad. Phukan was later removed from the post of party Working President and was finally expelled from AGP in 1997 following differences with party president and the then Chief Minister of Assam Prafulla Kumar Mahanta. Another leader of NAGP, former state Education Minister Brindaban Goswami later on became the president of AGP.

The Plain Tribals Council of Assam is a political party in the Indian state of Assam. In 1966, the PTCA launched a militant agitation for a separate tribal state called 'Udayachal'.

Rashtriya Democratic Alliance (National Democratic Alliance), was a front of five political parties contesting the 2001 state legislative assembly elections in the Indian state of Assam. RDA included Nationalist Congress Party, Asom Jatiya Sanmilan, Asom Gana Sangram Parishad, Purbanchaliya Loka Parishad and Janata Dal (Secular). RDA should not be confused with National Democratic Alliance.

Trinamool Gana Parishad (Grassroots Peoples Association) was a political party in the Indian state of Assam.

TGP formed as a splinter-group of Asom Gana Parishad in 2000. The party was led by Atul Bora, then Public Works Department Minister in the Prafulla Mahanta Cabinet. The party was allotted "Cup & Saucer" as election symbol.

In the state assembly elections of 2001 in Assam, TGP made an alliance with Bharatiya Janata Party. In the Lok Sabha elections of 2004, TGP put up one candidate, Deben Dutta from Guwahati. Dutta received 14,933 votes (1.69% of total votes polled).

United Minorities Front, Assam is a regional political party in Assam, India. UMFA was set up in 1985 by the All Assam Minority Students Union, as a response to the militant "anti-foreigner" agitations of All Assam Students Union and the signing of the Assam Accord. The support of UMFA comes mainly from Bengali Muslims.

The president of UMFA is Hafiz Rashid Ahmed Chowdhury, who has been the last founding member of the party to stay till it is merged with AUDF.

United People's Party of Assam, a political party in the Indian state of Assam. UPPA was an ally of Asom Gana Parishad and took part in an AGP-led government in the state. On December 17, 2000 UPPA merged with Samajwadi Party.

United Tribal Nationalist Liberation Front, a regional political party in Assam. UTNLF was launched by the PTCA (Progressive) (splinter group of Plain Tribals Council of Assam) in 1984. UTNLF demands statehood for the Bodo areas.

The UTNLF led a violent campaign during the 1990s against both the Assamese and the Indian military units in the area.

Though there are number of regional political parties in Assam, these parties have no significant roles in state politics of Assam.

Pressure Groups

The development of pressure groups in Indian political system is generally considered a vitalizing factor in the process of political modernization. In democratic system pressure groups operate to represent a segment of public opinion.

In North East India, particularly in the hill areas the students are the most formidable and strong force to work as an extra-constitutional organized group to articulate the grievances of public. The students of Assam have launched three important movements on economic issues. They are—Oil Refinery Movement, 1957, Food Scarcity Movement, 1966 and

Second Oil Refinery Movement in 1969. The Oil Refinery movements mainly focused on the industrial backwardness of Assam and reflected the anxiety of the Assamese middle class over the unemployment problem of the state. Though some political parties played important role in these three movements, the actual power came from the All Assam Students Union.

The students of Assam launched another three important movements for the protection of the linguistic and cultural identities of the Assamese people. The first in 1960 on the issues of official language of Assam; the second in 1972 on the issue of medium of instruction; and the third one against foreign nationals. In all these agitation they have been able to mobilize a large sunk of the Assamese population.

The All Manipur Students Union (AMSUO) was formed in 1965 following the food crisis in the then Union Territory of Manipur, AMSU tried to pressurize the Chief Minister to take corrective policy decision on food crisis in Manipur and acted as pressure group. In fact in 1965 government and traders without taking stock of rice stores into consideration sent rice outside the state for marketing which resulted in non-availability of rice stocks in godowns. It affected general and poorer sections of people who could not afford to have two square meals because of price hike and non-availability of rice in the market. This policy went against the interest of general public. As a reaction the student organization, i.e. ANSU took to streets to highlight the issue.

The AMSU took active interest was also in the foreigner's issue. Following the civil war between the then Eastern and Western Pakistan millions of refugees crossed the border and entered most the North-eastern part of India. During February 1980, AMSU took up foreigners issue and showed great concern on the demographic changes in the state which had occurred due to influx of foreigners in the region. In Assam foreigners issue was first taken up in April 1979 and this issue was soon picked up by AMSU in Manipur in February 1980. Different dates were put forward specifying the cut off year for identification of foreigners such as 1951, 1971 and 1976. Apart from this, students also demanded that foreigners should not be allowed to purchase or sell land or to seek jobs in the region. They also demanded effectuating the existing inner-line permit such system to prevent entry of foreigners in the state. Ultimately the Government of Manipur had to accept the demand of AMSU and signed an agreement on 9 November, 1994 with AMSU at the Raj Bhavan in Imphal. The AMSU met the Union Minister of state for Home affairs and urged the Union Minister to expedite the matter of detecting and deporting of foreigners from Manipur before the Parliament election of 1996.

The AMSU again expressed their concern too in the language issue. In

1987 it formed a Language Demand Committee to press the state government to put pressure on the Central Government to include Manipuri language in the eighth schedule of the Constitution. Ultimately, they succeeded in helping to get Manipuri language included in the eighth schedule of the Constitution.

The "Mizo Students Association" although came into existence on 27 October, 1935, it could not function properly during the Second World War. It was again activated in 1947 and worked effectively till 1966. From 1966 to 1970 it again remains inactive because of the independence movement launched by Mizo National Front headed by Laldenga. Since 1970 it again started working.

Since its emergence the Mizo Students Association (MSU) associated itself in many welfare activities of students and also participated in many social and political issues of the state. The MNF insurgency of 1966 resulted in food shortage all over Mizoram. The MNS immediately took up the issue and decided to observe fasting in places inhabited by the Mizos outside Mizoram. It also resolved to collect a sum of money equivalent to one meal for the help of the distressed people.

Prior to the attainment of Union Territory by Mizoram in 1972 the Students Association hardly interfered in the Government policies. It for the first time expressed its resentment on the government's intension to convert Mizoram into a Union Territory. The students found fault with the move and submitted a memorandum to the Prime Minister on 31 July, 1971. The memorandum stated: "Permanent and peaceful settlement in Mizoram could only be attained through peace talks and negotiations between the Central Government and the underground Mizos. The Union Territory will not solve, but multiply the Mizo problems."

As MacIver says a pressure group can be defined by its techniques when most people think about pressure group they tend to concentrate on efforts of influence in the process of legislation. The choice of techniques employed by a group is determined not only by the structure of the political system but also by the various attitudes or interactions within society. Number of pressure groups are playing significant role in Assam. Some of them are:

Assam Sahitya Sabha

The Assam Sahitya Sabha, through long period of history has taken up a number of issues in the interest of the Assamese people.

One of the most important demand of the Sabha is the question of Assamese as an official state language of Assam. Its effort on this issue is remarkable in the history of the organisation. The first resolution of the

Sabha on this question was adopted on March 11-12, 1950. An all Assam 'State Language Day' was observed on 16th July, 1950, throughout the state with unprecedented enthusiasm. The Sabha presented a Memodandum before the Official Language Commission of Government of India in 1955 and indicated 1960 as the 'dateline' within which the Government was requested to take measure to recognize the Assamese. The representatives of the Sabha personally met the Chief Minister of Assam on three occasions (1-5-59, 14-5-59, 7-11-59). The Sabha observed 'the State Language Day' 12-9-59 and published a book 'Rajyik Bhasa Asamiya' which was distributed among the Cabinet members, Speaker, Deputy Speaker, members of the Legislative Assembly. Again, the Sabha called for observance of 'State Language Demand Day' on March 11, 1960, followed by meetings in various places, and publication of a book entitled. 'Assam's State Language' by the Sabha. Further, a delegation of the Sabha met the Prime Minister Nehru and submitted him a Memorandum at Jorhat on 19-7-60 and another Memorandum to the delegation of M.Ps. on 15-8-60. A delegation of the Sabha met the Chief Minister, Finance Minister, the A.P.C.C. Chief and the Hill Leaders Conference on 1-10-60 and clarified its stand. In the All Party Conference of 4-5 October, 1960, the delegation of the Sabha proposed that the Assamese should be recognized as the only language of the state and expressed strong resentment against the bilingual Bill put forwarded by the Chief Minister on 10-10-60 in the Assam Assembly. The Sabha expressed dissatisfaction with the Assam Official Language Bill which contained: (1) provision for the use of the Assamese and English and thereafter of the Assamese and Hindi in the Secretary and the offices of the Head of Department of the State Government, (2) provision for the adoption of the Assamese (or any other language) by the Autonomous Region or the Districts only if a majority of not less than two-thirds of the members present and voting decides in favour of such adoption, (3) In spite of the solid demand for the declaration of Assamese along as the State Official Language made by the Nepali people and considerable proportion of Muslims of the Cachar provision has been made for the adoption of Assamese for administrative and other official purposes upto and including the district level in Cachar only if the Mahakuma Parishads and Municipal Boards of the District if a Joint meeting decide in favour of such adoption. Again, the Sabha had put heavy pressure into effect by submitting a Memorandum to the Union Home Minister on June 4, 1961, which clearly expressed the unreasonableness of the Shastri Formula to have Bengali recognized as the second official language of the State. The Sabha submitted another Memorandum to the Union Home Minister on June 29, 1969, which mentioned, the decision to amend the Language Act in the light of the Shastri Formula will neither be conducive to the stabilisation of the situation nor in any way facilitate final peaceful settlement fair to all. The three member delegation of the Sabha submitted the Home Minister a Memorandum on 12-9-61 whereby they pointed out to the Articles 345-347 of the Constitution of India which envisages the adoption of a minority language. Thus, right from 1950 onwards the Sabha has made consistent efforts at the question of Assamese as only the official language of Assam. The Sabha launched the movement under the leadership and inspiration of late Ambika Giri Roy Choudhury who may rightfully be regarded as the 'Father of the Movement.'

The Assam Sahitya Sabha has greatly sought for Assamese as the medium of instruction from 1965 onwards. The Executive Committee on September 1967, demanded from the two Universities of Assam practical measures to make Assamese as the medium of instruction at the University level and to take up measures for the publication of books and other literary materials in Assamese at an early date. The Sabha participated in the Protest Day on 29-9-68 and the Assam Bandh on 5-10-68 in this connection. A representative body of the Sabha met the Vice Chancellor of the Guwahati University and submitted him a Memorandum on 25-9-78 mentioning that the Assamese should be introduced as medium at the Doctorate level in support of the Dongerkerry Committee.

Further, the Sabha made a very strong move on the issue of State Reorganisation. As early as March 1955, the Sabha decided to send a delegation to the State Reorganisation Commission which envisaged the reconstitution of the States. On arrival of the three-member Commission, the Sabha submitted a Memorandum which stated the modest and legitimate claims for the reconstitution of Assam from the historical, Cultural and linguistic view points, (1) by keeping the present area of the state of Assam as at present constituted intact, (2) by completely integrating the NEFA with the state of Assam as originally proposed by hills Sub-Committee of the Constituents Assembly, (3) by amalgamating the district of Jalpaiguri and Darjeeling with Assam subject to the will of the people, (4) by amalgamating the district of Cooch Bihar with Assam, (5) by integrating the present Part C states of Tripura and Manipur with Assam provided that their people so desire. It also laid down that the ill-conceived plans of separate states on this frontier like Purbanchal and Hill state be not countenanced. The Sabha justified these claims on the polyglot character of Assam which presents a picture of unity in diversity—a brilliant fusion of Indo-Aryan and Mangoloid cultures.

However, the Sabha played a significant part in the movement against the Federal plan conceived by the Government of India. The Union Home

Minister on 13-1-67 announced in the Lok Sabha of regional federation in Assam, composed of federating units having equal status not subordinate to one another. The Sabha believed that such a proposal is unconstitutional, undemocratic and unfeasible by all standards which seem to have been improvised to placate fissiparous and recalcitrant tendencies. Considering the geographical and imperative needs of security and co-ordinated development of the region as a whole the Sabha opposed to any clevage that might be conceived of in the body of this frontier state. A delegation of members went to Delhi and submitted to the Prime Minister on 11-2-67 which contained that—(1) the Reorganisation of Assam on the basis of the Federal Plan will be opposed at any cost, (2) the sixth schedule of the constitution should be given up and on the contrary the people of the Hill Districts should be given equal status with the other people, (3) if necessary, the sixth schedule should be amended which may help full, autonomous states, and (4) fully autonomous administration may be advised on the principles of the Pataskar Commission etc. The Sabha also observed a demand day on 11-2-67. By second Memorandum to the Prime Minister on 11th May, 1967, the Sabha stated that in consideration of the various statements made by the Chief Minister of Assam, APCC, Hill Leaders, Political parties, the All Assam anti-Federation Action Council, the Sabha disapproved the idea of the formation of a Hill state as demanded by the All party Hill Leaders Conference on the ground that it would very readily encourage the division of Assam. Neither is the demand acceptable on democratic principle because two of these districts, namely North Cachar and Mikir Hills and Mizo Hills have unequivocally opposed such a demand. This was followed by another memorandum by the Sabha to Y.B. Chavan, Union Minister for Home Affairs on 21-5-67 which reiterated the humble and strongly felt demand that Assam must not be reorganized or disintegrated any further and that the people of the Autonomous District may be given the widest scope for social, economic and political development in the line of the sixth schedule. It approved the proposed Round Table Conference. The Sabha also sponsored the All Assam Anti-Federation Action Council which demanded withdrawal of the two proposals, namely Reorganisation of Assam on the basis of federal structure and the creation of separate Hill States—which may have disintegrated the state. While pleading to maintain amity, integration and composite culture of Assam, the memorandum expressed strong sentiments of the Assam people like security, national integrity and emotional integration.

The issue of Foreign Nationals in Assam is another important problem in recent history of the Sabha. Truly speaking, it can be tacked back to the Margherita Conference of 1950 which demanded from the State government that the non-Assamese residents should never be termed as Assamese in the next Census. This was repeated at the annual conferences in 1975 and 1979. The constitution of the Karma-Parishad is an innovation to tackle the present situation. The Sabha observed a 'protest day' on 30-10-79. Further, a delegation of members submitted Memorandum to the President of India on 5-11-79, to the Union Home Minister Y.B. Chavan at Guwahati on 1-11-79, to the Chief Minister of Assam on 2-11-79. These memorandum laid down certain historic facts like the continuous flow of immigrants from East Bengal to Assam from pre-Independence period till present time, the pressure of population on agricultural land in Assam, entry of foreigner's names in the Electoral roll by vested interests—which have threatened to shake not only the foundation of Assam's language and culture but also striking at the very sovereignty of India. Therefore, the Sabha demanded that the election can be held only after correction of the voter's list by deleting the names of foreign nationals and save Assam. In this connection, the Karma Parishad formed a "legal advisory committee", a "publicity wing", published a book in English on December 1979, a "fund collection committee" as well as a "Karma Parishad Fund", published and distributed a few pamphlets and bulletins, made extensive tours within the state to explain to the people and drew the attention of the Government for any consequence which may come out of any division, pressure or the like.

In this way, the Sabha has made genuine efforts for the protection and promotion of Assam's national interests throughout its existence. During the course of different movements it has resorted to various technique like sending resolutions to government, observance of protest day, Demand Day, Lobbying, submitting Memoranda, sending delegations and representatives, organization of meetings, publication of books, sending letters, telegrams, filling legal suits, participating in Satyagraha, mass picketing and hunger strike with other organizations. Of these, the memoranda constitutes the most strongest and effective part. They speak out very clearly the historical perspective of Assam's problems and their constitutional and legal validity. The methods applied may be classified as peaceful and non-violent. It has all along reiterated its stand for 'communal harmony' and 'larger interests of the people'. Its approaches are always direct, constitutional and logical whenever there is any dispute about the language, culture or territorial integrity of Assam, the Sabha has been useful to draw the attention of the significant in the national life of Assam. Since all progress depends on the mass support, the Sabha is always expected to keep its door open for the public to play a creative part and make it succeed.

All Assam Students' Union

The students in Assam have played a role extremely well in all concrete issues of importance to Assam's national life. Right from the freedom movement down to the present time—the labour, the unselfish sacrifices of the students in upholding the social, economic and cultural values of Assam is unparalleled in Assam's history to begin with, the Assam Chatra Sanmilan 1916, an early organization of the students of Assam played glorious role in the nationalist movement through peaceful and non-violent means. So well did they take part in Congress tactics that student's participation in politics could not be avoided till the country achieved its independence? The Assam Students' Federation 1940, also appealed to the students to take part in the movement for India's freedom, establishment of world peace based on justice and emancipation of nations, participated in a protest demonstration at Guwahati against the Imperialist War, staged a protest against the Government scheme of opening a Branch system University in Assam. The students all over the Brahmaputra valley observed 16th August, 1941, as "The Assam University Day". The Assam Students' Union 1945 celebrated the INA day at Dibrugarh, collected funds for INA men, held 'Anti-Repression Day' on 15th December, 1945 all over the valley and later the 'Anti-partition Day' in February, 1946. After independence, the students led the Refinery movement in 1957. The All Assam Students' Association, 1959 was seriously concerned with the growth of regional sentiments in Assam. On the convention of 19-9-59, the members organized a forum in connection with the recognition of Assamese as the official language of Assam. The organization observed 11-3-60 as 'State Language Day' and July, 12, 1960 as students 'Protest Day'. During the Chinese aggression of 1962 the students expressed their firm determination written in blood to face the challenge. Students activity was very much stimulated during the flood movement. The students observed August 4, 1966, as the 'Protest Day' against the artificial scarcity and high prices of food, gharoad the M.L.A. at Nalbari etc. Further, the students of Assam observed February 4, 11 and 15 as all Assam Students Protest Day. 'Hartal Day' and 'Promise Day' respectively. However, the present organization constitute in 1967 under the banner of All Assam Students' Union (AASU) has demonstrated some strong and remarkable group methods to influence the Government to begin with, the AASU initiated in 1972 a movement for Assamese as the medium of instruction which was really striking. The All Assam State Convention of 25-10-72 formed a 'Karma Parishad' to initiate the movement.

The Charter of 21 Demands 1974 is a landmark in the group activities of the students. It was submitted to the Chief Minister of Assam on 21-2-74, which constitutes the main foundation of solving the various complex problems of Assam through gradual socialization of our economy. Therefore, the demands have been stressed as marks of great social change.

However, the techniques displayed by the AASU in dealing with the foreigner's problem are remarkable. Since, pressure group techniques are based on attitudes of the Government as well as interactions within society the techniques of AASU here lie in a number of peculiar historical perspectives. The flow of immigration into Assam, the Bengal Famine of 1943, the system violation of Law and order, inclusion of the names of the migrants in the electoral roll, failure to guard the international boarder by the Government etc. The students wanted the basis to be the National Register of Citizens 1951 and the Assam Census of 1952. The NRC is the first enumeration of the citizens after the Constitution of India came into force. However, the Prime Minister and the Home Minister offered 25-3-71 as the cut of date. So, herein lays the conflict.

For the effective solution of the problems, the AASU submitted some proposals to the Prime Minister on 8-1-80 for acceptance and implementation. The proposals were highlighted in the Memorandum submitted to the Prime Minister on June 2, 1980. Since, then, AASU has a series of discussions with the Prime Minister, Home Minister and at various Government levels. The tripartite talks which started on 18-1-82 between the Government and the opposition parties and the movement leaders continued through 1983. The AASU opposed the election in 1983 because the electoral Roll consisted of lakhs of foreigners' names. It was followed by a peaceful movement with various programmes like *bandhs*, road blockades, Janata curfews, blackout, non-co-operation etc. over the last four years. Various other techniques resorted to. These included submitting memorandum. Boycott of Nominations, Statewide *Hartal*, Hunger strike, Mass picketing, Assam *Bandh*, Mass Rallied, Demonstration, Employees strike, All-Assam Gana Satyagraha, Procession, Non-Co-operation, *Dharna*, Stoppage of Crude oil, stoppage of rail movement, ban on Truck movement, anti-oppression day, anti-oppression of women day, Black Day, Boycott of MLAs, Ban on export of forest produce, peace and harmony processions, *sankalpa sikha*, courting of arrest, anti-repression meetings and processions, surrender of Tamrapatras, Gherao of forest officers and SDOs., anti-conspiracy campaign, Air-Rail Blockade, Warning against Census Operations, Mass March to Dispur, Boycott of Dispur Secretariat, Boycott of Children's Day, Public meetings, Black flag demonstration, Silent processions, Protest Day, Road Blockade, Ticketless Travel, Poster Campaign, Transport Blockade, Mass Defiance of prohibitory order, Black out, Total non-Co-operation, Janata Curfew, All Assam Blackout, Wearing of Black Badges, Bazar and Cinema *Hartal*, Burning Effigies, Boycott of Buses, Display of Cartoons, Street Corner meetings, Programme meetings, 15 minutes slogan shouting, hunger strike by women, Beating of Drum, cycle processions by volunteer etc.

As regards the basis of techniques, the AASU was committed to pursue the cause with sense of deep conviction on the principals of non-violence, democracy and secularism. A sense of disciplined and solidarity marked the movement. Determination to maintain peace and harmony is written on the face of everybody participating in the movement.

The Assam College Teachers' Association (ACTA)

The ACTA, over the years has made ceaseless efforts in putting forth a number of suggestions particularly for the spread of higher education as well as safeguarding the rights and interests of non-government college teachers of Assam. Under the inspiring guidance of the first president Late R.R. Thomas, this organization started a peaceful and constructive movement for the promotion of the standard of education, improvement of the lot of non-government college teachers and for defending their rights and interests wherever these were threatened and solution of the financial and other problems of the non-government colleges. Immediately after its formation, the Association placed before the Government of Assam and the Gauhati University the demands like better pay scales, well defined condition of service, reorganization of the governing bodies with a view to secure proper representation of non-government college teacher in different bodies of the University.

However, the most effective role played by the organization was with regard to the question of pay scales. It moved the Vice-Chancellor of the University to utilize his good office in recommending to the Government of Assam a better pay scale with similar allowances as were admissible to the Government College teachers. In the last part of November 1954, the ACTA met the State Education Minister and Finance Minister at Shillong and requesting them to implement the recommendation of the University Grants Commission and those of the Executive Council of the Gauhati University. In 1955, the ACTA submitted a memorandum to the pay committee demanding improved pay scale with dearness and other allowances, followed by a meeting with the chairman of the U.G.C. at Guwahati. During 1964-65, the delegations of the Association made representation to the UGC, Central Ministry of Education, the Government of Assam, and Central Finance Minister. The ACTA, however, took up a programme of more positive action beginning with a Protest Day or the 5th February, 1972 by holding meetings in the colleges, putting protest badges and then a mass demonstration before the Assam Assembly. Further, the Association submitted a detailed memorandum to the Pay Commission on 10-2-72. The Association also observed the protest Day on 15-2-72, followed by the observance of one day strike on 28-7-72. On 24-9-74 a delegation of about 500 members submitted a memorandum to the Speaker of the Assam Assembly expressing resentment at the apathy and indifference of the Government in implementing the UGC pay scale. Discussions with the Government was repeated on 18th November, 1974. The notice of Boycott of examination under Gauhati and Dibrugarh Universities for the year 1975 by the ACTA on the 19th March, 1975, is indeed a very bold step. It was submitted to the Vice-Chancellors and Registrars of the two Universities, the Chief Minister and Education Minister of Assam, Education Secretary and the D.P.I. of the Government of Assam. In fact, the organization was successful in paralyzing the examination.

Another outstanding demand of the Association has been the taking over of the degree colleges under the deficit system. The colleges receiving grant-in-aid under the deficit system can pay the teachers according to the approved scale and other benefits extended to them as the deficit under this head is made good by the Government. But colleges receiving grants on *ad hoc* basis are to face great difficulties in maintaining their staff causing great anomaly and consequent resentment among the teachers. In order to ensure greater coordination between the politics of the Universities and the Government in respect of granting affiliation and grant-in-aid to colleges, the 18th Conference, 1968, recommends that a combined survey committee by the Government and Universities be constituted, There were discussions between the Government of Assam and the ACTA representatives on 30-10-71. Thereafter, the Association organized a demonstration in front of the Assam Assembly on 5-4-72. The above demand was reiterated in the conferences of 1973 and 1974. The Association again submitted a memorandum to the Chief Minister and Education Minister of Assam on 2-4-74, followed by representation to the Education Minister of Assam on 14-6-74, and pressed for definite commitments. Discussions were again repeated on 18-11-74 and 1-2-75. The demand for the inclusion of the non-deficit colleges affiliated up to Degree standard under the Deficit System of grant-in-aid was made by the notice of Boycott of Examination under the two Universities by the members of the ACTA on 19-3-75. Thus, in view of the hardship of the teachers of the non-deficit colleges, the ACTA strongly feel that full Justice to higher education and unflinching devotion to the cause of education are impeded if the teachers are not paid their due.

The management and service conditions of the affiliated colleges were another outstanding problem which invoked the attention of the members for pretty longtime, involving efforts at many points. The dual control of the colleges by the Government as well as the University resulted in uncertainties in the vital matters of security and conditions of service of teachers, the snapping of the organic link between the University Centre and its affiliated colleges and ultimately, undesirable political influence making inroads into the colleges. The ACTS has been all throughout against this system of diarchy. It is true beyond doubt, that the healthy growth of higher education can be propagated when the affiliated colleges, methods of appointment of teachers and service rules are determined and controlled by the University. The ACTA representatives hold a demonstration on 5-4-72 in front of the Assam Assembly in Shillong to express their demands to democratize the organization and management of higher education by amending the University Acts. The above demands were further revived in the Memorandum submitted by the Association to the Chief Minister and Education Minister of Assam on 2-4-74, which rightly demanded the amendment of the Gauwahati and Dibrugarh University followed by memorandum to the Vice-Chancellors of the two Universities, memorandum to the Speaker of the Assam Assembly on 24-9-74.

The attention of the organization was also drawn to the problem of foreign Nationals in Assam. A delegation of the ACTA on 30-11-79 met the President of India and submitted a Memorandum urging that the Election should not be held on piecemeal basis. Since, the Centre was not sympathetic to the demand, it appeals to the people of the state to boycott the polls in early 1980. It supported the mass movement in connection with the deportation of foreign nationals which is a national problem and demanded the Central Government to start without delay the tripartite talks etc.

The ACTA also played its role in the movement of medium of instruction and provincialisation of the colleges etc. Further, in view of the necessity for economic development, rapid industrialization, solution of unemployment problem the Association strongly urged upon the Government of India to establish a Second Oil Refinery in this state under the Public Sector and also to create necessary skilled man power to be employed in immediate future. It has urged the State Government to check the Assam-Nagaland border incident, to check imposition of Hindi on the non-Hindi speaking areas which is potentially threatening national unity and emotional integration.

Of the techniques resorted to by the ACTA it can be remarked that it has more often, preferred the methods of negotiations. In particular, it has accepted more peaceful measures like adopting resolutions, sending them to the Government, sending letters and representations at Government platform sending delegations, Notices, submitting Memorandum holdings of talks at Government level. Only on rare occasions or rather as an extreme step it has been forced to adopt some sort of direct action which included demonstration before the Assam Assembly, and Boycott of Examination. In this connection, it is remarkable that the Association has been able to secure a best pay scale without resorting to much agitation programme and methods. It has never been used to hasty action or violent attitude on the other hand, it is known for its sober thinking, an understanding with the Government as well as the public with a dispassionate mind. As a matter of fact, the high level of discussions on various educational problems as well as the educational symposia during the ACTA annual conferences are rather some of the highlights which have truly influenced the course of its action or rather the techniques.

Indian National Trade Union Congress (INTUC)

The INTUC is the biggest spokesman of the tea labourers of Assam. It was originally organized with the tea plantation labour of Assam and in fact, from the beginning till now it has greatly endeavoured and made tremendous effort in safeguarding the interests of the tea labourers. The special interests of the garden labourers became the first and foremost issue.

In fact, the INTUC has dedicated itself to two different aspects of the labour interests. The first is with regard to the improvement and consideration of the economic status by fulfilling basic needs. To begin with, its main interest was confined to increase the wages. In the Tripartite Conference held in Nainital in 1946-47, B. Bhagawati, President of the Labour Cell of the APCC raised the question of wage increase. Following the tea crisis in 1951 and disagreement between the Employees and the Assam Government regarding application of the Minimum Wage Act, the Labourers of Itakhuli T.E. Tinsukia under the leadership and guidance of Tingrai Branch of the INTUC refused to work as a result of which the garden was closed for 10 days. This was followed by one week strike by the Tea gardens of Golaghat and Jorhat Sub-Divisions in February-March 1953. The strike of about 27 gardens in Mangaldoi in April 1953 continued for 25 days. The reasons of these strikes have been ration cut and non-implementation of the Minimum Wage Act.

Further, the INTUC in Doom Dooma, Tinsukia and Panitola Circles also introduced for the first time a demand for Puja Bonus. This also demanded the application of the plantation Labour Act, 1951 which was not implemented in Assam till 1956. In 1956, the INTUC had discussions with the ITA, ABITA about the Bonus payment in the tea gardens of the North

East India. The INTUC had also put pressures on Government to raise the unclaimed wages of the labourers and form a welfare scheme to be spent in education and practical training of the garden youth.

Subsequently, the Assam Chah Mazdoor Sangha has submitted a memorandum under the leadership of Sri Mahendra Sarma, President, INTUC (Assam) to one man Inquiry Commission demanding additional benefit like gratuity, Provident Fund benefits, free housing, Medical facilities etc. It contained scientific principles and formulas regarding many points.

The INTUC also greatly helped in removing the social disabilities of the labour groups and thereby, promoting social uplift. An important difference between the INTUC, Assam and that of other states is that here the organization has seriously taken note of the social factors involving the labourers. This was partly because of the social drawback of the labourers and partly because of the impact of Guardian principals of social reforms. Therefore, as its very inception, INTUC bought a house at Rowrich, Jorhat, to open a worker's training centre. The INTUC built unions on the pattern of Gandhiji's Ashram for developing the capacities of the garden youth. In particular, they were trained on handloom, handicraft, carpentry, adult education, sanitation etc. Ideas on prohibition was also very much published by the INTUC.

In this way, the INTUC has all along championed the special interest, of the labourers. It has greatly collaborated and contributed in advancing the cause of the plantation labour in Assam. The motive behind is to create a great social and economic contribution of the labour force.

The INTUC is also a great spokesman of the grievances of the Assam State Transport Worker's Association and has greatly fought to improve the economic status of the workers. In 1955, the Association submitted a Memorandum to the Secretary, Pay Committee, Government of Assam, Shillong, for favour of receiving due considering and sanction of a pay scale. Besides, the memorandum demanded for more holidays, better medical facilities, free housing, ration allowance, provident fund, pension, share of the profit by the employees.

The Association under the leadership of Sri Mahendra Sharma, general Secretary, INTUC, gave evidence to and a Memorandum to the pay Committee on 21-6-56. Again, in August of the same year the Association requested the Chief Minister to fix up the pay scales of the workers at the government level. The position of the workers was reiterated by a second Memorandum which was submitted on 6-9-56 to the chairman, State Road Transport Board, Assam. It urged the Board to put into effect the revised scales of pay that would be proposed with effect from 1-10-56. Because of the apathy of the Government, the Association decided to hold a 'strike ballot' within 25 August, 1957. Afterwards, from the 18th September to 23rd September, 1957, the Association under the leadership of Sri Sarbeswar Bordoloi made a series of discussions with the Chief Minister and the Transport Minister. Further, the Executive Committee prepared a 24-point Demand chapter on 16th March, 1958 and the workers representative convection which was held on 9-11-58 at Rowriah, Jorrhat threatened a strike from 15-2-59 in case the demands are not fulfilled.

During 1959-60, several rounds of discussions and joint meetings were held.

The one-day strike of the workers was held on 15-8-62 by Cease work in Shillong-Guwahati Route. The worker's demands were non-payment of double wages for working on 15th August and 26th January, abnormal delay in granting annual increments and leave, irregular calculation of overtime wages, non-payment of arrear accumulation as per Minimum wages notification, non-payment of substance allowance etc.

The STWA forwarded to the Director, State Transport, Assam, a charter of grievances on 16-7-69 and a separate Memorandum to the Chief Minister of Assam on 30-7-69 which contained clauses like confirmation, decasualization, promotion, deteriorating Industrial Relation etc. Again, on 14-3-70 the STWA under the leadership of INTUC President prepared a 10-point charter of Demands and submitted it to the Government of Assam. It was followed by a strike notice on 6-6-77 for non-fulfilment of their 10-point charter of Demands.

The INTUC also made great efforts in promoting the interests of the Colliery labourers of A.R.T. Co., Margherita. In 1952, the INTUC recommended to the Government to increase the wage to Rs. 3.50-Rs. 4.00. For the increase of wages the Colliery labourers went on strike for 20 days in 1952. The INTUC also pressed for the nationalization of the Colliery organization by raising the question in Assam Assembly as well as the national parliament.

Besides, the INTUC has spoken for improving the living conditions, housing and wages of the Dhubri Match Factory from 1950 onwards.

Again, the INTUC was the only organization to repeal the essential Services Maintenance Act, 1980.

Finally, the INTUC gave pressures on the Government to improve the conditions in the rural sector.

As regards techniques, the condition lays down (Section 4) that the means to be adopted for the furtherance of the objects shall be peaceful and consistent with truth. In fact, it gives emphasis on redress of grievances by means of negotiation and conciliation and failing these by arbitration and adjudication. Where such methods are not applied or not available, the workers shall recourse to other legitimate methods like strikes to Satyagrahas. The machine of arbitration is the most important part of the techniques employed by the INTUC so far. It is influenced by the Gandhian tradition of voluntary arbitration. The essence of Gandhian method is its emphasis on persuading the employers rather than coercing them and the strict adherence to non-violence. The Ghandian approach is an important contribution to industrial relations. It is regarded as indigenous and uniquely Indian. The way of consensus rather than conflict is believed to have its root in India. Further, the belief in accepting the judgment of a respected arbitration reflects a traditional Indian attitude to authority. In this way, the Ghandhian influence is very much seen in the methods of the INTUC, Assam.

A comparative study of the techniques applied by the groups makes it evident that the groups sometimes agree, sometimes not. Each of them has put mush emphasis on discussions, negotiation and amicable settlement. Of the methods common to them, the memorandum constitutes the most important. Much attention has been paid to dialogue. Yet, on all issues they had to take recourse to agitation and direct action like Satyagraha and strike. This means that the peaceful methods like discussion and negotiation were proved inadequate or unable to have any governmental response, as a result, agitations in some form or other in indispensable to advance pressure group activity in Assam. The groups, no doubt, speak about 'peace' and 'non-violence', but they are forced by circumstances to initiate in agitational programme which sometimes reaches points of threatened peace. Unlike the Sabha, the students and the teachers, the INTUC is in a much better position with regard to the application of the techniques. Since, the Constitution specifically mentions the means to the adopted for the furtherance of the objects namely conciliation, arbitration etc. failing which resource shall be taken to strike or Satyagraha, the organization can adopt clear cut methods. Thus, the INTUC legalizes strike and Satyagraha. In the other three organizations we do not find any constitutional sanction of direct method.

MODEL QUESTIONS

Very Short Questions (1 mark each)

1. What is the basic issue closely related with Contemporary Electoral Politics of North East India.
2. What model is the basis of Indian Parliamentary System?
3. Who conduct the election of North East India?
4. Is there Provision of Separate State Election Commission in India?

5. What is the Minimum Age for a Voter in India?
6. Write the name of one element responsible for the Growth of Middle Class in Assam?
7. Why Middle Class have an important role in the State Politics of Assam?
8. Write the name of one National Political Party has been occupying significant position in state politics of Assam?
9. Name the Political Party who given support to Indian National Congress to form the government in 2006 and 2011?
10. Write the name of one Pressure Group that have been playing significant role in Assam?

Write short note of the following (4/5 marks for each)

1. Electoral Politics in North East India.
2. Formation of North Eastern States.
3. Role of tea plantation in the emergence of Assamese Middle Class.
4. Role of Government Service in the emergence of Assamese Middle Class.
5. Importance of National Political Parties in State Politics of Assam.
6. Importance of Regional Political Parties in State Politics of Assam.

Essay Type Questions (10/12 marks for each)

1. Discuss the background of emergence of Middle Class in Assam?
2. Discuss the role of Middle Class in the state politics of Assam?
3. Discuss the role of National political parties in the State Politics of Assam?
4. Discuss the role of Regional Political Parties in the State Politics of Assam?
5. Discuss the role of Pressure Groups in North East India in the context of Assam?

UNIT-V
Border Dispute in North East India

The North East Region of India comprising eight states—Assam, Nagaland, Meghalaya, Manipur, Arunachal Pradesh, Mizoram, Tripura and Sikkim—a region poorly connected to the Indian mainland by a small corridor, and surrounded by many countries such as Bhutan, Myanmar, Bangladesh and China, is the setting for a multitude of conflict that undermines the idea of India as a prosperous and functioning democracy.

In a country like India which has a continental size and its inhabited by people speaking different languages, belonging to different religious and racial groups the problem inter-state conflict on various issues cannot be ruled out. Considering this point the framers of the Constitution inserted Article 3 for resolving the Boundary disputes. But, in spite of these provisions of the Constitution a number of inter-state disputes regarding boundaries still remain unsolved. They have not only created inter-state tensions because of agitations launched by certain groups but also have done great harm economically. Though linguistic reorganizations of states were done in 1956 and the process continued even thereafter the problem created by the linguistic reorganization of states still persists.

However, it must also be mentioned that internal conflicts have been a permanent feature of the Asian political landscape since 1945, of which post-colonial India is no exception. Currently, most of the states in the region are affected by some form of conflict, expect for Arunachal Pradesh, Mizoram and Sikkim in which the situation is at the moment relatively stable. The reasons for the respective conflicts are wide ranging from separatist movements, to inter-community, communal and inter-ethnic conflicts.

Before British rule in North East India different areas of this region were ruled by different kings and traditional local chiefs maintaining independent sovereign status. During the British rule most of the areas of this region were brought under one administrative unit. And even after Independence, most of these areas remained as a single administrative unit in the name of Assam. But, after independence the process of reorganisation of the states in North East India started and consequently the States and Union Territories such as Nagaland (1963), Meghalaya (1972), Arunachal Pradesh (1972), Mizoram (1972) have been carved out of the original state of Assam. All these newly formed States and Union territories cover a wide range of hill areas inhibiting various hill tribes with different traditions, culture and social system characteristically distinct from the people of the plains who occupied the dominant position in the undivided Assam. The hill states were mainly created in order to fulfil the socio-political aspiration of the hill people. They felt terribly insecure of their interest within the greater Assam. After independence, the sense of deprivation and exploitation by the plains reached its extreme point in the minds of hill people which ultimately led to the formation of afore-said Hill States and Union territories. But after creation of separate state on the basis of hill sentiment, the same attitude and feeling still persists among a section of the hill people which manifest in different border disputes and in the exploitation of anti-Assamese feelings in the hills. In north east region, interstate conflict mainly refers to the conflict of the plains of Assam with the neighbouring Hill States particularly Nagaland, Arunachal Pradesh, Meghalaya and Mizoram in the form of border disputes and anti-Assamese movement in these areas. The inter-state conflict in this region may therefore be understood in terms of conflict between the hills and the plains which has a legacy of the past.

During the British period hill tribes had very little scope of mingle with the people of the plains. The political demarcation and the separate system of administration in the hills had always been a factor of division between the hills and the plains. Non-tribals were not given admittance to the tribal areas without special permission. Such restrictions deepened the isolation of the hills from the plains and accentuated the economic backwardness of the hills.

Hence, their allegiance to the newly formed Indian nation-state was lacking from the beginning—accentuated by the creation of East Pakistan (today's Bangladesh)—which meant the loss of a major chunk of the physical connection between mainland India and North East India. Interestingly, 99 per cent of the North East's boundaries is international and only one per cent is domestic boundary.

Unfortunately, the data and information on the region is not sufficiently analyzed and communicated between the region and the Centre, contributing to further misinformation, mismanagement and alienation. At another level, conflict in the region has been an all pervasive phenomena, and in its violent form, it has not only affected the territorial and political sovereignty of the Indian state, but also the life of the various people living in the region in incomprehensible and inexplicable terms. In a drastic and dreaded sense, there is a "culture" of conflict and unfortunately, people have submitted to such an existence. However, amidst the widespread sense of helplessness, there is also an overwhelming desire and force to be free from such a situation of conflict which cripples the people from all sides.

It appears that the British took full advantages of the existing differences between the hills and the plains in order to perpetuate imperialist exploitation in this region. The British administration widened the difference between the people of the plains and the hills.

As already mentioned in the earlier units and particularly in the Unit–I, the diversity of North East India can be compared with a 'salad-bowl' where the different ingredients of the salad represent its diversity in the form of various communities and tribes as well as various geographical entities. But at the same time, the same 'salad-bowl' is not perfect enough (as nothing is altogether perfect in this earth) as desired for the integrity of the region as well as for the nation. The over concern for separate identity of the people of North East Region (NER), resulted in the inability to evolve a common imaginary and say 'we'. However, the people only can not be blamed for this present inability to evolve a common imaginary as historical facts and incidents have played a great role in this regard. There are disputes, differences and conflicts among various communities or tribes as well as among the various states of NER. It has been observed that conflict or dispute in NER has been an all pervasive phenomena. In a drastic and dreaded sense, it can be argued that there is a culture of 'conflict' in NER and unfortunately people have submitted to such an existence. A reference may be made about the Naga aspirations to the unification of all Naga inhabited areas. From the very initial period, they had a clash with Government of India (GOI) regarding their independent homeland. This conflict began with India's Independence in 1947 when the Naga leaders rejected the idea that their land, which is under a special dispensation during British colonial rule, could simply pass into Indian hands at the end of British colonial rule (Baruah, 2003: 321). The Naga leaders believed that it was unfortunate and it led to an era conflict in NER including border conflict. This Naga conflict in a sense was the initial seed sown for growing demands like separate state for various ethnic groups of NER and thereafter the creation of boundary dispute.

It is well known that a number of states were created from time to time by carving out the erstwhile state of Greater Assam in the wake of rising demands for separate state. But even after the creation of separate states, there are still number of boundary issues among various states of NER, particularly the states of Nagaland, Meghalaya and Arunachal Pradesh have boundary issues with Assam. Hence, the Assam-Nagaland border dispute is as old as the state of Nagaland; and similarly the Assam-Meghalaya and Assam-Arunachal Pradesh border disputes is as old as the state of Meghalaya and the state of Arunachal Pradesh respectively.

Dispute between Assam and Nagaland

Since Nagaland, Meghalaya, Arunachal Pradesh and Mizoram have been carved out of Assam, hence, all these states have their boundary disputes with Assam in one form or the other. For example, there is a dispute between Assam and Nagaland regarding the Rangapani area of the Rengana Reserve Forest, and Nagaland Government has claimed 4,973 sq.km area of Assam. To settle this dispute the Government of India set up a committee under V.K. Sundaram. The Sundaram Committee rejected the claim of Nagaland. But Mr. Vizol, the then Chief Minister of Nagaland rejected the report as he called it a highly biased report. Again in February 1977, armed Nagaland police attack the Assamese in this area and as a result thereof, twenty thousand people left their homes in fear. In all 469 houses were burnt in 13 villages. Again there was a clash between Assam police and Nagas in Desoi valley on the same border dispute on February 20, 1982. Even there were violent clashes in 1985 in Merapani sector of Golaghat district resulting in loss of lives and property. When the Election Commission set up seven booths in the disputed area claimed by Assam in November 1987 for Nagaland Assembly Elections, the Assam government objected to it and the all Assam Students Union organized an economic blockade against Nagaland for five days. Considering these all in April. 1989, an accord was signed between the then Chief Ministers of the states and it was hoped that the problem has now amicably been solved, but soon after violent clashes again broke out resulting in the loss of more than 20 lives. In a bid to resolve the issue the two Chief Ministers decided to erect boundary pillar to defuse the tension and to find out a solution of the problem once for all. But it has been seen that the Border problem between the two states still continues and a solution is not in sight.

The Nagaland State Act of 1962 had defined its borders according to the 1925 notification when Naga Hills and Tuensang Area (NHTA) were integrated into a new administrative unit and made an autonomous area. Nagas, however, did not accept the boundary delineation and demanded that Nagaland should comprise the erstwhile Naga Hills and all Naga-dominated area in North Cachar and Nagaon districts, which were part of Naga territory according to the 1866 notification. Since Nagaland did not accept its notified borders, tensions between Assam and Nagaland soon flared up resulting in the first border clashes in 1965 at Kakodonga Reserve Forest. Since then, violent clashes along the Assam-Nagaland border have become a regular feature, with major armed conflicts reported in 1968, 1979 and 1985. The latest in this series occurred in June 2007 in Sibsagar district when three villages—Sonapur, Dhekiajuri and Borholla—were attacked by Nagas resulting in the death of two people.

The Nagaland-Assam border dispute at Merapani area has been a cause for worry. Burning of houses and killings has been occurring occasionally.

Geographical Status of the Assam-Nagaland Border Area

On the Northeast corner of the Republic of India lie the States of Assam and Nagaland. Assam extends from latitude 24.1°N to 26.0°N in breadth and longitude 89.67°E to 96.04°E in length. As such it is the most populated State in the North East. The seven States of the North East (Arunachal Pradesh, Assam, Manipur, Meghalaya, Mizoram, Nagaland and Tripura) are surrounded by Bhutan, Tibet and China to the north, Myanmar to the east and Bangladesh to the south. Assam has common borders with all the States of the region as well as with Bhutan and Bangladesh. At Independence, Assam included the present States of Mizoram, Meghalaya and Nagaland. It was even bigger prior to the Partition. A substantial area of the province went to East Pakistan. However, by 1980, its area of 2,55,000 sq. km. was reduced to 78,438 sq. km. After the Yandaboo treaty with the Burmese emperor in February 1826 the British regime took over the political control of Assam and gradually consolidated its administrative control over its fertile plains. Within this territory lived many tribes whom the British administrators considered wild and hostile. The tribes who occupied the Hill tracts of Assam are collectively known as Nagas. The British rulers did not succeed easily in taking control of their areas. Several conflicts followed and ultimately they were brought under the single administrative unit of the Naga Hills District through a Notification dated 15 November, 1866 that read: "It is hereby notified that, with the sanction of the Government of India, the Lieutenant Governor has been pleased to abolish the sub-division of North Cachar in Assam, and to constitute a separate district, consisting of that part of the district of Nowgong which lies on the right banks of the river Doyang. The name of the district will, for the present be the Naga Hills, and its headquarters will be Samoogooting. It will be administered by a Deputy Commissioner under the control of the Commissioner of Assam.

The description of the territories included in the new district of 'Naga Hills' was vague and lacked clarity and specification. However, this order of the British Government paved the way for the inclusion of large tracts of land along the foothills into Assam. The British Government tried to rectify the loopholes on the notification of 1866 through another order dated 28 June, 1875. In the meantime the tea industry received a boost in Assam and the attention of the regime was drawn towards this lucrative business.

The eyes of the tea garden management fell on these tracts of land and it got due permission to grow tea in this area. Since the inclusion of certain reserve forests of the foothills in the Naga Hills District created impediment on their way, the administration felt the need to reorganise the district boundaries. As a result changes were effected in the boundary line from time to time including the transfer of the reserve forests on the foothills to the administrative control of the Sibsagar district of Assam (Present Sibsagar, Jorhat and Golaghat District). In 1913, Dimapur was included in to the Naga Hills District. Having undergone several alterations the boundary of the Naga Hills District received what was considered a final settlement in 1925 through Notification No 3102R dated 25 November, 1925. It was supposed to supersede all previous notifications. It demarcated what it called the permanent boundary line between Assam and the Naga Hills District. According to some claims, except for a short stretch of about 20 kilometres towards the north from the Taukok Nadi to the Tiok Nadi, this boundary line was defined accurately and in great detail in a notification dated 25th November, 1925, and was not altered subsequently. The British regime claimed that the notification was based on a survey conducted between 1916 and 1923. In the Notification natural boundaries like hills, rivers, streams etc. are not mentioned. Instead, numbered boundary pillars in the documents of the Survey of India are mentioned. These pillars have either perished or have been removed deliberately. Because of this lack of clarity, the notification took more the form of guidelines than demarcation on the ground. As a result, the ground reality remained vague though both sides agreed to follow the guidelines. It remained unchanged till 1947 when Nagaland had two administrative units known as the Naga Hills District and the Naga Tribal Area inhabited almost entirely by the Naga Tribes. On 1st December, 1957, they were combined into one to form the Naga Hills-Tuensang Area and administered as a 'Part B Tribal Area'.1947 marked both independence and the emergence of A.Z. Phizo under whose leadership the Naga National Council raised the issue of sovereign Nagaland. Much before that the Nagas had begun dreaming of development and prosperity of the Nagas. In 1918, the 'Naga Club' was formed consisting of some government employees and village Headmen. This was the pioneer and major organization of the Nagas. On 16 January, 1929, the members of the Naga Club met the Simon Commission and raised the issue of independence of the Nagas. In June 1947 the Commission had already signed a nine-point charter with Sir Akbar Hydari the Governor of Assam. In 1957, the first sitting of the 'Naga People's Convention' was held at Kohima and Mokokchung. On 30 January, 1980 these Naga organisations together formed 'The National Socialist Council of Nagaland' (NSCN) committed to the cause of Naga integration. Apart from the NSCN, also the Naga Students Federation, Naga Hoho and other non-political organisations favour the creation of Nagalim. The NSCN has taken the cause to "Unrepresented Nations and People's Organisation" (UNPO) in 1993. They have successfully raised the issue of 'Independence' in this and other international platforms. In 1947 began the armed struggle for a Naga Nation that the Indian army suppressed with an iron hand. The Government of India banned the Naga National Council and announced a price on Phizo's head. There are allegations that in the name of suppressing insurgency the Indian army committed atrocities on the Naga youth, burnt down Naga villages, raped women and committed other atrocities. Thus, the Naga issue stood as a serious challenge to the Government. Mahatma Gandhi seems to have understood the Naga cause better than most other Indian national leaders did. When the NNC leaders met him on 13th July, 1947, he is reported to have said: "Nagas have every right to be independent". However, the conflict continued. In the midst of turmoil a peace process began in the Hills. One section of the Naga nationalists agreed to a solution within the framework of the Indian Constitution. At its second meeting on 20 and 21 May, 1958 held at Amang village in Mokokchung district the Naga people's convention demanded a new Nagaland State. In its support it also prepared a 16-point charter of demands for the Indian Government. After a series of negotiations the Indian Government conceded the demand of a new state comprising the Naga Hills District and the Tuensang region. Thus, Nagaland became the sixteenth State of the Indian Union on December 1, 1963 based on the state of Nagaland Act, 1962, whose Clause 3(1) read: 3. Formation of the state of Nagaland (1) As from the Appointed day there shall be formed a new state to be known as state of Nagaland comprising the territories which immediately before that day were comprised in the Naga Hills-Tuensang area and thereupon the said territories shall cease to form part of the state of Assam. Thus the boundaries of the new state were exactly the same as the boundaries of the combined Naga Hills District and Naga Tribal Area before 1957. However, the dispute continued with another section of the Naga Nationalist Movement continuing their armed struggle for a sovereign Nagaland. In recent years they speak of 'Nagalim' or Greater Nagaland comprising the Naga inhabited areas of Assam, Manipur, Arunachal Pradesh and Myanmar. That can bring much territory now forming part of

Assam under Nagalim. However, the border dispute pre-dates this claim and is not linked to it directly. The border dispute keeps lingering and has to be solved.

Main Disputed Area

To the west of Nagaland in Assam lie the districts of Sivasagar, Jorhat, Golaghat, Karbi Anglong and North Cachar Hills. This boundary has a total length of 434 kilometre. The entire 434 kilometre stretch of the Assam-Nagaland border, predominantly plains land, has long been disputed by the two sides. Much of the land of this sensitive area comes under Reserve Forests which, of course, are now being encroached upon by settlers from both Assam and Nagaland. Under Golaghat District, along the disputed border, practically no traces of Reserve Forests exist. The rich flora and fauna of yesteryears have been replaced by huts and the land turned into cultivable fields yielding rich crops. This change has attracted migrants from every corner of Assam, Nagaland and even nearby Bangladeshi nationals. The main disputed area is on the border of Golaghat district. The district had a population of 9,46,279 in 2001. Golaghat became a full-fledged District on 23rd October, 1987. The district situated at a height of 71 metres above MSL is rich in flora and fauna. Famous for its one horned Rhino in the Kaziranga National Park, it is bounded by River Brahmaputra in the north, Nagaland in the south, Kakadonga River and Jorhat district in the east and Nagaon and Karbi-Anglong districts on its western boundary. The entire patch of the Assam-Nagaland border under Golaghat district covers approximately 125 kilometres including Reserve Forests, viz.

(1) Diphu Reserve Forest
(2) Nambor Reserve Forest
(3) Rengma Reserve Forest
(4) Doyang Reserve Forest

2. As already mentioned, ever since the formation of the Nagaland State, Nagaland has been demanding some portions of Assam's territory which the Nagas believe as historically belong to them. Since the inception of the dispute not less than 300 people killed in these conflicts (Siddique, 2014). The Assam Assembly once reported in an official report that over 86,886.12 hectares of land of Assam have been encroached upon. Nagaland alone has been accused of encroaching 59,159.77 hectares (ibid). The following image will be helpful in explaining the demarcated as well as demanded Assam-Nagaland border.

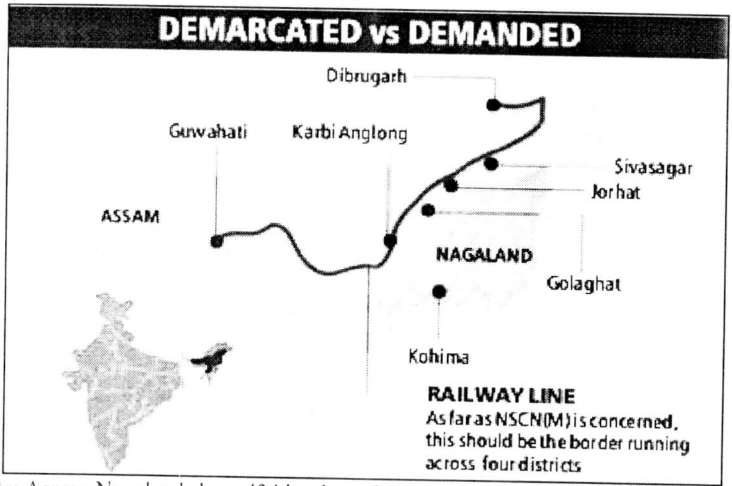

Note: Assam-Nagaland share 434 km boundary.
Source: http://indianexpress.com

3. The allegation from the side of Assam is that Nagaland has been encroaching upon over 66,000 hectares in Sivasagar, Jorhat, Golaghat and Karbi-Anglong districts. This includes over 42,000 hectares in Golaghat alone. Recently, in August 2014, nine people have been killed allegedly by the Naga miscreants in the border villages of Assam in the Golaghat district and thousands of villagers were displaced. Assam's chief allegation was that Nagaland has set up three civil sub-divisions on Assam territory. Nagaland, on the other hand, insisted that more tracts under Assam occupation belong to Nagaland. Moreover, the NSCN (National Socialist Council of Nagaland) (IM) wants the entire Assam tract south of the Guwahati-Dibrugarh railway track for fulfilling their dream of 'Greater Nagalim'.

4. Besides, the 2014 Golaghat incident, there has been a series of border clashes since the Nagaland was created. Two major incidents took place in 1979 and 1985, leaving at least 100 persons dead between them. On January 5, 1979, 54 Assam villagers were killed in a series of attacks by armed men from Nagaland in Chungajan, Uriamghat and Mikirbheta of Golaghat district, while over 23,500 persons fled to relief camps. In June 1985, a major flare-up at Merapani, also in Golaghat, left 41 persons dead on the Assam side. These included 28 Assam Police personnel. In both incidents, Assam claimed that the attackers included Nagaland Police personnel.

Causes of the Territorial Dispute

Several causes can be attributed to the territorial dispute between Assam and Nagaland. They can be divided chiefly into the following heads:

(a) Insurgency: Some link the dispute to Nagalim. However, as stated above, this demand is recent. The dispute existed much before even the demand for a sovereign Nagaland which was under the aegis of the NNC and later NSCN. One cannot deny that today most Nagas dream of a greater Nagaland just as they spoke of a sovereign Naga State in the past. But, it is difficult to state with any certainty that is the main cause of the dispute. However, they as well as other militant outfits seem to have intensified the conflict. The NSCN in particular has been running a parallel government in Nagaland and has a large number of cadres and supporters. They as well as other militant outfits require big amounts to run their administration and to look after the well-being of their cadres. These budgetary demands are met by collecting "taxes" both within Nagaland and in other Naga inhabited areas. It can thus be called a force that intensifies the conflict and does not create it by itself.

(b) Governments' Failure to Solve the Border Dispute: The vagueness of the borders and the Central Government's failure to bring about an amicable and permanent solution to the vexed border dispute between Assam and Nagaland is its immediate cause. The Centre as well as the State governments of Assam and Nagaland does not look sincere and serious in their efforts to bring about a permanent solution to this problem. They have appointed Commissions but as their reports as well as agreements signed between the States of Assam as Nagaland remain only on paper. The political parties in power look at the problem only in terms of political gains and losses, very often in the form of a vote bank. As a result, the inhabitants of the boundary have to pass their lives in tension, fear, uncertainty and as second class citizens. The failure of the Border Commissions is another reason and that too can be attributed to the priority given to the political interests on both sides of the border.

(c) Encroachment of Reserved Forest Land: Some think that the Assam government's negligence has led to the encroachment of the Reserve Forests along the Assam-Nagaland border in Golaghat District. Others are of the view that their present inhabitants were encouraged to settle thereby some political leaders in order to create a vote bank. One of its results is that once a home to rich flora and fauna, now it is the most densely populated area of the District. Instead of the forest, there are small huts all over interspersed with agricultural fields and some scattered trees remaining in the name of Reserve Forests. People from both Assam and Nagaland have settled here with the sole purpose of earning their daily bread and

claiming the area as their own. This brings about friction among the people and aggravates the territorial dispute.

(d) Breach of Interim Agreements: Four interim agreements were signed between the two State Governments in the presence of Shri KVK Sundaram, the then Chairman of the Law Commission, as Adviser in the Ministry of Home Affairs. Two of them were signed by the chief secretaries on 31 March, 1972 at Shillong, the third on 2 May, 1972 at Kohima and the fourth on 23 May, 1972 at Shillong. The agreements sought to maintain the *status quo* in the border areas until the border dispute was resolved. In principle, the agreements stand even today but in reality, there is constant breach of these agreements. Violating the ground rules, the state governments of both Assam and Nagaland have been undertaking developmental works through their official agencies. Construction of permanent structures such as schools, community halls and churches, supply of electricity, water supply schemes and roads are in progress.

(e) Seed Farm: A Bone of Contention between Assam and Nagaland: In the east, Kakadunga river; in the west, Doyang river; in the north, Ghiladhari Mouza and in the South Naga Hills more than 200 sq. km in Golaghat District is the Doyang Reserve Forest. It is also known as sector D. The controversial seed farm is situated in this sector at Bhelowguri near Merapani. The seed farm is of recent origin, after 1973 when it began to be talked about and was started after the 1985 armed conflict of Merapani. In reality there is no seed farm here but only cultivation done by engaging paid workers. The seed farm is spread over 1,000 acres that are managed by the Nagas. It has become a major irritant between Assam and Nagaland since both claim this plot. Assam claims that it is situated in Assam but it is under the patronage of the Nagaland government. The Naga effort to gain control over it meets with vehement opposition from the Naga side. The State governments have often engaged in conflict over this issue. So Nagaland has set up a Nagaland Armed Police camp, to safeguard its interests.

(f) The Landlords, Militants and the Neutral Forces: The people on the Assam side of the border claim that they have become victims of tax collection by the Naga landlords and militants but it is difficult to attribute all the tension to them. What is clear is that the gun dominates and taxes are collected in cash or kind from those cultivating land in the Reserve Forests. Those refusing to pay them have to face the gun or abduction for a heavy ransom. Also house tax is collected. The people have no choice but to surrender before the sophisticated arms. Those who claim to represent the landlords and the insurgent outfits have a free access to tax collection. The role of the neutral forces deployed in the area often sends wrong signals to the public. The people on both sides allege that they are not neutral.

Instances of these forces harassing innocent people put a question mark on their neutrality. The disdain and fear with which most people look at them is detrimental to the peace process. People on the Assam side allege that the neutral forces support the Nagas but the latter state that they support the Assamese. Thus they are the centre of accusations and counter accusations.

(g) Suspected Bangladeshi Nationals: Alleged Bangladeshi migrants are a major issue in the North East. This border belt has not been spared either. There are allegations that it has become their haven because of the uncertainty around the border areas. They are said to receive the support of some political leaders and government officials who have a vested interest in their presence. The original encroachers resent their presence. They claim that some of them have got their names enrolled in the electoral roll with the help of influential police and government officials. We were told that most of them are found around Merapani in Sector D and Bidyapur and Koraghat in Sector C and that their presence often leads to conflicts. However, we could not verify their presence and got no details of conflicts. Most, however, consider the political parties the real cause of the conflicts and the unresolved border dispute between Assam and Nagaland. The inhabitants of the area feel that the political parties are not sincere in finding a permanent solution to the vexed problem. The common people allege that they only ignite tension for their political gain and treat the people only as vote banks. They entice the people with empty promises before elections but do not keep them. So the problem persists. A 'cause and effect' relationship is clear but one should probably attribute the situation to a combination of causes rather than a single one. That is one of the reasons why the issue has become very sensitive. As a result, fear and tension are escalating. Violent and unpleasant incidents are a serious threat to law and order. No amount of peace talks will bring about any fruitful and amicable settlement, unless the causes are dealt with. Hence, the state governments of Assam and Nagaland together with the Centre need to take serious measures and plan positive and constructive action in order to get out of this border tangle.

Efforts to resolve Assam-Nagaland border dispute—There were a series of meeting at various level. In 1971, the Centre appointed KVK Sundaram, the then Chairman of Law Commission, as adviser in the Ministry of Home Affairs for matters of Assam-Nagaland. He as a solution to the dispute suggested a joint survey of the border, which Nagaland did not agree to. Moreover, since 1971, the Central Government forces like Central Reserve Police Force (CRPF) have been employed in the region. However, the two states signed four interim agreements in 1972 to maintain *status quo*. Moreover, on January 25, 1979, the Prime Minister wrote to the

Nagaland Chief Minister to take firm action against miscreants on the Nagaland side of the boundary.

In March 1981, the Union Home Minister asked both Chief Ministers to sort out the issue through discussion while strictly adhering to basic constitutional aspects. Accordingly, several meetings of the Chief Ministers of both the sides have been held, but the problem remained unresolved. In 1988, the Assam government filed a title suit in the Supreme Court to determine and delineate the constitutional boundary of each state. In September 2006, the Apex Court set up a three-member Local Commission headed by a retired SC judge to identify the boundary. The Commission has submitted its report to the Court, but a final decision has not yet been made.

Dispute between Assam and Meghalaya

The state of Meghalaya as a separate autonomous Hill State with the provision for a Legislative and Council of Ministers was inaugurated on April 2, 1970 within Assam. But, this arrangement has not satisfied the aspirations of the people and as such the Meghalaya Assembly unanimously resolved on September 30, 1970 to request the Government of India to convert the state into a full-fledge state which the Government of India conceded in January 1972. Soon after the creation of Meghalaya as a separate state out of the territory of Assam, Assam again faced the boundary problem with Meghalaya. The boundary dispute between Meghalaya and Assam is in the Langpih and Hakumari areas and the Jingiram river areas of Garo Hills. When the Election Commission set up seven election boots in the disputed area claimed by Assam in February 1988 for the Meghalaya Assembly Elections it was objected to by the Assam Government. Moreover, the Karbi Anglong sector also remains as a disputed area between these two states. A two member committee headed by justice Chandrachud was appointed by the Central Government to find out a solution of the boundary problems between two states. Justice Chandrachud made recommendations on this issue in July 1987, but the report of the committee did not made public.

The border problem between Assam and Meghalaya has persisted for decades now. It started when Meghalaya challenged the Assam Reorganisation Act of 1971, which bestowed Blocks I and II of the Mikir Hills to Assam (presently the Karbi-Anglong district). Meghalaya contends that both these blocks formed part of the erstwhile United Khasi and Jaintia Hills when it was created in 1835. At present there are 12 points of dispute along the 733 kilometre Assam-Meghalaya border. At a time when the India-China border dispute is hogging the limelight and causing unease in the Indian establishment, many festering inter-state border disputes in the North East that are sowing seeds of discord seem to elude the attention of policymakers at the Centre. The issue of inter-state border disputes came to the fore recently, when tensions erupted along the Assam-Meghalaya border following the Assam government's attempt to lay a foundation stone for a primary health sub-centre at Langpih, a border village claimed by both Assam and Meghalaya.

Langpih is the subject of a long-running dispute between the Meghalaya and Assam state governments, one of twelve such disputed territories. According to Meghalaya ex-Chief Minister Donkapur Roy, the British annexed the village to Assam's Kamrup district, but then after Indian independence, it was assigned to the United Khasi and Jaintia Hills district, a district in today's Meghalaya state. The Meghalaya government claims that Assam's 1951 demarcation shows the area as part of a district in what would later become Meghalaya state. However, in 1972, Assam's new demarcation showed the area as part of its own Mikir Hills district (now Karbi-Anglong District).

In 1974, government forces from the two states had a face off in the village after Meghalaya policemen allegedly expelled Nepalese grazers, leading Assam policemen to arrive and investigate. Link magazine described the situation as "explosive". Hopingstone Lyngdoh claims that Assam "encroached on the village in 1979" and since then encouraged further Assamese settlement there. In 1988, it was claimed in the Lok Sabha that the government of Meghalaya had proposed to set up an electoral constituency, 34-Nongstoin, which covered Kamphaduli, Hakumari, and Langpih.

The Langpih incident occurred on 14 May, 2010, when clashes broke out between the Nepalese and tribal Khasi and Garo communities, leading to shootings by police. National media reported that four Khasi villagers died of the gunshot wounds: Columbus Hujon, Charles Lyngkhoi, Dennis Nonsiej, and Ekros Rani. Reports of the total number of injured varied between twelve and twenty-six. The Governments of Assam and Meghalaya have each reported the death toll as two; even this death toll has become an object of political controversy, with authorities of each state moving the corpses around across state borders to manipulate the number. A monument was constructed in memory of the dead villagers.

Repercussions of the 2010 incident continued to be felt in 2012, when Pynskhemlang Nongshlong of neighbouring Rambrai village planned to lead a hunger strike in memory of the four slain men. Nongshlong and thirteen fellow activists took to a stage constructed by local people specially for their fast. Two hours after the fast began, the Assistant District

Commissioner of Kamrup and 150 police of Assam State arrived at the site. However, Langpih villagers formed a human chain to deny access to police. By the eighth day, eight of the fasters had been retired to Shillong Civil Hospital due to ill health; Nongshlong and five others remained, but were clearly suffering from the effects of dehydration.

Nongshlong declared an end to the fast on 13 July, giving the government a deadline of two months to fulfil a list of demands which the villagers would later announce. However, on 16 July Nongshlong and four women resumed their fast at Nongstoin. Around the same time, the Meghalaya People's Human Rights Council sent a delegation to the 20th Session of the United Nations Human Rights Council in Geneva, Switzerland. MPHRC General Secretary Dino Dympep met with UN Special Reporter James Anaya regarding the 2010 killings, following which Anaya sent a communiqué to the Government of India. However, by the following month the Government of India had failed to respond.

Assam and Meghalaya took a sensible stand on solving their disputes on the basis of the demographic composition of border villages but have failed to make any headway. Meghalaya Chief Minister Mukul Sangma has sought the Centre's intervention to solve the dispute over Langpih village, which both Assam and Meghalaya claim belongs to them. The former claims Langpih on the basis of the Y.V. Chandrachud Committee Report, something the latter has rejected. Last year, four Khasi inhabitants were killed when police fired on demonstrators and presently a number of people are on a hunger-strike.

Sangma favours a boundary commission to go into the dispute, arguing that it will be "a win-win situation for both the states". Not many, however, may share his views. And no state is prepared to back down on its claims. A boundary commission will be effective only if the states concerned agree to the terms and references and accept that its recommendations are binding and mandatory.

To settle the long border dispute with Assam, Meghalaya Chief Minister Mukul Sangma has now sought the constitution of a boundary commission. Earlier, he and Assam Chief Minister Tarun Gogoi had favoured a mutual agreement.

Mukul Sangma met Union Home Minister Sushil Kumar Shinde at the national capital yesterday and urged him to expedite the constitution of a Boundary Commission to "re-examine and re-define the inter-state boundary between Meghalaya and Assam" in line with the all party committee recommendation last year. Mukul Sangma also handed over a letter to Shinde where he sought a feedback from the ministry on a resolution which was adopted for the purpose last year.

The Chief Minister said various efforts have been made to find an amicable solution to this vexed issue but was left without any tangible outcome. "This has caused immense hardship to the people living along the border and has also led to violent incidents at times", Mukul Sangma said.

Assam legislators had voted against the constitution of such a commission in the last budget session citing that a previous commission's report was rejected by Meghalaya since it was "not" in their favour. The borders of the two states have witnessed a spate of unrests in recent past with the chief minister saying he wanted an expeditious resolution to this issue. Assam and Meghalaya have 12 areas of difference which are often termed as "disputed" areas along the inter-state border. In 2010, four Meghalaya youth were shot dead by Assam Police in a clash at Langpih, one such disputed area.

Both states have, on several occasions, engaged on a dialogue to end the crisis, both at the secretariat and the chief ministers' level. Thus the boundary disputes between the two states not yet been solved.

Causes of the Dispute—The following causes may be regarded as responsible for the Assam-Meghalaya Border Dispute.

1. As already mentioned that once, inter-district boundary dispute between the Kamrup and the United Khasi-Jaintia Hills is one of the main causes behind the Assam-Meghalaya border clash. While Meghalaya was created by carving out the two hill districts of Greater Assam, viz. the United Khasi-Jaintia Hills and the Garo Hills, the Kamrup remained in Assam. These districts, viz. the Kamrup and the United Khasi-Jaintia Hills of Greater Assam were adjacent one and hence, claim from both the sides on areas in its common boundary frequently roused. Particularly, Meghalaya always claim the semi-hilly area of Khanapara by arguing that it belongs to the district of United Khasi-Jaintia Hills.

2. Another important cause behind this border dispute is that Meghalaya refuses to accept the demarcation of boundary laid by the North-Eastern Areas (Reorganization) Act, 1971, which granted Blocks I and II of the Mikir Hills (present the Karbi-Anglong) to Assam. Meghalaya contends that both these blocks formed part of the erstwhile United Khasi and Jaintia Hills when it was created in 1835 (Das, 2008).

Dispute between Assam and Arunachal Pradesh

Assam and Arunachal has a 704 km long common boundary. A part of this boundary is already demarcated. The dispute is now confined to only a portion of the boundary. The total length of this portion is officially stated to be 316 km. The areas where the boundary is very sensitive and were frequent boundary disputes takes place are Jonekorong, the Debing-Depi, Talen-Deka Pam and the Likabali. The dispute between Assam and Arunachal Pradesh has assumed serious importance in recent years and create a threat to the people living in boundary line of both states. The dispute has let to occasional bitterness between the people of the two states and several boundary incidents of serious nature, in the past. Even now the boundary is very sensitive at several places and a solution to the problem has not yet been found out, in spite of best efforts of the two governments.

Background of the Dispute

The present boundary between Assam and Arunachal Pradesh owes its origin to the British Raj. The British, after annexing Assam and establishing their rule, there undertook a series of expeditions to the adjoining hill areas and gradually extended their administration into these areas. Such newly acquired territories of present Arunachal Pradesh were made part of Lakhimpur district of Assam but were kept separate from the plain areas of the district by an Inner Line introduced under the Inner Line Regulation, 1873. This line extending from the trijuncture of Bhutan and the Kamrup and Darrang district of Assam to Nagaland forming an area around the present Darrang, Lakhimpur and Dibrugarh districts of Assam formed the basis of present Assam-Arunachal Pradesh boundary. In 1914, the hill areas of Lakhimpur district were separated by creating the Central and Eastern Section and the Western Section of the North East Frontier Tracts of Assam. The notifications issued to create these two Sections of the North-East Frontier Tracts, described in details their boundaries with their adjacent plain districts. The boundary ran, more or less, along the inner line than in force, and served as the boundary between the Frontier Tracts and the plain district of Assam till Independence. At the eve of the Independence, the Constituent Assembly of India constituted a Sub-Committee for the North-East Frontier (Assam) Tribal and Excluded Areas to examine the future administrative setup of these areas, in independent India under the chairmanship of Gopinath Bordoloi. The creation of North East Frontier (Assam) in 1954 and Arunachal Pradesh in 1972 did not alter the boundary line of the former frontier tracts. They only redefine the same line described in 1914 modified in 1934 and 1951. Thus the legal position of the boundary between Assam Arunachal Pradesh today is as described by Notification No 977 EB and 979 EB of 25th September, 1914 modified *vide* Notification No 6779 AP of 2nd November, 1934 and read with Notification No. TAD/R/35/50/109 of 23rd February, 1951. This boundary is also described partially in Assam Government Notification No. RSS, 296/51/126 of 5 March, 1957 which described the boundary of the then Lakhimpur District of Assam. However, the boundary remained mostly un-demarcated on the ground leaving scope for future disputes.

Rise of the Dispute

Although Assam Arunachal Pradesh boundary problems assumed importance only in recent years, due to emergence of a numbers of factors the boundary dispute between the then NEFA and Assam early years of our Independence in some form and other. The people of Arunachal Pradesh, at least a section of them, did not reconcile to the transfer of certain areas of former frontier tracts to the plains district of Assam in 1951.

A meeting of senior officials from the Assam and NEFA was held in Shillong to discuss the problem. The political officer of the Siang Frontier Division and the Deputy Commissioner of Lakhimpur district jointly toured the area. It was not considered necessary to appoint a committee to enquire into his matter.

The Assam government is understood to have decided to extend the same privileges as are enjoyed by the people in the transferred areas of Assam to the Adi village under their jurisdiction. They have also confirm that the right of the Adi village from NEFA possessing cultivable lands in Assam will not be affected in any way by the demarcation of the Inner Line. An officer each from Assam and NEFA have been deputed to remain in the area to settle the differences on the spot till the demarcation is completed.

Nature of the Problem

Assam and Arunachal Pradesh has a 704 kilometre long common boundary making it the second longest interstate boundary in the North-Eastern region. A part of this boundary is already demarcated and there is no dispute regarding this portion of the boundary. Recently some more parts of the boundary between Lohit district of Arunachal Pradesh and Dibrugarh district of Assam have also been fixed. The dispute is thus confined to only a, portion of the boundary. The total length of this portion is officially stated to be 316 kilometres. The actual areas of dispute stretch of the boundary are divided into several sectors. They may be placed under two categories according to nature of the dispute. In certain sectors the dispute is, more or less, confined to claims and counterclaims for certain areas with no or very rare boundary incident. For example the Balijan-Banderdewan Sector in Lakhimpur-Suwansiri area or the Kanubari Sukanjuri-Nagakhat Sector in Dibrugarh-Tirap district area. Secondly, there are areas where the boundary is very sensitive and where frequent boundary incidents take place. For example the Jonekorong, the Debing-Depi, Telam-Dekapam and the Likabali Sectors of the boundary. In the former category the dispute is mostly regarding a village or a reserve forest while in the later category the dispute mostly involves cultivable lands on the boundary. The actual areas disputed are not very big at any given site.

It involves a plot of or a patch of cultivable land or a commercially important site from less than an acre to few hundred acres. The nature of the boundary dispute in these sectors is, therefore, essentially that of a land dispute with all the complexities that go with it. Sometimes lands traditionally cultivated by the people on one side are claimed by the people on the other side on the ground that it lies on their side of the boundary. Sometimes lands reclaimed by the people of one side are occupied by the people living on the other side because they think that it is on their side of the boundary. At other times a tenant tilling the land of his landlords for several years suddenly claims the land to be his own when somebody tells him that the land is on the other side of the boundary.

Other Causes of Dispute

(i) Absence of enough flat arable land: The most important factor aggravating the boundary problem between Assam and Arunachal Pradesh appears to be the growing pressure for flat arable land in Arunachal Pradesh. Traditionally the people of Arunachal Pradesh practiced Jhooming cultivation in the hilly slopes that abound the territory. But, in recent years due mainly to governmental efforts, the primitive and unremunerative method of cultivation has increasingly been replaced by permanent wet rice cultivation. Due to its comparative economic advantages more and more people in Arunachal Pradesh are taking to this new method of cultivation. This has led to a spurt in the demand for flat arable land in the territory. Although Arunachal Pradesh is very large in size it does not have enough flat land to meet this growing demand. Most of its flat lands lie in the foothill areas along the Assam-Arunachal boundary. The pressure for more land is, therefore, felt more in this region. There is a tendency on the part of the villagers of Arunachal in this region to occupy all suitable land available in the area. This frequently leads to clashes and quarrels over lands, at times such as quarrels take place between parties across the boundary. Lack of any demarcation of the boundary on the ground in certain sectors leaves ample scopes for such quarrels to develop into boundary dispute.

(ii) Improvement of Transport and Communication: Improvement of transport and communication facilities and extension of Railway line up to Jonai along certain portion of the boundary has also served as a factor emphasizing the problem. In fact the most sensitive sectors of the boundary lie along the newly extended Railway line from Lakhimpur to Murkongseick station of N.E. Railway. Before the opening of the Railway

line and later the road that runs parallel to this line, transport and communication in this area were very poor. The population in the area was very sparse and the farmers from both Assam and Arunachal Pradesh were more so less free to cultivate any patch of land they chose. People recognized the rights of each farmer to the land he reclaimed irrespective of the boundary and there was no interference from any quarters. It is no wonder that the people seldom bothered for the Assam-Arunachal boundary. But the extension of Railway line to the area has completely changed the situation.

(iii) Construction of Police Outposts along the Boundary: Construction of police outposts along the boundary is also another factor of the border problem. During the last few years a number of new police outposts have been established along the boundary, specially by the Assam government. It is alleged that the police personnel of these outposts instead of maintaining peace and amity in the boundary area contributed more in creating tension among the people across the boundary.

(iv) Ethnic Composition of the Boundary: The ethnic composition of the population in the disputed areas has a direct bearing on the nature of the boundary dispute. The population pattern on the disputed areas of the boundary present two distinct patterns. A homogenous population belonging to a single tribal group living in the area since long. They are found in the disputed areas mentioned in the first category. Here the main cause of the dispute appears to be the desire of a village to come within the jurisdiction of the state where the majority of their tribe lives or to gain the right to use a forest or so. Secondly, mixed population of several sub-tribes of a tribe or tribals and non-tribals who have migrated to the area from different places in the respective states. This is the pattern found in the more sensitive areas of the boundary.

(v) Influx of New Settlers in the Assam: Following devastations of flood in successive years and facilitated by the opening of the rail and road communications up to the Jonai area, a stream of new settlers, mostly Boro tribals from Kamrup and Goalpara district of Assam and also some immigrants from Nepal, poured into the area. They have increased the pressure for land in Assam side as well, changed the demographic picture on the boundary area and disturbed the equilibrium among the indigenous population living on the boundary. Since the new settlers are ignorant about the rights of a person over a particular plot of land which due to the nature of heavy growth of vegetation in the area looks like jungle land if it is left follow for a year or two, and new settlers have a tendency to reclaim the most suitable lands, this influx lead to frequent land clashes and boundary incidents. They also added to the complexity of the problem by increasing

the number of claims and counter-claims over a plot of land.

Although Arunachal Pradesh was created only recently the Assam Arunachal boundary has a long history early as 1914. The boundary was a line arbitrarily drawn by the Britishers. There was no boundary dispute in those days. The boundary dispute appears to have originated only after the 1951 notification transferring certain plains areas of Arunachal Pradesh to Assam. Of course, over the years a number of factors social, political, economic and demographic have made the issue more complex and the dispute more intense. As a result the boundary for the most parts remains unsettled undemarcated on ground till today.

Assam is the common strand that connects all these border disputes. The root cause of all these inter-state border disputes can be traced back to the decision to carve out new political entities out of Assam. It is necessary to point out that this decision was taken under compelling circumstances. The prevailing external and internal situation in the region during the 1960s highlighted the urgent need to effectively integrate this sensitive frontier area with the Indian Union. The 1962 border war with China and numerous ethnic insurgencies that plagued the region threatened the unity and integrity of the country. In this context, the Government of India decided to carve out new political entities, with the dual aim of consolidating its hold over this remote region as well as to fulfil the aspirations of various ethnic communities involved in separatist movements. Thus, the reorganisation of Arunachal Pradesh into a Union Territory in 1972 and its upgradation to full-fledged statehood in 1987 can be seen as a strategy of the Indian government to consolidate its position *vis-à-vis* China in the border negotiations. Similarly, the granting of statehood to Nagaland in 1963, Meghalaya in 1972 and Mizoram in 1987 were steps to accommodate the territorial aspirations of the Nagas, Khasis, Garos, and Mizos.

MODEL QUESTIONS

Very Short Type Questions (1 mark for each)

1. Which State of India is lastly comprises with North East?
2. Write a name of one Committee formed by the Government of India to settle border dispute between Assam and Nagaland?
3. Why did Indian government form Sundaram Committee?
4. In which state 'Doyang Reserve Forest' is belongs?
5. What is the most Popular Cultivation of Arunachal Pradesh?
6. When did Meghalaya become a full-fledgd Separate State?
7. Name two most disputed area between Assam and Meghalaya?
8. Write a name of one disputed area between Assam and Arunachal Pradesh?

9. What is the contemporary demand of government of Meghalaya regarding settlement of border dispute?
10. What is the main provision of Article 3 of the Indian Constitution?

Short Type Questions (4/5 marks for each)

1. Write a short note on Geographical status of Assam Nagaland Border Area.
2. Discuss briefly the causes of territorial dispute between Assam and Nagaland.
3. Why Jayantia Hill and Longpih become the most disputed area between Assam and Meghalaya?
4. Discuss the Background of dispute between Assam and Arunachal Pradesh?
5. Discuss the nature of problem between Assam and Arunachal Pradesh?

Essay Type Questions (10/12 marks for each)

1. Write a note on border dispute in North East India with reference to Assam, Nagaland, Meghalaya and Arunachal Pradesh.
2. Discuss the basic reasons of boundary dispute between Assam and Nagaland?
3. Discuss the causes of Inter-State Conflict between Assam and Meghalaya?
4. Discuss the causes of inter-state conflict between Assam and Arunachal Pradesh?
5. Give your suggestions for peaceful settlement of boundary dispute of Assam with Meghalaya, Nagaland and Arunachal Pradesh.

Appendix 1
The Assam Official Language Act, 1960

No. LJL.35/60.—The following Act of the Assam Legislative Assembly which received the assent of the Governor is here by published for general information.

Received the assent of the Governor on the 17th December 1960

ASSAM ACT No. XXXIII OF 1960

THE ASSAM OFFICIAL LANGUAGE ACT, 1960

(As passed by the Assembly)

[*Published in the Assam Gazette, Extraordinary, dated the 19th December 1960*]

An Act to declare the Official Language of the State of Assam.

Preamble—Whereas Article 345 of the Constitution provides that the Legislature of a State may by law adopt any one or more of the languages in use in the State as the language to be used for official purposes of the State and for matters hereinafter appearing;

It is hereby enacted in the Eleventh Year of the Republic of India, as follows:

1. Short title, extent and commencement.—(1) This Act may be called the Assam Official Language Act, 1960.

(2) It extends to the whole of the State of Assam.

(3) It shall come into force on such date as the State Government may, by notification, in the official Gazette, appoint and different dates may be appointed for different official purposes and for different parts of the State of Assam:

Provided that the date or dates appointed by the State Government in respect of any of the parts of the State of Assam shall not be later than five years from the date the assent to this Act is first published in the official Gazette.

2. Definitions.—In this Act, unless there is anything repugnant in the subject or context:

(a) "Autonomous District" means an area deemed as such under paragraph 1(1) of the Sixth Schedule to the Constitution of India.

(b) "Autonomous Region" means an area deemed as such under paragraph 1 (2) of the Sixth Schedule to the Constitution of India.

(c) "District Council" means a District Council constituted under paragraph 2 of the Sixth Schedule to the Constitution of India.

(d) "Mohkuma Parishad" means a Mohkuma Parishad, established under the Assam Panchayat Act, 1959.

(e) "Municipal board" means a Municipal Hoard establi-shed under the Assam Municipal Act, 1956 and shall include Town Committees established under the said Act.

(f) "Prescribed" means prescribed by rules made under this Act.

(g) "Regional Council" means a Regional Council cons-tituted under paragraph 2 of the Sixth Schedule to the Constitution of India.

3. Official language for official purposes of the State of Assam.— Without prejudice to the provisions of Articles 346 and 147 of the Constitution of India and subject as hereinafter provided, Assamese shall be used for all or any of the official purposes of the State of Assam:

Provided that the English language, so long as the use thereof is permissible under Article 343 of the Constitution of India, and thereafter Hindi in place of English, shall also be used for such official purposes of the Secretariat and the offices of the Heads of the Departments of the State Government and in such manner as may be prescribed:

Provided further that,—

(a) all Ordinances promulgated under Article 213 of the Constitution of India;

(b) all Acts passed by the State Legislature;

(c) all Bills to be introduced or amendments thereto to be moved in the State Legislature; and

(d) all Orders, Regulations, Rules and Bye-laws issued by the State Government under the Constitution of India or any law made by Parliament or the Legislature of the State;

shall be published in the official Gazette in the Assamese language.

4. Safeguard of the use of language in the Autonomous Region and in the Autonomous District.—Notwithstanding anything in Section 3, only languages which are in use immediately before the commencement of this Act shall continue to be used for administrative and other official purposes up to and including the level of the Autonomous Region or the Autonomous District, as the case may be, until the Regional Council or the District Council in respect of the Autonomous Region or the Autonomous District, as the case may be, by a majority of not less than two-thirds of the members present and voting decide in favour of adoption of any other language for any of the administrative or official purposes within that region or district.

5. Safeguard of the use of Bengali language in the district of Cachar.— Notwithstanding anything in Section 3, the Bengali language shall be used for administrative and other official purposes up to and including the district level in the district of Cachar until the Mohkuma Parishads and Municipal Boards of the district in a joint meeting by a majority of not less than two-thirds of the members present and voting decide in favour of adoption of the official language for use in the district for the aforesaid purposes.

6. The Use of English as official language in respect of examination conducted by the Assam Public Service Commission.—Notwithstanding anything in Section 3, any examination held by the Assam Public Service Commission which immediately before the commencement of this Act used to be conducted in the English language shall continue to be so conducted till such time as the use thereof is permissible under clause (2) of Article 343 of the Constitution of India:

Provided that a candidate shall have the right to choose the language in use in the State of Assam, which was the medium of his University examination.

7. Rights of the various linguistic group.— Subject to the provision of this Act, the State Government may by notification issued from time to time, direct the use of the language as may be specified in the notification and in such parts of the State of Assam as may be specified therein:

Provided that—

(a) the rights of the various linguistic groups in respect of medium of instruction in educational institutions as laid down in the Constitution of India shall not be affected:

(b) the State shall not, in granting aid to educational and cultural institutions, discriminate against any such institutions on grounds of language:

(c) the rights to appointments in the Assam Public Services and to contracts and other avocations shall be main. tained without discrimination on the ground of lan-guage; and

(d) in regard to noting in the offices in the region or district if any member of the staff is unable to note in any of the district language, the use of English shall be permitted by the Heads of Departments so long as the use thereof is permissible under Article 343 of the Constitution of India.

8. Powers to make rules.—The Slate Government shall have the power to make rules for carrying out the purposes of this Act.

IS. G. BARUA,
Secy. to the Govt. of Assam, Law Deptt.

Appendix 2
Assam Accord

15th August, 1985
(Accord between AASU, AAGSP, Central and State Government on the Foreigner Problem Issue)

Memorandum of Settlement

1. Government have all along been most anxious to find a satisfactory solution to the problem of Foreigners in Assam. The All Assam Students' Union (AASU) and the All Assam Gana Sangram Parishad (AAGSP) have also expressed their Keenness to find such a solution.

2. The AASU through their Memorandum dated 2nd February, 1980 presented to the Late Prime Minister Smt. Indira Gandhi, conveyed their profound sense of apprehensions regarding the continuing influx of foreign nationals into Assam and the fear about adverse affects upon the political, social, cultural and economic life of the State.

3. Being fully alive to the genuine apprehensions of the people of Assam, the then Prime Minister initiated the dialogue with the AASU/AAGSP. Subsequently, talks were held at the Prime Minister's and Home Ministers levels during the period 1980-83. Several rounds of informal talks were held during 1984. Formal discussions were resumed in March, 1985.

4. Keeping all aspects of the problem including constitutional and legal provision, international agreements, national commitments and humanitarian considerations, it has been decided to proceed as follows:-

Foreigners Issue :

5.

(1) For purpose of detection and deletion of foreigners, 1-1-1966 shall be the base date and year.

(2) All persons who came to Assam prior to 1-1-1966, including those amongst them whose names appeared on the electoral rolls used in 1967 elections, shall be regularized.

(3) Foreigners who came to Assam after 1-1-1966 (inclusive) and upto 24th March, 1971 shall be detected in accordance with the provisions of the

Foreigners Act, 1946 and the Foreigners (Tribunals) Order, 1939.

(4) Names of foreigners so detected will be deleted from the electoral rolls in force. Such persons will be required to register themselves before the Registration Officers of the respective districts in accordance with the provisions of the Registration of Foreigners Act, 1939 and the Registration of Foreigners Rules, 1939.

(5) For this purpose, Government of India will undertake suitable strengthening of the governmental machinery.

(6) On the expiry of the period of ten year following the date of detection, the names of all such persons which have been deleted from the electoral rolls shall be restored.

(7) All persons who were expelled earlier, but have since re-entered illegally into Assam, shall be expelled.

(8) Foreigners who came to Assam on or after March 25, 1971 shall continue to be detected, deleted and expelled in accordance with law. Immediate and practical steps shall be taken to expel such foreigners.

(9) The Government will give due consideration to certain difficulties express by the AASU/AAGSP regarding the implementation of the illegal Migrants (Determination by Tribunals) Act, 1983.

Safeguards and Economic Development:

6. Constitutional, legislative and administrative safeguards, as many be appropriate, shall be provided to protect, preserve and promote the cultural, social, linguistic identity and heritage of the Assamese people.

7. The Government takes this opportunity to renew their commitment for the speedy all round economic development of Assam, so as to improve the standard of living of the people. Special emphasis will be placed on the education and Science & Technology through establishment of national institutions.

Other Issues :

8.

(1) The Government will arrange for the issue of citizenship certificate in future only by the authorities of the Central Government.

(2) Specific complaints that may be made by the AASU/AAGSP about irregular issuance of Indian Citizenship Certificates (ICC) will be looked into.

9.

(1) The international border shall be made secure against future

infiltration by erection of physical barriers like walls barbed wire fencing and other obstacles at appropriate places. Patrolling by security forces on land and riverine routes all along the international border shall be adequately intensified. In order to further strengthen the security arrangements, to prevent effectively future infiltration, an adequate number of check posts shall be set up.

(2) Besides the arrangements mentioned above and keeping in view security considerations, a road all along the international border shall be constructed so as to facilitate patrolling by security forces. Land between border and the road would be kept free of human habitation, wherever possible. Riverine patrolling along the international border would be intensified. All effective measures would be adopted to prevent infiltrators crossing or attempting to cross the international border.

10. It will be ensured that relevant laws for prevention of encroachment of government lands and lands in tribal belts and blocks are strictly enforced and unauthorized encroachers evicted as laid down under such laws.

11. It will be ensured that the law restricting acquisition of immovable property by foreigners in Assam is strictly enforced.

12. It will be ensured that Birth and Death Registers are duly maintained.

Restoration of Normalcy :

13.The All Assam Students Unions (AASU) and the All Assam Gana Sangram Parishad (AAGSP) call off the agitation, assure full co-operation and dedicate themselves towards the development of the Country.

14.The Central and the State Government have agreed to :

a. Review with sympathy and withdraw cases of disciplinary action taken against employees in the context of the agitation and to ensure that there is no victimization;

b. Frame a scheme for ex-gratia payment to next of kin of those who were killed in the course in the agitation.

c. Give sympathetic consideration to proposal for relaxation of upper age limit for employment in public service in Assam, having regard to exceptional situation that prevailed in holding academic and competitive examinations etc. in the context of agitation in Assam:

d. Undertake review of detention cases, if any, as well as cases against persons charged with criminal offences in connection with the agitation, except those charged with commission of heinous offences.

e. Consider withdrawal of the prohibitory orders/ notifications in force, if any :

15. The Ministry of Home Affairs will be the nodal Ministry for the implementation of the above.

Sd/-
(P.K. Mahanta)
President
All Assam Students' Union

Sd/-
(R.D. Pradhan)
Home Secretary
Government of India

Sd/-
(B.K. Phukan)
General Secretary
All Assam Students' Union

Sd/-
(Smt.P.P.Trevedi)
Chief Secretary
Government ofAssam

Sd/-
(Biraj Sharma)
Convenor
All Assam Gana Sangram Parishad
In the Presence of
Sd/- (Rajiv Gandhi)
Prime Minister of India

Date : 15th August, 1985
Place: New Delhi

1. Election Commission will be requested to ensure preparation of fair electoral rolls.
2. Time for submission of claim and objections will be extended by 30 days, subject to this being consistent with the Election Rules.
3. The Election Commission will be requested to send Central Observes.

Sd/- Illegible
Home Secretary

1. Oil Refinery will be established in Assam
2. Central Government will render full assistance to the State Government in their efforts to reopen.
    i) Ashok Paper Mill
    ii) Jute Mills
3. I.I.T. will be set up in Assam.

Sd/- Illegible
Home Secretary

Select Bibliography

Baruah, Sanjib. *Politics of Territoriality: Indigeneity, Itinerancy and Rights in North-East India*. Obtained from https://www.academia.edu/4805185/_Politics_of_

Baruah, Sanjib. "Confronting Constructionism: Ending India's Naga War." In *Journal of Peace Research*, 2003.

Chaube, SK. *Hill Politics in Northeast India*. Patna: Orient Longman Limited, 1999.

Choudhury, Lutfur Rahman. "Ethnic Identity Question and the Autonomy Movement in Karbi Anglong." In *Pratidhwani, the Echo—A Journal of Humanities and Social Science*, 2014.

Das, Pushpita. "Interstate Border Disputes in the Northeast." In *Institute for Defence Studies and Analyses*, 2008.

Dutta, Akhil Ranjan. *Human Security in North-East India: Issues and Policies*. Guwahati: Anwesha, 2009.

Formation of Autonomous District Councils as a Part of Administrative Reforms KanglaOnline accessed from http://kanglaonline.com/2010/08/formation-of-autonomous-district-councils-as-a-part-of-administrative-reforms on 28/09/2015.

Gochhayat, Artarana. "Regionalism and sub-regionalism: A theoretical framework with special reference to India." In *African Journal of Political Science and International Realations*, 2013.

History of Mizoram accessed from www.mizoram.nic.in/about/history.htm on 28/10/2015.

Hussain, Monirul. "Tribal Movements for Autonomous State in Assam." In *Economic & Political Weekly*, 1987.

Kabaw Valley obtained from http://en.wikipedia.org/wiki/Kabaw_Valley

Karbi Anglong: A Journey from District Council to Territorial Council accessed from http://ijellh.com/karbi-anglong-journey-from-district-council-territorial-council/ on 23/10/2015.

Madhab, Jayanta. "North- East: Crisis of Identity, Security and Underdevelopment." In *Economic & Political Weekly*, 1999.

Mizoram accessed from https://en.wikipedia.org/wiki/Mizoram on 16/11/2015.

Meghalaya accessed from https://en.wikipedia.org/wiki/Meghalaya on 11/01/2015.

Mohrmen, HH. "The North East Interstate Border Dispute." accessed from http://www.Theshillongtimes.com/2014/05/12/the-northeast-interstate-border-dispute/

Ngaihte, S Thianlalmuan. "The Reality of North-East as an Entity." In *Economic & Political Weekly*, 2013.

Nuntham, C. "Sociological Reflections on Peace Process in North East India." In *Peace in India's North-East: Meaning Metaphor and Method*. edited by Prasenjit Biswas and C. Joshua Thomas. New Delhi: Regency Publications, 2006.

Prabhakara, M.S. "Separatist Movements in the North–East: Rhetoric and Reality." In *Economic & Political Weekly*, 2007.

Raj, Hans. *Indian Government and Politics*. Delhi: Surjeet Publications, 2004.

Rocky, Raile. "Tribes and Tribal Studies in North East: Deconstructing the Philosophy of Colonial Methodology". In *Journal of Tribal Intellectual Collective India: Critical Articulation of Lived and Shared Experience from within*.

Roy, Hirokjeet. "Politics of Janajatikaran: Koch Rajbanshis of Assam." In *Economic & Political Weekly*, 2014.

Siddique, Nazimuddin. "Assam – Nagaland Border Violence: Role of Militants and the State." In *Economic & Political Weekly*, 2014.

Sixth Schedule – Constitution Society accessed from www.constitution.org /cons / india /shed06.htm

Upadhyay, Archana. "Terrorism in the North-East: Linkages and Implications." In *Economic & Political Weekly*, 2006.